AF685847

Psychic Trauma

Dynamics, Symptoms, and Treatment

IRA BRENNER, M.D.

JASON ARONSON

Lanham • Boulder • New York • Toronto • Oxford

Published in the United States of America
by Jason Aronson
An imprint of Rowman & Littlefield Publishers, Inc.

A wholly owned subsidiary of
The Rowman & Littlefield Publishing Group, Inc.
4501 Forbes Boulevard, Suite 200, Lanham, Maryland 20706
www.rowmanlittlefield.com

PO Box 317
Oxford
OX2 9RU, UK

Copyright © 2004 by Jason Aronson, Inc.

All rights reserved. No part of this publication may be reproduced, stored in a retrieval system, or transmitted in any form or by any means, electronic, mechanical, photocopying, recording, or otherwise, without the prior permission of the publisher.

British Library Cataloguing in Publication Information Available

Library of Congress Cataloging-in-Publication Data

Brenner, Ira, 1950–
Psychic trauma : dynamics, symptoms, and treatment / Ira Brenner.
p. cm.
Includes bibliographical references and index.
ISBN 0-7657-0365-3 (cloth : alk. paper)
1. Psychic trauma. 2. Psychic trauma—Treatment. I. Title.
BF175.5.P75B74 2004
616.85'21—dc22 2004014281

Printed in the United States of America

The paper used in this publication meets the minimum requirements of American National Standard for Information Sciences—Permanence of Paper for Printed Library Materials, ANSI/NISO Z39.48-1992.

Contents

PART III TREATMENT

To the memory of
JUDITH KESTENBERG, M.D.
Pioneer, mentor, dear friend

ILLUSTRATIONS

"Mary"

ACKNOWLEDGMENTS

I would like to thank Jason Aronson and Norma Pomerantz for their encouragement in writing this book. The chapters have gone through numerous revisions that have been expertly typed and retyped by Deborah Szumachowski. My wife, Roberta, has seen the piles of paper come and go on my desk, but she has been a constant support. My mentors, peers, and supervisees are an ongoing source of intellectual stimulation, which helps me clarify my thinking and better understand my clinical experience, so I can write about it. In particular, I would like to thank Drs. Salman Akhtar, Richard Kluft, Moises Lemlij, Nadia Ramzy, and Vamik Volkan. It is truly a privilege to work with patients like those described in the following pages, and I hope that this volume will help others in their daily efforts, too.

INTRODUCTION

During one of those silent, mind-numbing, ferry rides away from Ground Zero, the site of the former World Trade Center in New York, I sat with an utterly depleted family who had just witnessed the devastation that killed their son. The mother bitterly fought back her tears and declared, "They'll forget this too!" A faint European accent caught my ear as I listened to her reference to a recent article in *The New York Times* reporting that many Americans either forgot or never knew that anyone had died in the first terrorist attempt to destroy the World Trade Center back in 1993. As I heard myself automatically reassure her that this disaster would most certainly always be remembered, I began to wonder if she was also alluding to yet another more distant catastrophe.

This woman was a child survivor of the Holocaust who begged her son not to accept his new job because she feared, indeed, that it would happen again. It did, and she could not save him. With the bravado of a young man with a bright future ahead, he reportedly shrugged off her overprotective worry and laughingly told her she wouldn't be happy unless she was there with him holding his hand. Now, all she could do was cry and convulse as her losses from almost 60 years ago merged into the hopelessness of the present. She, the survivor, with nightmares of her own ordeal, was truly inconsolable at that moment. The past, the present, and the future collapsed into a black hole of despair, rage, and guilt. I am not sure there could ever be any textbook that could really teach psychotherapists how to work with someone like her. Yet, when we are able to reach someone who has suffered enormously, we want to share it with others. It is with this hope that I humbly offer this book.

In an important series of pre-millennium editorials written by several prestigious leaders in psychiatry who were asked to predict the future of our field, not one of these experts addressed the issue of psychic trauma (Michels 1999, Sharfstein 1999, Tischler and Astrachan 1999). One might have concluded from this curious omission that they did not see it as a major problem worthy of emphasis in their vision of the evolution of psychiatry. Though we are not known for our expertise in predicting the future, it would have been very difficult to imagine the events of September 11, 2001, nonetheless. Since then, the epidemic of posttraumatic symptoms and the renewed interest in the recognition, treatment, and prevention of complications of traumatic events has become a top priority. As someone working in the field of psychic trauma for more than two decades, it is clear to me that the far-reaching and long-lasting effects of severe recurrent trauma are indeed a public health priority. While it still remains unclear to what extent psychoanalytically oriented treatment can be modified to be of the greatest help in the acute phases of severe trauma, it undoubtedly offers an excellent model for the long-term consequences.

This book offers a clinical study of psychic trauma through the perspectives of time and depth. These dimensions provide a framework in which to understand the myriad long-term effects of overwhelming life experiences. I draw on my work with two different but sometimes overlapping populations—those affected by severe early physical and sexual abuse, and those affected by genocidal persecution during the Holocaust. The extensive case material is presented as accurately as possible, given the safeguards necessary to protect patient confidentiality (Gabbard 2000). An attempt at synthesis without arriving at premature closure, this book adds to my previous contributions, *The Last Witness: The Child Survivor of the Holocaust* (coauthored with Judith Kestenberg, American Psychiatric Press Incorporated, 1996) and *Dissociation of Trauma:*

Theory, Phenomenology, and Technique (International Universities Press, 2001). Readers familiar with my work will find new ideas to complement and corroborate earlier ones, whereas readers who are unfamiliar with these topics will find helpful background discussion and clinical material.

The text is divided into three parts, within which each chapter examines an aspect of trauma from a different vantage point. Part I addresses dynamics. Chapter 1 summarizes my theory about the range of dissociative character pathology. An extended vignette illustrates how I work with patients on the severe end of the spectrum, which is officially known today as dissociative identity disorder (DID). This chapter is a revised and expanded version of a paper I presented in September 2000 in Izmir, Turkey, at the Second Izmir Conference on Psychoanalysis and Psychotherapy. It also contains segments from a previously published paper that were excerpted with permission (Brenner 1999a). In keeping with the theme of the book, Chapter 1 also looks at the long-term effect of severe early trauma on personality development in which dissociation becomes a central defensive operation instead of repression or splitting. Chapter 2 discusses a rarely reported aspect of sexual exploitation that is kept so secret that the patient may prefer to die rather than reveal it: mother–daughter incest persisting into adulthood. Three case reports are offered of patients with major dissociative psychopathology. Their sexual relationship with their mothers continued well past the time one generally envisions when thinking about "child" abuse. The profound effects on their development and the challenges in treatment are discussed. Chapter 3 examines from a research perspective the elusive phenomenon of "switching" from one alter personality to another in DID. Applying the model developed by Lester Luborsky to elucidate the contexts in which symptoms manifest themselves during the course of a therapy session, this short-lived and controversial mental event can also be studied and better understood. Results from a pilot study funded by a small grant from the '76 Fund of Pennsylvania Hospital are presented along with excerpts of sessions of two patients with profound dissociative psychopathology.

Part II addresses symptoms, and discusses the Holocaust and its aftermath in the three major subgroups of adult survivors, children of survivors, and child survivors. Chapter 4 documents the lifelong persistence of symptoms in adult survivors. It includes a case report that describes a concentration camp survivor whose repetition compulsion was evident throughout his life and continued through the terminal phase of his illness until his death. [This chapter is an expanded version of a paper entitled "Returning to the Fire: Surviving the Holocaust and 'Going Back,'" which was presented at the "At the Threshold of the Millennium" Conference in Lima, Peru, in April 1998, and is reprinted with permission from the *Journal of Applied Psychoanalytic Studies* (Brenner 1999c).] Chapter 5 offers a view of the passing on of traumatic effects of genocidal persecution from one generation to the next in both children of survivors and children of Nazis. A seminal contribution of Holocaust research, the notion of intergenerational transmission was originally termed by Kestenberg as transposition and is now applied to other situations resulting in massive psychic trauma. The effects of the Holocaust may continue to be deeply felt by the children more than half a century later even though they were never there in the first place. [Comparing and contrasting the legacies, superego problems, and therapeutic challenges found in both second-generation groups, this chapter was originally published in German as part of the proceedings of a historic conference held in Dusseldorf in 1999. *Das Ende-der Sprachlosigkeit?* (*The End of Speechlessness?*) was organized by a study group of German children of survivors and children of Nazis under Vamik Volkan's supervision. "Stacheldraht in der Seele" ("Barbed Wire in The Soul") is reprinted with permission from Psychosozial-Verlag (Brenner 2000a)]. Chapter 6 considers another long-term effect of severe early trauma, unresolved grief, and development of the manic defense. A case report is presented of a child survivor who as a young girl lost everyone in her family except her mother. A remarkably resourceful and resilient individual, she emigrated to the United States and realized the American dream of material prosperity. Her seemingly boundless energy was in part fueled by manic defense against unresolved loss. [A shorter version of this chapter was presented as a keynote address at the Virginia Psychoanalytic Society's annual meeting in April, 2001.]

Part III addresses treatment, including some of the technical issues and the experiences of the analytic therapist. Chapter 7 explores the effect of the analyst's own trauma as it comes to bear on the therapeutic stance and countertransference issues. An illustrative case is presented of a second-generation analyst treating a sexually traumatized patient who inadvertently discovers his background. This loss of anonymity presented both an anxiety-provoking challenge and a technical dilemma. [An earlier version of this paper was presented at the International Psychoanalytic Association meeting in Santiago, Chile, in July 1999.] Chapter 8 returns to the subject of defensive altered states and addresses their effect on the analyst and the possibility of becoming sleepy and actually falling asleep during the session. Following a review of the literature, a detailed vignette describes the mutual influences such an event had on a therapeutic dyad. The formulation that a dream within a dream was being enacted in the transference helped explain the surprising aftermath and furthered the understanding of the pathogenesis of DID. Chapter 9 discusses a temporal issue as old as psychoanalysis itself: the length of treatment. Even in this managed-care era, long analyses are not unusual, especially for those with a history of significant trauma and character problems resulting in disturbances of appreciation of the passage of time. Yet the pressures of the life cycle, such as the aging process, the "biological clock" for a woman's childbearing years, and the growing up of her children, exert their influences. In addition, the revolution in health care has resulted in intrusive micro-management of frequency and duration of mental health visits, which may prevent significant changes to occur for patients staying in treatment long enough. Regardless, Freud himself thought it a worth idea to contemplate how to shorten the length of an analysis. His debates with Ferenczi over "active techniques" continue to echo in the current debate over the relational aspects of the analytic encounter. This chapter considers the possible interface between psychoanalysis and eye movement desensitization and reprocessing (EMDR), a controversial new treatment involving activity on the therapist's part. This modality has been enthusiastically embraced by its proponents as a breakthrough in the treatment of psychic trauma. Three vignettes are presented of patients with dissociative pathology where guided eye movements were introduced into treatment. One patient, an artist, has graciously permitted her artwork over the course of treatment to be reproduced here. Psychodynamic and possible underlying neurophysiologic mechanisms are considered to explain some of the effects seen in these patients. The reader is asked to consider whether such an active technique could be used as a parameter as per Kurt Eissler (1953), and have any value in certain circumstances, or whether it is yet another fad that will eventually be cast aside.

I

DYNAMICS

1

Trauma and Dissociation

> ". . . a double malformation something like the so-called teratoma, which harbours in a hidden part of its body, fragments of a twin-being, which has never been developed."
>
> [Ferenczi, 1930, p. 123]

Sigmund Freud wrestled with the problem of psychic trauma for almost half a century. From his earliest work on hysteria to his final essays, he tried to reconcile the mutual influences of one's internal and external worlds. In *Moses and Monotheism* (Freud 1939), which was written toward the end of his life when his own survival was threatened by the Nazis, he summarized his views as follows:

> The effects of trauma are of two kinds, positive and negative, the forms are attempts to bring the trauma into operation once again—that is, to remember the forgotten experience, or better still to make it real, to experience the repetition of it anew, or, even if it was only an early emotional relationship, to revive it in an analogous relationship with someone else. We summarize the efforts under the name of "fixation" to the trauma and as a "compulsion to repeat." They may be taken up into what passes as a normal ego and, as permanent trends in it, may lend it unalterable character traits. [p. 75]

> The negative reactions follow the opposite aim: that nothing of the forgotten traumas shall be remembered and nothing repeated. We can summarize them as "defensive" reactions. Their principal expressions are what we call "avoidances," which may be intensified into "inhibitions" and "phobias." These negative reactions too make the most powerful contributions to the stamping of characters. . . . This . . . opposition between the reactions sets up conflicts which in the ordinary course of events can reach no conclusion. . . .
>
> All these phenomena . . . have great psychical intensity and at the same time exhibit a far reaching independence of the organization of the other mental processes, which are adjusted to the demands of the external world and obey the laws of logical thinking. . . . If . . . domination by an internal psychical reality over the reality of the external world . . . [then] the path to a psychosis lies open. [p. 76]

These observations have essentially stood the test of time and have become the foundation of contemporary thinking about Posttraumatic stress disorder. For example, in the *Diagnostic and Statistical Manual of Mental Disorders*, 4th edition (DSM-IV) (American Psychiatric Association 1994), Freud's positive symptoms are described as "recurrent and intrusive distressing recollections . . . images, thoughts, or perceptions . . . in young children, repetitive play . . . recurrent dreams . . . as if the traumatic event were recurring" (pp. 209–210). The negative symptoms are characterized as "persistent avoidance of stimuli associated with the trauma and numbing of general responsiveness . . . [such as] efforts to avoid thoughts, feelings, or conversations, . . . efforts to avoid activities, places, or people, . . . inability to recall, . . . detachment or estrangement" (p. 425).

The twentieth century saw more than its share of natural and man-made disasters, sadly providing endless opportunities to learn more about psychic trauma and massive psychic trauma. In his hierarchy of human suffering, Freud (1930) pessimistically concluded in *Civilization and Its Discontents* that "we are threatened with suffering from three directions: from our body, which is doomed to decay . . . , from the external world which may rage against us with overwhelming and merciless force of destruction, and finally from our relations with other men. . . . This last source is perhaps more painful to us than any other" (p. 77). Freud continues,

> Men are not gentle creatures who want to be loved and who at most can defend themselves if they are attacked; they are, on the contrary, creatures among whose instinctive endowments is to be reckoned a powerful share of aggressiveness. As a result, their neighbor is for them not only a potential helper or a sexual object, but also someone who tempts them to satisfy their aggressiveness on him, to exploit his capacity for work without compensation, to use him sexually without his consent, to seize his possessions, to humiliate him, to cause him pain, to torture and to kill him. Homo homini lupus (man is a wolf to man). [p.111]

Of particular interest here are Freud's observations that man-made atrocities leave the most powerful traumatic imprint, that trauma can greatly affect character development, that the effects of trauma can result in an independent area of the mind, and that one may become psychotic if psychical reality takes precedence over external reality. I will present a psychoanalytic perspective on the understanding and treatment of patients who have been severely traumatized in childhood and who employ defensive altered states of consciousness. In contrast to the classic views regarding the organization and structure of the mind—(1) the structural theory of id, ego, and superego, and the central role of the defense of repression; and (2) the object relations theory and the role of defensive splitting—I hypothesize an additional model of the mind. In this model, dissociation is the central defensive operation along a continuum of what I term the "dissociative character." At the most severe end of this spectrum would be the lower level dissociative character, which is generally known as multiple personality.

Throughout his career, Freud struggled with the notion of a split in the psyche, an idea first put forth by Janet (1889), known as "disaggregation," or dissociation. In his earliest work with Breuer, Freud described a "splitting of consciousness" in hysteria, which was replaced by his theory of repression. However, he later returned to this concept, and described splitting in perversion (1923b), neurosis (1940a), and psychosis (1940b). Unfortunately, the ambiguity over this term and the term *dissociation* has resulted in much confusion, which persists to this day.

There is an important connection between dissociation and posttraumatic symptoms. It is well known, for example, that two of the immediate psychological responses to sudden, unexpected life-threatening shocks may be an alteration in the perception of time and disturbances of memory. Furthermore, the presence of such altered states has been correlated with the severity of posttraumatic syndrome and prognosis for treatment, which supports the link between trauma and dissociation. Many writers have therefore concluded that in the absence of organicity, dissociation is invariably associated with trauma.

From a descriptive standpoint, dissociation is defined in the DSM-IV as "a disruption in the usually integrated functions of consciousness, memory, identity or perceptions of the environment" (APA 1994, p. 231), that "is not due to direct physiological effects of the substance (e.g., a drug of abuse, a medication) or a general medical condition (e.g., temporal lobe epilepsy)" (APA 1994, p. 230). This definition however is based on the predominant psychiatric view that dissociation is a symptom. But since the psychoanalytic principle of multiple function (Waelder 1936) assumes that all psychic products have multiple meanings, then it follows that symptoms may also serve defensive purposes and vice versa. This blurring of the distinction between symptom and defense is important for the deeper understanding of dissociation because if seen as a compromise formation that incorporates the demands of the id, ego, superego, and external reality (C. Brenner 1982), the dynamic significance of dissociation can then be explored in psychoanalytically informed treatment.

For the past two decades, I have been involved in the psychoanalytic study of the effects of massive psychic trauma on mental functioning. My work started with adult survivors of the Holocaust and the transmission of their trauma to their children, that is, the second generation. My research then extended into the realm of child survivors, as I participated in an international interviewing project, collecting data on the longitudinal effects of profound early trauma in development. During this time, I fortuitously met Richard P. Kluft, M.D., at the Institute of Pennsylvania Hospital, whose historic work with dissociative disorders had already come into prominence (Kluft 1984). His patients had also reported severe early trauma, but more often it was associated with domestic physical and sexual abuse, not the deprivation and atrocities associated with genocidal persecution. Furthermore, their seemingly bizarre altered states, different selves, amnesia, and suicidal aggression presented a different set of challenges to the treating clinician.

Adding to the complexity of these patients, many of whom seemed somewhere between borderline personality and schizophrenia while also suffering from substance abuse or anorexia, was the fact that they were being treated by a different approach. This was a cognitively and psychodynamically informed hypnotherapy, which used a different language to describe the structure and function of the mind. Since a number of Kluft's patients were admitted to my inpatient unit before he started his dissociative disorders unit (DDU), it was not only an extraordinary opportunity but also an administrative necessity to try to understand what was going on with their care. It was bewildering and overwhelming at first, since I did not understand the paradigm being used and could not readily apply my psychoanalytic model of the mind to this psychopathology.

My background in Holocaust research taught me to tolerate my own pain while listening openly to horrendous stories of unspeakable atrocities, and to become aware that human beings are indeed capable of inhumane sadistic behavior. With this "preparation," my exposure to a large number of suspected cases of dissociative identity disorder (DID) in the inpatient setting enabled me to eventually see that one of the most enigmatic patients in my own practice back then was also a "multiple." Since I was not looking for it, since the patient was very secretive about it, and since the patient had not read about it, had no contact with such patients, and had not been treated by any recovered-memory therapists, I had no choice but to become a believer in the legitimacy of the diagnosis. Afterward, I devoted considerable energy trying to understand it and had the opportunity to work on the DDU—until the hospital became a casualty of the cutbacks due to managed care. My experience grew exponentially, and over the years I have had clinical contact with hundreds of such patients, ranging from administrative management, consultation, supervision, and inpatient treatment to long-term, five-time-a-week analytic therapy.

TOWARD AN ANALYTIC UNDERSTANDING OF DID

The essence of my approach to DID is based on three assumptions:

1. Dissociation is multiply determined and may be utilized as a defense against anxiety in the here and now through the reactivation of altered states associated with earlier trauma. It may be seen as

   > a defensive altered state of consciousness due to autohypnosis, augmenting repression or splitting. It develops as a primitive, adaptive response of the ego to the overstimulation and pain of external trauma, which depending on its degree of integration, may result in a broad range of disturbances of alertness, awareness, memory and identity. Dissociation apparently may change in its function and may be employed later on as a defense against the perceived internal danger of intolerable affects and instinctual strivings. [Brenner 1994a, p. 841]

2. DID, contrary to the prevailing view, may be understood as being at the severe end of a continuum of character pathology, that is, a "lower level dissociative character" (Brenner 1996a,b) whose predominant defense is dissociation.

3. There is a pathognomonic psychic structure at the core of DID, whose function is not only to disown intolerable memories, affects, and drives (Brenner 2001), but also to personify these conflicts through the creation of so-called alter personalities. This structure therefore transcends and fuels these alter personalities, or to use Fairbairn's (1952)

term, the *personifications*, and is referred to as the dissociative, or the "It's not me!" self. It is an unconscious construct that essentially creates the alters, while tricking the patient into believing that they are not part of her/him, much the way the man behind the curtain wanted to be ignored while he created the illusion of the Wizard of Oz. It is elusive and evades engagement in the therapeutic alliance, as it is the core of the dissociative defense armamentarium. This dissociative self needs to be dissolved in order for integration to occur, and has at its disposal several organizing influences that help in the creation and maintenance of the conviction of separateness (Brenner 2001). Freud's (1923a) view that different identifications might take over consciousness at different times is necessary but not sufficient to explain the unique and at times bizarre quality of the alters. The elucidation of these organizing influences, therefore, may further our understanding of this phenomenon.

The influences that have come to light so far through analytic exploration are (1) the fragmenting effects of internalized aggression on mental states; (2) perverse sexuality, that is, different personifications encapsulating different traumatic memories, aggression, and anxiety by traversing various sexual developmental pathways, such as sadomasochistic heterosexuality, homosexuality, and transsexualism; (3) intergenerational transmission of trauma, that is, the abuser's own trauma history becoming incorporated into the biography of certain alters; (4) near-death experiences in childhood, that is, out-of-body, telepathic-like phenomena; and (5) the ego functioning seen in the dream state. It appears that the mind's capacity to anthropomorphize altered states of consciousness, such as in hypnogogic and hypnopompic states, may also occur during traumatic autohypnotic states. Recurrent dreams of such experiences may then help to reinforce and solidify a sense of separateness. The common origin of both dreams and alters may be seen in such patients who report dreams of witnessing unknown children endure the identical experiences that their alters report firsthand in the awake dissociated states. A reciprocal amnesia is often present in that the patient, when reporting the dream, has no memory of the dissociated state, and while in the dissociated state has no memory of the reported dream (Brenner 2001). Because this particular manifestation of the dream ego is a relatively unfamiliar one, the similarities between the dream state and the altered state in DID may be recognized but not fully appreciated.

Most analysts would agree that it would surely be a sign of progress if patients started to remember their dreams and report them in the treatment setting. It would be seen as even further progress if those patients associated to them and made connections to their past and how their minds work. This attitude is based on a century of study and observation of this "royal road" to the unconscious (Freud 1900). Indeed, Freud's recognition of the importance of dreams led him to hope one day to unite the psychology of dreams with psychopathology. Is DID that missing link (Brenner 1996b)?

But imagine for a moment what it would be like for patients to report their dreams to a therapist who doubted the dreams' existence and who had no understanding of their role in the patients' inner lives! In such a situation, the patients' expanding dream life might be misdiagnosed as a serious regression of psychotic proportion.

To complicate matters further, suppose there are others who believe that dreams are a dangerous by-product of the therapeutic interaction. So instead of just confusing dreams for psychotic decompensation, the additional error would be to blame the clinician for iatrogenically inducing dreams to develop! Could an analogy then be drawn to the misunderstandings and confusion about the dissociative disorders, especially DID? While it certainly may be that exploitation of patients may occasionally occur for perverse reasons or secondary gain by deviant therapists, there is not one documented case of iatrogenic DID to my knowledge.

Extreme anxiety about the reality of severe trauma or skepticism about the legitimacy of the condition predisposes one to embrace iatrogenic theories of causation and airtight circular reasoning that may then result in premature closure on thinking any deeper about the subject. Indeed, it is a double irony that the now legendary case of Anna O., Josef Breuer's patient who was treated by the "talking cure" that inspired psychoanalysis, was not only considered a case of *double personality*, one of the many archaic terms for DID (Breuer and Freud 1893–1895, Jones 1953), but has also been more recently decried as a massive case of fraud (Borch-Jacobsen 1996). It is for these reasons and more that I have found it imperative to explore in depth how the various personifications, the hallmark of this condition (APA 1994), are created and what function they serve in the psyche. In so doing, I have been able to develop a basis of understanding, which seems to have predictive value for what may emerge in the therapeutic situation. The nature of this clinical interaction, however, depends on the goals of treatment that may range from palliative, supportive care to vigorous intensive efforts to achieve a cure. Crucial factors include not only the theoretical approach employed, but also the therapist's ability to tolerate, contain, and empathize with the patient's subjective internal experience and behavior. From a broader perspective, what therefore may be judged as decompensation or iatrogenic causation when, for example, new alter personalities emerge may become more comprehensible with a better understanding of the psychic structure and the impact of the therapeutic relationship, which provides the opportunity to articulate that which has not been symbolized or verbalized before (Bromberg 1998).

A Historical Note

Although there are many excellent reviews describing the history of the condition (Ellenberger 1970, Greaves 1993, Ross 1989, Ross and Lowenstein 1992), the contributions of Sandor Ferenczi, the Hungarian psychoanalytic pioneer, are generally minimized or overlooked. A disagreement over his emphasis on the magnitude of the problem of sexual abuse may have contributed to Ferenczi's break with Freud and the other members of the inner circle at the end of his career. Like a parent's attempt to squash the child's revelations of incest, Ferenczi had been discouraged from presenting his landmark "Confusion of Tongues" (Ferenczi 1933) paper to the International Psychoanalytic Congress in Wiesbaden, Germany in 1932 because it was seen as a heretical step backward by reviving the seduction theory of neurosis. Freud dismissed it as "harmless and dumb," but the furor it stirred up enabled Ernest Jones, Ferenczi's longtime rival for Freud's affection to block its publication in English until 1949 (Blue 1994). It was not even available in his native Hungarian until 1971 (Rachman 1997)!

Ferenczi, who was dying of pernicious anemia, was discredited as being psychotic because of a deteriorating brain (Rachman 1997), but a modern rereading of this remarkable essay shows not only great clarity, but it "presaged a widened interest in the analyst's analyzing functions, unconscious communication, countertransference, and the interplay of reality and fantasy inside and outside the analytic situation" (Blum 1994, p. 871). Regarding his insights into sexual abuse, Ferenczi described the importance of (1) domination by the adult perpetrator, resulting in emotional surrender and robotlike obedience, that is, becoming an automaton; (2) the correlation between defenses like dissociation to cope with severe early trauma and later characterological problems; (3) the child's renouncing his/her own reality testing in order to conform to the needs of the parents; (4) the presence of pervasive confusion as an overriding state, resulting in the belief that the abuse is an act of love rather than exploitation for the adult's own sexual gratification; and (5) identification with the aggressor resulting in the shared pseudo-delusion that they are in a mutually tender and beneficial relationship (Rachman 1999).

Sounding rather contemporary in his attempt to reconcile Janet and Freud, Ferenczi (1933) observed:

> If the shocks increase in number during the development of the child, the number and the various kinds of splits in the personality increase too, and soon it becomes extremely difficult to maintain contact without confusion with all the fragments, each of which behaves as a separate personality yet does not know of even the existence of the others. . . . I hope even here to be able to find threads that can link up the various parts. [p. 165]

It may be that the suppression of Ferenczi's work was a factor in the "Dark Ages" before the renaissance of analytic interest in DID in the late 1970s and early 1980s (Berman 1981, Laskey 1978, Marmer 1980). In other words, the "lost tribe" of these disturbed and disturbing patients may be seen as returning to the fold, but they remain rather enigmatic.

Nearly seventy years later, despite all the advances in theory, technique, and pharmacology, DID remains the most controversial psychiatric entity and perhaps still one of the most challenging to treat.

AN INTERNATIONAL PERSPECTIVE

In a search of the world literature on dissociative disorders, one of the countries seen to be actively doing research is Turkey. It is a country beset with both natural and man-made disasters. As I understand it, the Turkish psychiatrists learned from the Dutch, read what the Americans had written, and then proceeded to make their own contributions in the areas of epidemiology, phenomenology, and treatment (R. Kluft, M.D., personal communication, 2000). Skeptics of these conditions are prone to view them as culturally influenced phenomena indigenous to North America, but the experience throughout the world in places like the Netherlands, Norway, and Turkey suggest otherwise. For example, Tutkun and colleagues (1998) reported a prevalence of at least 5 percent of all their newly diagnosed inpatients fulfilling criteria for DID. And this statistic does not even include all the previously diagnosed cases. Apparently, many such individuals may initially receive the diagnosis of hysterical psychosis, a category used by many Turkish clinicians even though it is not part of any official nomenclature (Tutkun et al. 1996).

> One such case reported in the literature was that of a 45-year-old woman who lived 40 kilometers from downtown Istanbul in a semi-urban area. In her dissociated self states, she revealed and enacted a history of physical abuse by her mother as well as sexual abuse by an older brother and uncle. After her father died when she was 14, she was forced into an arranged marriage that she experienced as a perpetuation of the sexual abuse. Nine of her fourteen children died shortly after birth and she carried on extramarital affairs in amnestic altered states for many years. She decompensated after the death of her mother when after decades she returned to her hometown of Bursa, which triggered forgotten

> memories of her childhood. When she presented to the emergency room she appeared to be in a psychotic state, experiencing visual and auditory hallucinations ordering her to kill family members. She exhibited rapidly labile affect, amnesia, headaches, and suicidal urges. Twenty-one personalities were identified during her treatment, which was conducted in both the inpatient and outpatient settings for over two years.

The authors speculated that the patient's relatively rapid integration was possible because she had considerable ego strength to have encapsulated her traumas for as long as she had and because she was both geographically and temporally removed from the traumatic environment. They noted that in rural areas of Turkey in families where the father dies early or where the mother is negligent, the eldest daughter is often sent to live with other families to assume adult responsibilities at too early an age and to be forced into arranged marriages. Although such customs have long been known, the associated risk of sexual abuse and its psychological sequelae were not appreciated in Turkey until the last decade (Sar and Tutkun 1997). However, the role of unresolved grief in cases similar to this one may be an additional traumatic factor that is not always appreciated when the emphasis is exclusively on the descriptive and psychiatric aspects. Such factors emerge when one has the opportunity to work in depth with these individuals.

I address some of these deeper issues through the following case report of a woman in treatment for a number of years, focusing on the therapeutic alliance, transference, countertransference, and certain interventions unique to this population. I present the material according to the stages of treatment that I have found to be useful in this work:

1. Therapeutic alliance
2. Delineation of the mosaic transference

3. Challenging the "It's not me!" self
4. On the road to integration
5. Consolidation and working through

CASE REPORT

Mrs. A., a married woman in her late thirties and the mother of two children, was referred for treatment after a series of hospitalizations over the previous five years failed to help her get control of her mental deterioration and suicidal despair. She had had a professional career that put her in contact with hazardous materials, and she had been intentionally mishandling them, putting herself at great medical risk. In addition, her long-standing eating disorder had been exacerbated, so she was bingeing, purging, abusing laxatives, and becoming addicted to toxic emetics. She had consulted numerous therapists of various disciplines with varying degrees of expertise and had even been admitted to some of the most prestigious institutions in the nation, but to no avail. What was concluded, however, was that the suicide of a male relative may have been a precipitant to her decompensation. Mrs. A., however, denied this connection to her problems, and instead ascribed her progressive decline to her therapists' encouraging her to talk about her never-forgotten memories of early sexual abuse by this dead relative. Her strategy for years had been simply to not think about it and pretend that it did not happen. She was oblivious to the fact that she would lapse into trancelike states for minutes or even hours at a time, and would return to her usual state of mind without realizing it. However, she was convinced that her condition had deteriorated at an accelerated pace once she explored her memories of childhood and a brutal gang rape in college after which she was left for dead.

The youngest daughter of three children born to an egocentric, troubled, and unavailable woman whose military husband was away for long periods of time, Mrs. A. grew up alone and lonely. Her mother was addicted to sedatives and frequently left her unsupervised or in the care of an uninterested older sibling. A male relative spent much time with her and sexually abused her on a regular basis. Not all of her sexual experiences with him were forced and painful, however, leaving her with profound guilt, doubt, and confusion. A review of her previous hospital records described intermittent agitated outbursts and periods of time curled up in closets sucking her thumb. In each situation she seemed disoriented and psychologically unreachable. In this former state of mind she was terrified and screamed, "Get away from me!" whereas in the latter state she was either mute or cried quietly like a little girl. Mrs. A. had amnesia for these episodes, thought the staff was lying about her, and absolutely refused to talk about these reports. In her usual state of mind, she was generally sullen, sad, secretive, and silent. Interestingly, not only was the diagnosis of DID not considered, but even the term *dissociated states* was rarely used.

Coupled with her conviction that therapy only made her worse and the growing specter of litigation resulting in huge monetary settlements for false memories allegedly implanted by her former therapists, Mrs. A. had no faith in doctors and had nothing to say. To her, I had nothing new to offer except perhaps continuity of care. I sensed her utter hopelessness about being deemed a treatment failure and had my own doubts about what anyone could do for her. So I proceeded slowly and with great caution with this catastrophically ill woman. Because she had made several serious suicide attempts in the past and was convinced she did not deserve to live, I informed her and her family at the outset that whatever we were dealing with was a potentially lethal condition. I made no promises that I could help her but said I would be willing to work with her if we could agree on some basic ground rules: (1) the patient's making every effort to stay alive from one session to the next; (2) our meeting four to five times per week, inpatient or outpatient; (3) the patient's saying everything that comes to mind including thoughts, feelings, emotions, and bodily sensations; (4) our deciding on a mutually acceptable fee. My emphasis was on the fundamental rule for such a patient, that she needed to include reporting all sensory input, that is, what she felt in her body and what she saw, heard, smelled, or tasted.

The Therapy

STAGE 1: THERAPEUTIC ALLIANCE

Mrs. A. worked hard to get me to give up on her, sabotaging treatment by not talking, by being evasive, and at times by lying. She insisted that she was untreatable, and her frailty due to starvation and dehydration made her extremely sensitive to the hypotensive effects of virtually every class of psychoactive drug. Nothing really helped her except benzodiazepines in acute panic states. Furthermore, she insisted that it was necessary to have the safety valve of purging because any effort to stop it would only result in more serious self-destructive behavior. Cutting and burning with her ever-present cigarettes (smoking was her only acknowledged passion in life), left her already-disfigured body even more scarred. She flatly stated that she was determined to make her body look as disgusting on the outside as she felt on the inside, and she was equally determined to prove to me that there was no such thing as a talking cure. In her disintegrated mind, she was a disgusting, contaminated whore, who, because she was unable to fight off her assailants, would have been better off dead. Her fantasy life was consumed by planning the perfect punishment for her crimes, ranging from burning and cutting to amputation of her limbs or any bodily part that failed to protect her or was involved in the sexual activity.

A typical session in the early months of treatment was characterized by her anxious silences, total lack of curiosity, evasiveness, intentional deceptiveness, and trance-like withdrawal. Since her sense of morality generally did not permit her to lie outright, if asked the right question she would give an honest answer. Mrs. A. would spontaneously drift into her reveries and at times even when I tried to redirect her with banal conversation, she would lapse into a state where her eyes would glaze over and she would become mute and unresponsive. These stuporous states would continue well after the end of the session, and when she regained her alertness she would have no recollection of her former state. On occasion, when I would share my observations with her, she conveyed a total lack of interest ("la belle indifference" to an extreme) and refused to discuss the matter further. In my efforts to develop a therapeutic alliance I felt as though I were groping for a foothold on a slippery mountain because what little rapport we had during her usual state of alertness would completely evaporate during her absences. My work with previous patients taught me the necessity of developing a therapeutic alliance in all states of consciousness as a prerequisite for continued work. I observed but did not comment on certain subtle behavioral differences in her states, such as her wearing a special hat on some days, and her insisting on sitting on the floor on some days but being garrulous and jocular and sitting in a chair on other days. Throughout this phase, I assured her that my interest in her day-to-day safety took precedence over hearing the details of her horrible experiences throughout her life. I tried to focus on her here-and-now functioning, essentially offering to be an auxiliary ego and memory bank. I also told her that it seemed that she had very little sense of continuity from one session to the next, which was based on my countertransference feelings and subjectivity from day to day. At times, I became sleepy, too, as though she were putting me into a trance also. If I were to become so relaxed, perhaps I too would become forgetful and spare her the agony of remembering. I also wondered whether she were unconsciously inducing me to enact her relationship with her drugged mother, who was oblivious to her early needs and to her danger.

Several months into treatment there was a brief opening in her defensive wall. It occurred at the end of our fifth session of the week when she tearfully confessed just how scared, confused, and out of control she often felt. Given the fragmentation of her previous care with a non-M.D. primary outpatient therapist, an outpatient psychiatrist, a family therapist, an inpatient primary therapist, and an inpatient psychiatrist, I wondered how the blockages in her mind might have been represented externally by her team of professionals who did not communicate with one another and left her feeling that no one was in charge. As if their internal worlds mirror their early relationships, such patients often report a family life of isolation, secrecy, indifference to suffering, and deceptive use of language that becomes a template for their personifications, who "behave" similarly.

Fairbairn (1952), the object relations theorist from the British Middle School, had an interest in multiple personality also and he favored the term *personification* instead of *alter personality*. He believed that fusion and layering of introjects helped explain this phenomenon. The renewed appreciation of Sullivan's (1953) interpersonal theory warrants further mention here also. He too used the term *personification* but not specifically in reference to DID. His emphasis was on both the internalization of people and of their interpersonal relationships. In addition, he conceptualized the "not me" in reference to dissociated mental contents, but his purpose was to explain what was projected in paranoid states. In DID, by contrast, the patient employs a pseudo-externalized displacement so that what is disowned or "not me" is attributed to one's inside people instead. It is this function that I ascribe to the dissociative self.

I suspected that Mrs. A. was close to inflicting major self-injury again and might be ready to take me into her confidence. I told the patient that unlike her previous therapists, I would be her doctor both in the hospital and as an outpatient, so she need not fear the same fragmentation of treatment as before. Though she seemed visibly relieved to be reminded of our arrangement, she dreaded rehospitalization and my concern for her safety prompted a discussion about involuntary admission. The possibility of my being induced into forcing her to do something against her will had the definite quality of a sadomasochistic enactment, which I tried to convey to her. While I doubted that she truly understood the significance of my comment, she did sign herself into the hospital of her own free will, where a medical evaluation revealed weight loss, dehydration, electrolyte imbalance, hypoglycemia, and numerous fresh burns on her emaciated chest and pelvic area.

While medically restabilizing, Mrs. A. lapsed into altered states and remained inaccessible. She made attempts to express herself artistically by making a collage depicting violence, sin, blood, and punishment, but abruptly stopped the activity each time she started. However, she made an important disclosure—that she felt that she was not being allowed to continue! This experience of feeling controlled by an inner power, reminiscent of schizophrenia, completely dominated her and prevented her from continuing any form of verbal or artistic expression. As if being held hostage by her inner censor, she reluctantly agreed to try to write me a note. Mrs. A. quickly scribbled a line saying that "the unknown one" would not let her say any more. Sensing that the patient disowned her mental functioning relating to will, action, and responsibility, and ascribed it to a mysterious inner force, literally known as "the unknown one," I was still uncertain as to the extent to which it was personified. Trying not to reify this state of mind any more than Mrs. A. already had, I was careful to use only her words and tried to empathize with her subjective experience. While I thought it a bit ironic to be concerned that a patient as negativistic and withholding as Mrs. A. might be unduly vulnerable to suggestion, much of her rebelliousness may have been a characterological defense to her susceptibility to being hypnotically dominated. In fact, Janet (1907) described this paradox as follows: "Suggestibility with them should not in fact be considered a simple exaggeration of docility or normal belief. Such persons are neither docile nor believing. They have an unsteady, undisciplined disposition; they themselves recognize that they do not succeed in believing" (p. 288). What I realized later was that while it was almost impossible for Mrs. A. to say no to her male relative and all her subsequent victimizers, her harshly unforgiving superego remained remarkably refractory to outside ameliorating influences. The patient at this point had little or no observing ego, no understanding, and no curiosity about how her mind worked. All that she did know was that she was very bad, that she was like a puppet on a string, and that she already knew too much. I told her that in my experience it was necessary for me to learn how to communicate with her in all states of mind, even those with which she had no knowledge, as I reminded her of the clinical observations that others had made about her over the years. I used the metaphor of building a bridge, which required solid foundations on each riverbank. She looked bewildered, but I informed her that an attitude of openness was more important than specific knowledge on her part. Furthermore, I told her that it was important to recognize that however strange and frightening things felt inside her mind, it all had meaning and was there for very important reasons. As a result, it was potentially understandable and needed to be respected, even if we could not decipher it yet. Essentially, I was speaking to her dissociative self or what DID therapists might called the "total human being." I was not talking just to Mrs. A., a construction perhaps related to Winnicott's concept of a false self who might be referred to as the "host personality," the mediator to the outside world. Mrs. A. was the social facade, as it were, who could not do her job if she was constantly overwhelmed with bad memories and the associated affects.

The patient's behind-the-scenes dissociative self tried to ward off anxiety by wanting to believe that whatever it was, maybe it didn't really happen, or if it did, it must have happened to somebody else. And indeed, this doubt and disowning were the predominant defenses expressed by Mrs. A., who tried to keep everything under control through the most stringently obsessive dietary restrictions. She would calculate the caloric content of every morsel of food, setting ever-lower daily goals of intake in order to discipline herself. When she failed, she would feel overwhelmed with disgust and feel forced to purge, which then increased her self-loathing and required more punishment of herself. Her idiosyncratic inner world of restrictions, rewards, and punishments was tinged with deep religious convictions, and totally consumed her attention, as she desperately tried to buffer herself from any other influences through this near-delusional preoccupation. Unfortunately, "the unknown one" part of her who demanded to remain unknown was full of rage, had remembered what had happened, and was unable to keep it all completely encapsulated. Essentially, her unmetabolized and unarticulated traumas threatened her with annihilation anxiety, and when this material broke through, Mrs. A. hurt herself as a punishment and to toughen herself up in preparation for the next time something might happen.

The situation was complicated by confusion over the

passage of time and the distinction between past and present, which was not amenable to any intervention at this time. So the patient's own strategy for coping was quite simple: "Don't talk, don't think, don't feel, and don't remember. Let what is 'unknown' remain unknown." I told her that from her perspective this philosophy made perfect sense and had helped her over the years, as it was the mind's natural way of coping with overwhelming situations. Furthermore, I empathized with her strong belief that talking about it was completely counterintuitive to her. Unfortunately, the efforts to suppress what had already been coming forth over the last several years was not working anymore and it appeared that, like Humpty Dumpty, she perhaps was not able to put all the pieces back the way they had been. Consequently, the only way I knew how to potentially help was for her to go forward and learn new ways to deal with her anxieties. Once again, the patient looked bewildered and doubtful, but I continued as I sensed that conveying a feeling of hope was more crucial at this time than the actual content of my words.

The patient's impulse control stabilized enough for her to be discharged from the hospital, but she was not able to stay safe for much more than a month and was repeatedly hospitalized. This continued pattern raised the perennial question about her treatability, and her insurance company contemplated curtailing reimbursement for acute care, pushing for a transfer to a state facility; she stated she would kill herself if she were sent there, which was more than just a manipulative threat. Mrs. A.'s vulnerability to retraumatization was so great that being in such an environment with so many disturbed people would likely have felt like another gang-rape situation to her. But I told the patient that there was only so much I could do, and by acknowledging my realistic limits, I tried to convey that I could not miraculously save her if there was no cooperation from "the other river bank," as it were.

A Crisis

The situation continued relatively unchanged, with the patient's enormous resistances, self-mutilation, and fears of engagement persisting into the second year of treatment, when a shocking incident in a session brought me face to face with "the unknown one." As the session proceeded, the patient revealed that once again her impulse control was waning and that she felt "the unknown one" to be very nearby. I asked if there was anything I could do to help her stay safe, and an instant later she reached into her pocket, pulled out a razor, and with a crazed look, started screaming that she had to toughen up Mrs. A., as she made a series of deep incisions along her forearms. I was stunned, and I sat there momentarily frozen, staring at the dripping blood and the exposed tendons, which resembled dissection from medical school. The patient raged on triumphantly as I, feeling helpless and transfixed, watched her butcher herself. She refused to relinquish the blade, which I feared might be used on me if I tried to wrestle it from her. When I regained a modicum of composure, which seemed like hours (although it was probably less than a minute), I realized that "the unknown one's" dramatic and bloody introduction signaled a new phase of treatment and left no doubt in my mind about the diagnosis. At that point, I asked Mrs. A. to come back immediately, but the bloodletting continued, so I asked if there was someone else inside who could come and help. This was the first time I tried to access an alter in this patient; within moments after my distress call, the patient's facial expression, body language, agitation, and rage subsided, and the other Mrs. A. emerged, quietly and innocently asking me what I wanted, and requesting that I whisper so as not to wake up Mrs. A.! I explained that there was a major problem with the left arm and that I needed her assistance immediately. She looked at it in surprise, said she felt no pain, and dutifully handed me the blade while I found some paper towels. Getting her permission to apply direct pressure to her incision, I slowed the bleeding. While I was ministering to her wound and trying to think of the next step, the other Mrs. A. told me that the Mrs. A. I knew would have been too upset to come back, and so she had to come out to help instead. She could not tell me how such a decision was made, but I agreed that as long as she could cooperatively handle the situation, it was fine with me. Arrangements were made for her to be taken to the nearest emergency room, after which time she was rehospitalized, where I got to know "the unknown one" a little better under safer conditions.

STAGE 2: DELINEATION OF THE MOSAIC TRANSFERENCE

Over time, other distinctly defined personifications identified themselves, such as the little girl who sucked her thumb in the closet, and several other androgynous selves who were much more forthcoming and at times actually seemed to enjoy the sessions. It seemed evident that the others felt and expressed what Mrs. A. could not, be it impotent rage and internalized aggression, a wish to be understood and cared about in the transference, or vivid, unchanging details of her repeated abuse by her male relative as well as the gang rape she had suffered in college. In addition, their diverse opinions expressed her intrapsychic conflict as a pseudo-externalized interpersonal conflict, as well as being different manifestations of her mosaic transference. For example, there was enormous conflict over the female anatomy, and "the unknown one" hated me for having a man's body. Convinced that it was a mistake of nature, "he" wanted a sex change in order to make things right. This dissociated transsexualism, a major organizing influence in the development of her separate selves, emerged as a central conflict throughout the treatment. Furthermore, the patient was haunted by recurrent dreams of watching somebody get defiled, and these nightmares corresponded to the first-hand account that "the unknown one" had raged about in the sessions. In these situations, there was reciprocal amnesia, and the patient would either wake up from the dream or come back after "the unknown one" was out, gagging from a gustatory hallucination of having feces in her mouth.

The neutralization of her aggression, the softening of her savage superego, and the development of her observing ego were the next steps in the long-term treatment of this patient. However, there were a number of subsequent self-inflicted violent regressions that were life threatening. They seemed to be related to the anniversaries of the rape and the death of her male relative, to secret sexual liaisons in altered states where she could not refuse the attention and the advances of unsavory men and women, and to the tensions arising in the transference. The intimacy of the consultation room was overwhelming at times, as her longings for protection, understanding, and love made her feel disgusting and sinful. Her separation anxiety was also crippling, as she manifested chaotic states during my absences. Consistent with recent findings correlating disorganized, disoriented attachment disturbances in childhood with later dissociative psychopathology (Liotti 1992), she was at great risk during these times. In sessions, she would spontaneously "switch" to stave off the anxiety. For example, her sexualized selves might emerge and become flirtatious after Mrs. A. would become sullen or withdrawn following vague associations related to her forbidden wishes. These alters also divulged their secret relationships as well as recollections of earlier abuse that Mrs. A. did not remember. Or she might lapse into the thumb-sucking child, hiding in the corner. Other times, she would scream and rage at me, having no memory of these demonstrations of her compartmentalized mind.

During her second year of treatment, around the time of the anniversary of the gang rape in college, she cut her left wrist several times, inflicting nerve damage and hoping to paralyze her hand completely. Her plan was to place her arm under the path of an oncoming train, but after lying on the tracks for several hours, she became impatient and sought other means. She never forgave herself for not being able to defend herself, and sought to punish her left hand for the sexual acts it was forced to perform. She was rehospitalized, at which time a severe self-induced osteomyelitis of her index finger almost required the surgeons to perform the amputation for her. When she learned that the antibiotics were helping, she went into a silent rage. One evening in the hospital, "the unknown one" emerged and severed the finger with the sharp edge of a soda can, flushing it down the toilet so it could not be reattached. When Mrs. A. "returned," she was blasé and somewhat relieved by the amputation, which shocked and traumatized the nursing staff. The "curative" effects of this drastic measure lasted several months, until an upsurge of uncontrollable urges to remove the rest of the hand necessitated a readmission. Despite efforts to protect her through a supervised living arrangement and to extract her promises not to do further harm, "the unknown one" and his inner assistant, "Billy," were preparing for another amputation, which occurred about a year later. It was skillfully performed with a hacksaw purchased from a hardware store, and once again, the digit was discarded before she calmly drove herself to the hospital emergency room.

Following the completed amputation of the second finger, the therapeutic alliance reached a new low. It was painfully clear that the patient's capacity to delay acting on her explosive urges was extremely poor, and when she did broadcast her desperation it was usually veiled. Evidence of premeditation was found after the fact with notes that had been written shortly before the bloody act as though on some level she knew it would be just a matter of time before she had to act. Despite her affirmed safety contract as well as her promise to notify me, ask for extra medication, and request hospitalization for her safety, she helplessly acknowledged that when things happened so quickly in her mind it felt like she were falling into a black hole. But it was a relief to have "the unknown one" take over and do whatever was necessary to stop the psychic pain. The flashbacks of her rape were so graphic that she was convinced that it was happening all over again. She experienced gustatory hallucinations of feces, pressure on her arms and legs, excruciating genital pain, indescribable terror, and the feeling of contamination so intense that no amount of bathing, scrubbing, or scalding hot water could ever get her clean. Her sense of humiliation, worthlessness, and utter degradation was so great that she was almost literally dying of shame. No treatment up to this point had been able to stop the constellation of symptoms that to an observer looked like a major motor seizure complete with tonic clonic movements, falling to the ground, extreme arching of her back, frightening choking noises, occasional cyanosis, and violent pelvic thrusting. However, her electroencephalogram (EEG) was negative, she never bit her tongue, and she never became incontinent. She seemed so unreachable during these hysterical episodes and experienced so much disorientation and amnesia afterward that this aftermath resembled a postictal confusion. The only solution that she knew would short-circuit this sequence was severe self-mutilation. In her "the unknown one" state of mind she created an autohypnotic anesthesia so that she could burn, cut, or perform surgery on herself quite painlessly. This toughening was seen as a strengthening exercise that was rationalized in order to live through the rape once again with impunity. In so doing, her body would not go through its motoric gyrations and the devastating emotional aftermath. As a result "the unknown one" and his protégé, "Billy," were ironically seen as protectors, not as the internalization of brutal torturers that they appeared to be to an outside observer. In her inner world, relief of psychic pain was paramount, and if parts of the body needed to be sacrificed for that cause, that was acceptable to her. Furthermore, her left hand was forced into performing sexual acts on the men so it was deemed an evil part that should be punished.

Another irony occurred during this time, when several members of her deeply religious Christian community were urging her to change doctors because she suspected that I was Jewish. I did not work on the Jewish high holidays that occur each fall, but she was too timid to ask me directly. When she further deteriorated, her friends told her about a special ceremony that could be performed in order to rid her body of the devil. Mrs. A. became very agitated and confused, not knowing what to do, and she revealed this dilemma to me. It was a challenge to my countertransference and my anonymity as I initially felt a bit of anti-Semitic discrimination in her comments. It seemed that exploring her fantasies of my religious affiliation, while enormously significant, would not have furthered the process at this time. So I handled her resistance on a reality-oriented basis and told her that I was Jewish and that I could understand how someone might find consolation in seeking help from someone of the same faith. I then added that I did not view her problem as one of demonic possession and had never seen an exorcism as being therapeutic. On the contrary, I was concerned that such a procedure might further jeopardize her mental disturbance. But being sensitive to the issues and to the utter gravity of her situation, I did tell her that if she insisted on such a consultation I would not oppose it as long as I could first assess her spiritual counselor's knowledge and competence in the treatment of mental illness. Interestingly, she seemed relieved that I did not simply accede to her wish on the grounds of my ignorance of her religious needs. A more open discussion about her loss of faith and disillusionment in Jesus Christ then ensued.

She did not pursue the exorcism and felt protected by me from her well-intentioned friends whose intrusiveness overwhelmed her. She then described how she was totally preoccupied with the Book of Revelations and how she was waiting for the end of the world as her only hope for salvation. She then expressed a rare showing of curiosity, asking questions about Judaism, resulting in one of our first free exchanges of ideas in over eighteen months of treatment. This islet of rapport enabled me to confront her in a way that both amused her and made her stop and reflect about how she was treating herself. I told her that her amputation of her fingers and her wish to sever the whole hand was more reminiscent of the Old Testament dictum of "an eye for an eye, a tooth for a tooth" than anything I knew of in the New Testament. I told her that she seemed more like an ancient Jew than I did! She chuckled softly as her mood temporarily lifted and while we both knew that no single verbal intervention would cure her, I sensed a deepening of her trust.

I subsequently learned from "Billy," one of her self-destructive protectors, that the instrument used in the amputation was not disposed of as originally claimed. In fact it was hidden in her car, so I asked that she contact her husband to retrieve it and deliver it to me. By this time I had met with her family several times during her repeated hospitalizations and saw how her young sons were appropriately terrified that their mother might die. It was heart wrenching to see them cry and beg her to get better and to see her husband helplessly retreat into a corner while she either lapsed into a trance or would gently but falsely reassure them in tender loving tones that everything would be all right. It was a bit sickening to see the blood-stained metal hacksaw that she used, a chilling testament to her capacity to unconsciously anesthetize herself, to the precision of her surgical skills (the hand surgeons had nothing to do after she presented herself to the emergency room except to suture and bandage the cleanly severed stumps), and to the depth of her internalized destructive aggression.

Because of the potentially lethal quasi-delusional tendency in such patients to disown the body and to believe that whatever one personification might do would not affect the others, I was hoping to incorporate the hacksaw into the treatment. I announced to Mrs. A. and to her "It's not me" self that it might be helpful if everyone had a chance to see what was used to remove the fingers. Mrs. A. was overwhelmed but listened and looked at the implement in a wide-eyed stare. I actively accessed "Billy," who gave me a mildly contrite but coldly detached account about how he and "the unknown one" had performed the different surgeries. Her inner allies "Sam" and "Danny," two androgynous helpers who would occasionally report the patient's suicidal plans but were helpless to stop the action, also inspected the saw. They became rather upset and promised to try harder in the future to warn me of such disastrous plans. The younger "inside children," I was told, were crying too much and were too scared to come out and view the hacksaw directly. It became clear from my own behavior that I felt angry with the patient and was forcing her to look at what she had done in the hopes of inducing enough conflict in her so that such behavior would become ego dystonic. In a sense, I felt like the mother of an anal stage child, forcing the toddler to look at the mess that she had made in order to teach her how to use the toilet. We were aware of my stern demeanor and solemnity at this time, and she listened carefully. I felt as though I was confronting the personification of her death instinct, and dealing with an unpredictable insurance company that might conclude that she was hopelessly chronically ill and refuse to pay for any further acute care. The threat of institutionalization in a state hospital where she would no longer be under my care and would be subject to predatory behavior by the unsupervised mass of patients hung over both of us as a variable that was out of my control. I simply told her that I might not be able to protect her from that fate, which might remind her of her mother's abandonment of her.

Winnicott's (1963) observations about working with severely character-disordered patients gave me some solace during this very uncertain time:

> The patient will from time to time be acting out and as long as this has a relation to the transference, it can be managed and interpreted. . . . In this work the failure of the therapist or of those managing the child's life will be real and they can be shown to reproduce the original failures in token form. The acknowledgement of the analyst's failure . . . enables the patient to become appropriately angry instead of traumatized. The patient needs to reach back through the transference trauma to the state of affairs that obtained before the original trauma. . . .The patient's experience of anger that is appropriate, frees the patient's maturational processes; and it must be remembered that the patient is in a dependent state and needing ego support and environmental management (holding) in the treatment setting, and the next phase needs to be a period of emotional growth in which the character builds up and closes the distortion. [pp. 208–209]

Indeed I very much felt like a mother who was unable to protect her child, and if I failed her, I would be replicating her childhood.

STAGE 3: CHALLENGING THE "IT'S NOT ME!" SELF

Sensing some movement in the patient's alters regarding the awareness of their shared fate, I wondered if this was the dawning of a collective observing ego. I tried to take advantage of what I feared was a fleeting new insight and offered her a series of interventions that I have termed a "revolving door" interpretation. It has been my experience with such profoundly disturbed patients that standard interpretations (Allegro 1992) often do not work even when clear transference phenomena are operative, because the subjective sense of separateness of the inner selves is so great. So, at a time when she seemed a bit curious, I told her that it might be helpful if she could temporarily experience the connectedness of the different parts of her mind, so she could begin to believe that there was a chance for her survival. She was skeptical but agreeable. I then employed a modest suggestive technique that enabled Mrs. A. and "Billy" to rapidly trade places with each other, so each would be in executive control of the body and conscious mind for very brief periods of time. The patient's head was almost literally spinning during this experience, as though the patient and her personification were going round and round in a revolving door and taking turns poking their heads outside whenever they could. During this time, both Mrs. A. and "Billy" were even briefly out at the same time, an experience that felt very weird, frightening, and a bit exhilarating. For the moment, Mrs. A. could not deny that she felt the psychical relatedness to her inner people, and her defensive structure, the dissociative or "It's not me!" self had dissolved. However, she was not ready to own her mental contents for more than a few minutes at a time, so her insight was lost shortly thereafter. Nevertheless, a new and more honest spirit of cooperation developed afterward, which renewed and strengthened the therapeutic alliance. This intervention was repeated several more times over the subsequent months, as the patient gradually began to accept the "others" as indeed part of her mind. She also seemed to have acquired a bit more ego strength, in that she could tolerate more frustration and could delay acting on her impulses long enough to ask for help.

STAGE 4: ON THE ROAD TO INTEGRATION

Although the risk of another amputation remained a continuing concern as we entered the fourth year of treatment, I had the distinct impression that much more of the patient's mind was engaged in the therapeutic process. She took more initiative to try and communicate with the other parts of her mind, writing almost daily in her journal that she often brought to the sessions and read to me. The fear of never seeing her children again seemed to be the primary motivation for her wish to get better, as marital strain and the progressive awareness of the seriousness of her condition could not be denied any longer. There were observable changes in her psyche that suggested some further progress, even if her tendency toward regression remained great. For example, "the unknown one" had become dormant and it appeared that the repository of her aggression had become localized to "Billy." This personification, although still quite potentially dangerous, was able to speak more freely with me and would even walk over to shake my hand each time he would emerge. However, he refused to talk about his transsexual conflict. Billy had become much more sympathetic to Mrs. A.'s plight regarding her children, whereas in the past they were seen as a major annoyance who might interfere with his plan to keep her tough and prepare her for the next rape. Furthermore, the patient had become a bit more able to refuse sexual advances. In addition, her motoric reliving of the rape, lying helpless on her back, was transformed into a screaming, frenzied flight. A more defined personification named "Sally" was identified as the one who would try to run away from the rapists. She was plagued by day with hallucinations reliving this assault and haunted by night with nightmares of the event, which seemed to be a condensation of all the traumas in her life.

From a descriptive standpoint, there was a symptom substitution as the hysterical seizures were replaced by fugue states. During these states, which came with alarming frequency as she was easily triggered by crowds, stimulating TV shows, and her anxiety in the transference, the patient was totally disoriented to her surroundings. This latest development resulted in repeated enactments of being caught and held down when it occurred during her hospitalizations. As an outpatient it became an untenable behavior because any attempts to physically stop her would only overstimulate her and intensify the panic that she already felt. On a deeper level it would also be quite gratifying for her to enact a chase, capture, and submission in the transference. The alternative, allowing her to simply run out of the office screaming for her life, was unacceptable also, not only because of the risks to her safety but because of the great disturbance it caused the other tenants in the building.

After several episodes of Sally's emergence in my office, I shared an observation with the patient. I pointed out to her that when I observed her seizure-like episodes in the past, she would eventually and spontaneously switch into "Sam," who was oriented to the reality of the situation, could regain control of the body, and not be afraid. I then wondered out loud with her if, in this current situation, we could enlist Sam's help somehow. It appeared that these episodes, while resembling abreactions with potentially therapeutic value, did not diminish in intensity over time and seemed refractory to change. They were not able at this time to be experienced with mature self-observation in an empathic therapeutic relationship. Instead they seemed more like a repetitive sensorimotor discharge of a fixed nature. My experience has shown me that, over time, even many of these states can become somewhat metabolized and incorporated into the psyche. But there was enormous terror in these apparently disconnected episodes. The emergence of this state, as dramatic and disorienting as it was, also had psychodynamic and defensive significance in that it removed her from the immediacy of the anxiety-laden situation. However, the nature of it jeopardized the continuity of work, and it was not amenable to interpretation. The patient stated that if "Sally" stayed inside she would feel safer. Unlike some alters who claim to feel left out if not permitted expression, Sally would prefer to remain dormant, that is, unconscious as much as possible. It then occurred to me that an interim step might be helpful until she acquired sufficient observing ego to help tame this raw hallucinatory state into a controllable narrative (Laub and Auerhan 1993). So I considered actively trying to shore up her repressive barrier instead of allowing a more naturalistic process to continue given her propensity for self-mutilation and depletion after each of these episodes. I reasoned that if such a barrier could be fortified, then her threshold could be increased and she would not be triggered as easily. Mrs. A. was initially skeptical about such an idea but was amenable to anything that might give her relief.

Once again, I employed a "revolving door" interpretation, but this time with Mrs. A. and "Sam." As they got closer, I asked that they come out at the same time and metaphorically stand next to each other. As she did, the patient immediately brightened and felt giddy, experiencing a sense of confidence and control she had not felt since I met her. It appeared that these two selves had become co-conscious. As I reminded the patient that all of her parts were truly part of her, she and Sam were free to join forces and strengthen the mind. I used the image of two raindrops coalescing to form a larger drop as a metaphor for the coalescence of the facet of her psyche. Mrs. A. and Sam were then free to share all thoughts, feelings, memories, and drives in order to form the nucleus of a more cohesive mind. Further dissolution of her "It's not me!" self occurred during this fusion, as the patient felt hope for the first time since I met her.

She wrote in her journal that she was optimistic about getting control of her mind and ending her torment, but the next day just before her appointment Mrs. A. panicked and pushed Sam away, arriving in a miserable and hopeless state. She felt like giving up and quitting treatment. I suspected that this negative therapeutic reaction was multiply determined and the prospect of improvement in her mental condition was something for which she was unprepared. Her shame, guilt, and continued need for punishment would not allow her to maintain a good feeling for any length of time. She was convinced that I was tricking her, that unification of her mind was impossible, and that perhaps there was nothing wrong with her at all! Indeed, the nature of the autohypnotic defenses lend themselves to hypnotic manipulation by others for their own purposes, and Mrs. A. became very suspicious of my motive. In my ongoing countertransference self-analysis, I've wondered quite often about my wish to cure her, and I did try to be aware of unrealistic expectations of the treatment. Such an intervention is so foreign to psychoanalysts that we all may tend to view it as nothing more than a positive suggestion that could have no lasting effect. So I interpreted to Mrs. A. that she was justified in her skepticism, but I felt that it bordered on paranoia. I pointed out the negative transferential element of her mistrust, and she associated to the man who would always promise that he would not hurt her ever again, only to catch her with her guard down each time. She felt naive, gullible, foolish, and helpless. I tried to reassure her that some unification of the mind was possible in my experience, but that all the alters involved needed to want it and see it for the greater good of the total human being. I also told her that the more she could do on her own, the better. I was merely a facilitator, like a switchboard operator, and could not have the best blueprint for her mind. For the moment however, "Sally's" distress was threatening another major regression that I hoped could be averted.

Significantly, Mrs. A. decided to give it another chance and wrote to "Sam" asking for forgiveness for rejecting him. By the next appointment, these two selves were closely allied, requiring only a simple request on my part that they rejoin. Once again the patient immediately brightened and her cowering body language changed into a more assertive position. The patient then oscillated from skepticism to idealism, wishing that she would become impervious to all emotional pain. This was a fantasy that evolved from the "toughening up" that she achieved through amputation. When she awoke the next day in a demoralized mood following the aftermath of her usual nightmares, I reminded her of her myth of invulnerability, and she regained her composure.

"Sally's" next emergence in a session followed the patient's describing feeling aroused by a handsome young man who had hugged her in a friendly gesture. Fortified by "Sam," Mrs. A. acknowledged more openly how easily she would get stimulated, how it filled her with shame and guilt, and how she felt the need to hurt herself. Shortly after this disclosure, her eyes glazed over, and "Sally" took over. In terror, she ran for the door but this time did not run out. Instead, she waited and stared at me quizzically, waiting for my response! So I reflected on her behavior, much the way the mother of a toddler might, and we began a brief dialogue for the first time in this state of consciousness. The internalization of such dialogues would become the foundation of the expansion of her observing ego. This time she slowly slid to the ground instead of violently falling, experiencing a much less intense, much shorter, and much less sexualized seizure that was easily interrupted. Over time and after countless repetitions of this paradigm, she would come to incorporate Sally into her psyche. Accompanied by in-depth exploration of how her anxiety in the transference could precipitate such a reaction, and an analysis of how her other alters played a role in this sequence, Mrs. A. would then be on her way to integration.

Following this stage of treatment, an extended phase of consolidation and working through of her developmental anxieties and her complex sexuality would then be necessary to help her more fully own what was in her mind.

Discussion

Mrs. A. suffered from the disintegrating effects of destructive aggression on her mental development due to early unpleasure (Parens 1979) associated with maternal neglect and sexual trauma. Her propensity toward autohypnotic defenses (Shengold 1989) may have originated in infancy as a disorganized/disoriented disturbance of attachment (Liotti 1992). Winnicott suggested that the template for dissociation was in the natural barrier between wakefulness and sleep and in the loss of mental continuity in childhood due to infantile amnesia and the development of the repressive barrier. It may be that those children with constitutional predispositions and severe early trauma develop a hypertrophied repressive barrier that relies on defensive altered states. This situation, like Singer's (1996) model in borderlines, may occur even when there is a lack of integration of aggressively and libidinally derived self and object representations. It is also known that the ego in the dream state may represent alterations in consciousness by symbolizing it in the form of people (Silberer 1909). Therefore, traumatically induced alterations of consciousness may be symbolized by different people in a dream and become an organizing influence in the creation of personifications in multiple personalities (DID).

Mrs. A.'s recurrent nightmare of an unknown girl being raped corresponded in detail to the first-hand account of her alters, a typical finding in such patients. In addition, the scenes in her dreams were often described from above, consistent with the out-of-body experiences often described by those who have had life-threatening trauma (Greyson 1983). Mrs. A. encapsulated and personified her memories of the gang rape in college in the form of "Sally," who appeared to be the most disturbed and disconnected part of her psyche. Yet Sally's torment affected everyone, resulting in the patient's most drastic measures to keep in control. In her effort to be impervious to pain, she proved to be nearly impervious to treatment, as she was deemed a treatment failure and enacted a long-standing "not good enough" mother transference. Unresolved grief complicated the preoedipal conflicts over separation and loss that predominated and increased the danger of her erotic longings in the transference to a suicidal degree. A long treatment course with an uncertain outcome is not surprising in such a severely disturbed individual where the larger holding environment of the hospital and supervised living has been necessary.

Freud (1923a) speculated that multiple personalities could be attributed to different identifications alternately taking over consciousness. This explanation is necessary but insufficient to explain the complexities of a patient such as Mrs. A. In a rather contemporary sounding description, Ferenczi (1933) almost seventy years ago observed, "If the shocks increase in number during the development of the child, the number in various kinds of splits in the personality increase too, and soon it becomes extremely difficult to maintain contact without confusion with all the fragments each of which behaves as a separate personality yet does not know of even the existence of the others. . . . I hope even here to be able to find threads that can link the various parts" (p. 165). Some of the threads that Ferenczi was looking for might be seen in the treatment approach in my work with Mrs. A. By means of the "revolving-door" interpretation, which helps dissolve the dissociative or

"It's not me!" self, the patient becomes able to experience other personifications as truly part of her. And by considering the dual notion of dissociation as both a symptom of trauma and a defense against anxiety in the here and now, it becomes possible to recognize the dynamic factors influencing the switch from one personification to another.

CONCLUSION

It is possible to work psychodynamically with catastrophically ill patients who employ personified dissociated states as a consequence of severe, early trauma. Indeed, it may be the treatment of last resort when all else fails. This work is very difficult for both patient and analyst, and requires ongoing countertransference self-analysis. Due to the extent of aggression and the risk of regression, it may be necessary at times to create a larger holding environment such as a hospital and supervised living facilities. An understanding of these conditions is based on three assumptions: (1) There is a spectrum of dissociative character pathology. (2) Dissociation may be used as a defense. (3) In the lower-level dissociative character more commonly known as DID, there is a unique psychic structure known as the dissociative or "It's not me!" self that creates the various personifications and perpetuates the illusion of separate people. Steps in the long-term treatment of these patients can be identified and may be helpful in understanding the process.

2

Mother–Adult Daughter Incest

Sexual abuse . . . is notoriously difficult to spot, especially when it is a closely guarded secret.

[*New York Times*, July 2, 1998, p. B1]

Sexual abuse is now recognized as a widespread problem, and it is regularly covered in the media and portrayed in popular literature and the fine arts. However, incest between parents and their grown children is rarely, if ever, talked about or considered. Little seems to be known about it, so it is not surprising that mother–daughter incest persisting into adulthood has not found its way into analytic discourse until recently (Hodge 2000). It does appear, however, that these grown women have been stimulated, seduced, and brainwashed (Shengold 1989) from a very early age—either it just never stopped or it resumed under certain conditions. They have, as one might expect, been prone to rather severe mental disturbances as well. Consequently, their entry into the mental health system would be more likely psychiatric than psychoanalytic and for chief complaints such as drug and alcohol abuse, suicidality, self-mutilation, eating disorders, and psychotic regressions. In many such cases, the history of incest never emerges. After all, in children (van Leeuwen 1988) and even in cases of adult women whose incest ended years before, their secrets are generally not revealed or reconstructed until the analytic process is well under way (Kramer 1983, 1991, 1994). The memories, sensations, and affects associated with it can be so overwhelming that when it continues far beyond the time when a person should know better or be strong enough to say no, the shame and guilt can easily precipitate a suicidal crisis. Therefore, the need to defend against the full recognition of the incest can be a matter of life-threatening importance, requiring the maximum conscious and unconscious effort to ward it off. In this context, it seems that in addition to the three most significant questions (Kramer 1994) incest victims ask—(1) "Did it really happen?" (2) "Was it my fault?" and (3) "Did I enjoy it?"—a fourth potentially lethal question must also be added: "When did it really stop?"

The psychopathology associated with maternal incest viewed developmentally has been ascribed to a lesion in the separation-individuation process because the mother's parasitic relationship makes it extremely difficult for the daughter to extricate herself. As a consequence of the failure to individuate, disturbances in the integration of self and object representations (Mahler et al 1975), intolerance of intimacy, defects in reality testing, and faulty superego formation have been noted. In addition, problems in learning and in the woman's relationship to her body may also occur (Apprey 1991, Blum 1996, Fischer 1991, Kramer 1983, 1991, 1994, Steele 1970, 1991). However, one of the more misunderstood and difficult-to-treat aspects associated with this syndrome is the way in which the mind may defend itself in catastrophic cases.

In addition to deep repression and primitive splitting, the employment of autohypnotic defenses (Shengold 1989) has been well described. But the theoretical bridge from the autohypnotic defenses to the realm of the dissociative disorders, including the controversial multiple personality, now known as dissociative identity disorder (APA 1994), has rarely been traversed by psychoanalysts until recently (Brenner 1994a, 1996a,b, 2001). Consequently, many analytic writers seem to hit a brick wall when describing their work with severely traumatized patients who go into a dissociated state, seeing it as a psychotic-like regression that brings exploratory work to a grinding halt. In my experience, it is a conceptual wall, not a clinical wall, although the work is arduous, complex, potentially dangerous, and very long-term. It is limited as much by the anxiety experienced by both members of the therapeutic dyad as well as by the lack of an accepted theoretical model. It may also require the larger holding environment of an inpatient setting at certain times in the process. Coupled with the secrecy and a conspiracy of silence endemic to this situation, it is no wonder we still have so much to learn.

In my role as an administrator, treating psychiatrist, consultant, and supervisor on an inpatient unit specializing in dissociative disorders, I have had the opportunity to see hundreds of such patients. This experience has enabled me to recognize such tendencies in my analytic practice and to adapt analytic methods to further elucidate the nature of dissociative processes in more disturbed patients. In the course of this work, a number of these patients, primarily women, have convinced me that incest persisting into adulthood occurs with both fathers and mothers more often than we would imagine.

To illustrate the complexities, potential dangers, and resistances involved when surreptitious incest is occurring during treatment, this chapter describes three cases, focusing on how the secret came to the fore and its effect on the process. I then discuss some common trends in all three cases, reviewing the insights from Ferenczi's (1933) controversial "Confusion of Tongues" paper and commenting on the enactments surrounding his own presentation of it in 1932. For the sake of confidentiality, this case material is disguised as per Clifft's (1986) guidelines.

CASE 1

Grace, an energetic woman in her late twenties, prided herself on her perky, upbeat image. This veneer put her in good stead in her sales career, but it belied an underlying intensity and rage that periodically gave way to self-mutilation and suicidal regression, which required hospitalization. A very secretive and coy woman, she communicated by innuendo and inference. This presented a major challenge to the development of a therapeutic alliance. Furthermore, she had significant memory lapses for both recent events and her troubled childhood, which was recounted in a fairy-tale manner. A major source of guilt was her powerful impulse to molest young girls, a problem that had required her to give up babysitting years before. An avowed lesbian, she eschewed men and went through a series of female therapists over many years after developing profoundly ambivalent maternal transferences that could not be managed. One day, Grace, in an altered ego state, described in a very childlike way how her mother would touch her in the same way that she in another altered state had wanted to touch other young girls. The patient became terrified of being punished because she had "told" and imagined that her mother "knew" she was revealing the dreaded secret. In her regressed state, she enacted being hit and threatened with torture if she were to tell anyone. As this material continued to come forth, Grace, in another dissociated state, became hostile and threatening to her latest doctor, Dr. Y., an attractive female analyst who had considerable experience treating severe character disorders. As Grace's pathology emerged, a clinical picture developed that was consistent with multiple personalities replete with terrified "children," a menacing "male" presence, hypersexual selves attracted to women and young girls, a suicidal "teenager," and the pseudocompliant, socially adept, perky personification who was essentially ignorant (amnestic) about the goings-on in the rest of her mind.

Therapy proceeded spasmodically with suicidal crises and hospitalizations of increasing longer duration that actually allowed more intensive, five-day-a-week therapy than her three- to four-time-per-week, outpatient routine. During this time, more material related to incest emerged and the patient seemed to be opening up much more. However, it also seemed to emerge almost too quickly, and the transference heated up to such an extent that Dr. Y. began to feel uneasy with both Grace's dissociated threats of violence to her and Grace's increasing overtures to kill herself.

It soon became clear that the patient's behavior made it too risky for her to be discharged to her apartment alone. She then, very mysteriously, declared that the only place where she should go would be back with her mother. Unbeknownst to the staff, the patient had been making daily telephone calls to her estranged mother, who insisted that they were brainwashing her and that the psychiatrists were trying to make her crazy. Therefore, the only safe place was with her mother, a prospect that filled Grace, the social one, with a vague sense of dread and automatic obedience. Efforts to discuss staff concerns were unsuccessful and Grace insisted upon this plan, so she subsequently did return to her mother.

Initially, Grace seemed to restabilize, presumably as a result of such age-old remedies as home cooking and TLC. However, several months later, she regressed again, became suicidal, and required hospitalization. This time, she was more belligerent, agitated, and evasive than before.

Again, the "scared child" reemerged in session, living out and narrating her mother's sexual intrusion into her body but with such a sense of immediacy in the here and now that it was eerie. There was amnesia for these defensive altered states and total unwillingness to delve any further. The continued suicidal feelings and insistence upon returning to her mother in order to recover was a pattern that repeated itself several times during the next year. Each time, Grace's hostility toward Dr. Y. escalated, requiring physical-limit settings for everyone's protection. It was ultimately hinted at by her teenage "self" that the sexual activity, including oral sex between mother and daughter, had actually resumed during her move back home. This veiled reference was seen as a desperate, albeit very ambivalent, cry for help in extricating herself from an erotically bound, symbiotic trap set by her mother. Violent behavior in the transference then became untenable, and after a series of extended consultations, a mutual decision was made for Grace to change doctors. Her new analyst, Dr. W., a man, initially helped quell the patient's anxiety, and a honeymoon period of idealization, impulse control, and improved functioning followed. Grace was then felt to be able to return to her own apartment once again and continue her work as an intensive outpatient with Dr. W. However, she eventually discovered Dr. Y.'s home address and began to stalk her. Dr. Y. felt menaced, vulnerable, violated, and at times in fear of a sneak attack. The patient's capacity to inject a pervasive sense of uncertainty and insecurity into Dr. Y. was a sobering example of the power of projective identification and what her own maternal experience must have felt like.

CASE 2

Mary, an enigmatic, shy young woman, first sought help during a suicidal, homosexual panic that delayed her wedding plans with a man who was determined to rescue her from a life of alcohol and drugs. Overwhelmed by the rush of intense sexual longings for a woman, Mary felt as though she were losing her grip on reality. During her first hospitalization, she said very little and appeared severely depressed. As was customary, a family meeting was arranged with all interested parties prior to her discharge. Her mother sat stony-faced, completely incredulous at her wayward daughter's decline into seeming insanity. Vehemently opposed to any psychiatric treatment, she counseled Mary to "get it together" on her own, expressing unending mistrust and criticism of all helping professionals. To Mary's credit and with the support of her fiancé, she regained enough composure to be discharged and made a clear commitment to at least twice-a-week psychotherapy. Although her attendance was perfect, she did not seem to know what to do and usually sat mutely for extended periods of time. She was unwilling and unable to stop her substance abuse, so treatment at this phase took on the quality of supportive alcohol rehab work. Despite her recalcitrance, Mary's devotion to the sessions was striking. She worked extra-long hours at her job and deprived herself of certain luxuries in order to finance her treatment, an endeavor that on the surface looked like it was going nowhere yet became her lifeline. However, a series of suicide attempts and dishonesty severely tested my commitment to her.

A nodal point occurred in the second year of treatment when, in the closing minutes of a session, she nonchalantly revealed that she had taken a massive overdose of her antidepressants. Instead of dying, however, she slept for several days, waking up to vomit and telling her fiancé that she was just suffering from a flu virus. Interestingly, the story was told with such a bland affect I was tempted not to believe her, a paradigm that would continue throughout her treatment. Mary refused to be readmitted and therefore forced me to use my authority to get her admitted involuntarily, a move that felt distinctly like a provocative sadomasochistic enactment. Unrepentant and unable to give a safety commitment at the end of a frustrating hospitalization where her spaciness following the drug overdose seemed to last far beyond what one would expect medically, there was no choice but to transfer her to a state facility. Unlike most patients in such circumstances, however, Mary did not fight her fate; it was as though she were facing a deserved jail sentence for an unspoken crime.

Her state hospitalization both embittered and mobilized her, following which she sought treatment elsewhere. However, she recognized that she missed my empathic, patient approach and my sincere, but unsuccessful, efforts to get her to become curious about herself. I agreed to see her in consultation and sought a second opinion before resuming treatment with her. The patient seemed contrite and sufficiently shaken up that when therapy resumed she was determined to be more honest in her reporting. However, while she was much more forthright afterward, her mysterious suicidal regressions continued for several more years and required medication and hospitalization until she regained control.

Over the years, the therapeutic alliance strengthened and a modicum of trust developed on both sides. Sessions, however, were typically characterized by terse comments, long silences, and blank stares punctuated by rare outbursts of bloody, sadomasochistic fantasies, blurred memories of date rapes during drunken adolescent escapades, and uncompromising hatred of her mother. Stories of being fondled and hurt by summer camp counselors at age 5 started to emerge, and she recounted becoming mute afterward. Mary could not articulate much more of her experience but demonstrated rather well how she lost her capacity for speech. One might say that she became tongue-tied (Ferenczi 1933). Despite this seeming lack of progress, she remained utterly devoted to treatment, continuing to work overtime to pay the fees and never missing a session. As she tried to reconstruct her life, a picture developed of a lonely, inhibited, maladjusted girl prone to rebelliousness and mischievousness. She never felt comfortable with boys and virtually all of her sexual experiences were under the influence of alcohol, sedatives, and marijuana. Efforts to stop the self-medicating were initially short-lived because she stopped in order to feel the intensity of whatever was bothering her deep inside but she could not tolerate it. She would feel as though she were under water, would be overcome by a mysterious, all-encompassing self-hatred, and then become suicidal. Loneliness and alienation from her siblings and peers would then drive her back to her strict, religious, and unforgiving mother. In total desperation, Mary described how, as a young teen, she cut her wrists and tried to get counseling from her minister, only to feel further misunderstood and hated by God.

In the transference, she was prone to intermittent, paranoid regressions characterized by a belief that I was in direct contact with her mother, who knew everything that was being discussed in the sessions. At other times, she had impulses to shatter the glass in the window and cut my throat with a shard. She just assumed that I would merely sit there, quietly and passively reflecting on the attack, the way I had always behaved with her. She was surprised and relieved to hear me say that I would do my best not to let her hurt me. Her anxiety temporarily lessened once she learned that I would help her try to control the inner forces that dominated and threatened to take her over from time to time. During one of her periods of abstinence, after almost a decade of treatment, she hinted that as a teenager her long-standing love of animals became excessive, causing profound shame and guilt. I cautiously and empathically then disclosed that I had just read an article on unusual human relationships with animals, assuring her that despite her deepest fears of being a complete freak, such things were not unheard of. Once again, she was surprised and relieved.

After several weeks of shame, mutism, and forgetfulness, Mary then described how she taught a neighbor's dog to perform cunnilingus on her, bringing her to orgasm on a regular basis while she was babysitting after the children had gone to sleep. Interestingly, my first reaction once again was of incredulousness, but her affects and consistency in recounting the story made it quite believable. She then linked her guilt over the dog with her seeking the religious counseling when she became suicidal. Since Mary's adolescent sexual satisfaction was derived from partners not of our species, she reasoned it was no wonder that she felt progressively isolated from the human race. Indeed, she felt like a freak of nature and found her only solace in alcohol, a pattern that reached back for generations in her family. As I listened to her private life begin to unfold, Mary was unable to answer the basic question of what gave her the idea of using a dog in the first place. All she could say at this point was that she was not afraid of being bitten and that she could trust animals more than people. Furthermore, the dog's large tongue, which fascinated her, was easily trained by her to lick her genitals as she had a natural affinity for animals. Shortly after this revelation, the patient lapsed back into a serious bout of alcohol and drug abuse that eventually led to another hospitalization.

During this hospital stay, she became very agitated over a benign picture of a woman straddling her daughter and grooming her hair. She had violent fantasies toward women, and during this explosive time first hinted that there may have been sexual contact with her mother at a young age. The more she alluded to the possibility of incest, the more she seemed to deteriorate. From this point on, Mary's conflict over remembering and revealing the nature of the incest assumed a central role in treatment, and her regression as a defensive avoidance had the quality of a negative therapeutic reaction (Renik 1991). Many weeks could go by with no mention of it at all as the daily chaos of her life was more than enough to consume a team of mental health professionals. Months later, she declared that she felt more comfortable with women and broke off her interminable engagement in order to explore homosexuality. This time, she assured herself, she would not become suicidal when she became aroused and would feel free from guilt. Discussion about her mother, a distant nightmare that she was prone to deny, was replaced by excitement over finding her true self in the lesbian world. Much to her befuddlement and pleasure, she felt a sense of acceptance and belonging in the gay world as she tried to find others committed to being drug- and alcohol-free.

Her new life seemed to give her new hope for a fresh start, but she could not stay sober. She finally confessed that she was hearing voices, another secret she had kept since treatment began. Her capacity to keep her knowledge of things concealed was so enormous that it was routine for her not to reveal an insight she had acquired or a tidbit she had overheard on the inpatient unit about me for months or even years after. Obviously, the nature of her paranoid transference fears, the auditory hallucinations, and her restricted affect raised important diagnostic questions about psychosis. Over the years, as a result of her multiple hospitalizations and my vacations, she had seen many other psychiatrists, only one of whom seriously considered a diagnosis of schizophrenia. All of the others essentially felt that severe, borderline character pathology with a substance abuse problem would explain most of the clinical picture, so I did not abandon hope for some psychotherapeutic benefit. Nevertheless, as the depth of her pathology revealed her complex sexuality and increasingly important trauma history, it became clear that there was much more going on.

Mary then disclosed that she thought of herself as a marionette whose strings were being pulled by unseen inside operators living in her mind. Furthermore, she acknowledged the presence of a forbidding, older woman who censored all of her outgoing comments, that is, the personification of the reason for her long silences. In addition, she acknowledged long-standing amnestic gaps that, although they had been evident in the sessions for at least a year, were denied until this point. In fact, she may not have been fully aware that she was so forgetful. Her walking out of stores forgetting to wait for her change from the cashiers and then being frightened when they chased after her with the money was further dramatic evidence of her fugue-like tendencies.

Then a self-inflicted laceration of the arm, deftly executed during an amnestic state with a razor that was hidden in her shoe, was a shocking display of her dissociative pathology. Significantly, this injury occurred in the presence of a staff member while waiting for hospital readmission but was done with such rapidity that it was not preventable. Afterward, Mary was in a daze and seemed to have no knowledge of the existence of the blade or any clear memory of the act itself. At this time, she identified herself as Doris. Later on, Mary felt haunted by a mocking laughter inside and was terrified that she would get attacked again, but it was not always clear whether she was actually deteriorating or whether her autohypnotic states were simply becoming more evident. However, the anxiety over revelations about her mother was mounting, and she was sensing that she was being punished for talking too much. She also felt the presence of a latency-age boy inside, a youngster whose name was told to her as Brian. She felt such an enormous affinity for this young boy that at times she hallucinated having "his" penis. At such times, she cross-dressed and even put a sock in her underwear which produced a bulge in her crotch and gave her a sense of completeness and calmness. Suspecting the presence of an older male personification also, Mary confessed that she was utterly confused over her anatomical gender, hating her breasts and despising herself each month during her menses. At such times, she had impulses to cut off her breasts, perform a hysterectomy on herself, and then surgically acquire a penis. She was intermittently convinced that "he" was a man trapped in a woman's body, a not unusual transsexual conflict in severe dissociative pathology (Brenner 1996a). The emergence and exploration of a number of other personified, defensive altered states, including those encapsulating perverse sexuality, that is, heterosexual sadomasochism, transsexualism, and homosexuality, took place over subsequent months. Each "inside person" had his/her own transference, and it appeared as though she experienced intrapsychic conflict as an internalized interpersonal disagreement.

Mary then reached a point during a hospitalization where she decided that she must move back with her parents. Her mother had remained aloof and uninvolved, offering no other advice except to quit therapy immediately and come home. The patient would not do the former but felt an irresistible pull to do the latter. She could not be deterred by the staff or me, and convinced herself that a few weeks there would enable her to save enough money to get a better apartment in a better neighborhood to get another fresh start. She had planned to "come out" to her parents and get on with her life. Not surprisingly, her plans went awry and she got stuck at home for almost two years. Mary's dissociative symptoms surprisingly improved for several months and she considered stopping treatment. She then was observed to have more amnestic episodes, suicidal urges, and bizarre somatic sensations. She seemed to live in a perpetual altered state where she could not differentiate between waking and dreaming. During the day, she was plagued by voices and a peculiar constellation of extreme shortness of breath, burning hands, and the feeling that the skin on her face, especially her lips, was melting and being pulled away from her skull like taffy. At night, she was visited by nightmares of her house being broken into by an unknown intruder who was intent upon doing her grave harm. She found herself sleepwalking and waking with a knife in her hand, contemplating using it on her mother and then on herself. At this point, the patient knew that it was necessary for her to leave the house and made plans to do so. Interestingly, she was unable to make any sense of her somatic symptoms, and not until she moved away did the intruder in her dreams become her mother, at which point she felt free enough to explore their relationship once again.

Over time, a picture of insidious and sadistic abuse was assembled from the enactments and accounts of her personifications. She had recurrent images of her bathroom and being in the bathtub as a child. Her mother insisted that her genitals were always dirty and needed scrubbing every day. At such times she would insert her finger into the young child's vagina to "remove" whatever dirt might be inside while rubbing her raw with a washcloth. Any attempts to resist were dealt with by being held underwater until she submitted. Recurrent sensations that plagued and mystified her until this reconstruction were a burning sensation in her throat and chest as well as blurry vision. In addition, she had musky olfactory hallucinations, shortness of breath, and images of her face being forcibly held against her mother's crotch. Terrified of being suffocated throughout this ordeal as well, Mary pieced together having to perform cunnilingus on her mother, whose self-absorption made her oblivious to her young daughter's plight. She also reported images of her mother's inserting painful objects into her vagina when she was older. By this time she was conditioned to become totally still and cooperative with whatever was demanded of her. Mary reported these scenes with an eerie detachment, feeling as though she were watching an old silent movie of herself. She then realized that silence prevailed throughout her sexual life with her mother. Words were never used, nothing was ever acknowledged and her mother seemed to be in a daze of her own at these times.

As an adult, Mary described a typical scenario with her

mother as follows: She would be invited over to the house for a visit. After a time, her father would leave or would simply pass out from drinking. While mother and daughter were in the kitchen, mother would tap her on the shoulder and silently gesture that she was going to the bedroom. Mary would wait several minutes, agonize over what to do and then follow suit. By this time, her mother would be lying naked in bed and Mary would obediently undress and join her. Her mother would then masturbate her and become very aroused, at which point they would perform mutual cunnilingus until her mother climaxed. There was no warmth, tenderness, stroking, eye contact, or verbalization. The women would then silently get dressed and return to their activities as if nothing had happened. Indeed, Mary questioned her own senses and doubted her reality testing when it came to this account, which was spliced together with the help of her alter personalities. During this reconstruction, there was an upsurge of violent threats in the transference that were issued by her adult male personification who was supposed to guard this dreaded secret. In addition, there was a desperate, conflicted plea by the young boy to help "him" break off this parasitic and crippling relationship.

CASE 3

Alice had been in various treatments for almost ten years for depression and an eating disorder with weight fluctuations of over 100 pounds. As a last resort, she consulted an analyst but was not ready to reveal the ongoing sexual relationship with her mother until she reached a point of despair and rage as well as the conviction that it was actually happening. She would experience depersonalization and numbness during their regular interludes but would then become amnestic and promptly disown the experience, attributing it to one of her "inside" people. Prior to her "knowing" (Laub and Auerhahn 1993) about the incest, her five-time-a-week intensive therapy came to a halt in the second year after she abruptly announced that she was planning to discontinue. She accused her analyst, Dr. T., of brainwashing her into believing that she was sexually abused as a child in order to dominate her and exploit her financially. There was a threatening quality to Alice's allegations of false memories, and her change in attitude was sudden and puzzling. While prone to mistrust men in authority after a serious boundary breach by one of her former teachers, Alice, up until this point, was surprisingly willing to give men in the medical profession a chance. The pronouncement of her termination and the paranoid transference that seemed to reach psychotic proportion was so sudden that it took Dr. T. by surprise. It was as though she had become a completely different person overnight. There was no negotiation possible and Alice's decision was final. However, she had a contradictory request that betrayed her ambivalence, although she could not verbalize it. Despite her vitriolic condemnation, Alice still wanted to meet every month to have her antidepressant medication renewed. When Dr. T. inquired why she would still want to have anything to do with him if she truly felt he was brainwashing her, she seemed stymied as though the opinion expressed earlier in the session did not apply to her. It seemed that she was "switching" rapidly and her different personifications were expressing rather varied feelings in the transference that the patient could not comprehend. Dr. T. felt that it would be destructive at this point to insist on the current schedule or nothing, sensing that an ultimatum could sever the suddenly strained alliance or even precipitate a regression. He had a peculiar sense of being held hostage and hoped that by staying on in whatever capacity she could tolerate, perhaps intensive treatment might resume and the mystery might be solved in the future.

After several monthly sessions with Alice, Dr. T. became even more mystified. Alice seemed to have gone into a peculiar remission of her severe dissociative symptoms. She did not appear to switch spontaneously during the session, her affect was superficially appropriate, and she did not lapse into the hallucinatory or flashback-like reliving of past scenarios that had characterized her earlier sessions. With her improvements, her anxiety seemed in check and she exuded a positive attitude about the future. She repeatedly questioned her diagnosis of severe dissociative pathology, convinced that her new health was proof that it was the therapy that had really made her ill. She insisted that she was doing just fine with her new program at home but would not elaborate. Indeed, she would not even answer any questions, preferring just to present herself as intact, well-functioning, and happy. This clinical change was similar but more dramatic than Mary's and Grace's improvements when they moved back home with their mothers. Despite Alice's guardedness, which made Dr. T. more than a bit suspicious, she nevertheless gave a most impressive appearance of having made a spontaneous recovery from the depths of suicidal despair and mental chaos. But how and why remained totally unexplained, raising a fleeting question or two in Dr. T.'s mind about the nature of the condition and the therapeutic process.

This veneer of normality shattered within months following a serious suicide attempt by Alice's beloved teenage niece. The girl, who was like a daughter to Alice, who was childless, had been deteriorating since puberty after a date rape, drug experimentation, and bizarre behavior at home. Until this event, her turbulent adolescent behavior was thought to be a phase that she would outgrow, but the girl's suicide note revealed otherwise. In it, she described profound sexual confusion and alluded to a series of molestations by her grandmother. Alice, upon learning of the girl's brush with death and the allegation of abuse by Alice's mother, felt as though she were cracking apart again. Interestingly, the girl's mother, Alice's sister, did not believe the accusations, which were vehemently denied by the mother, and this lack of verification pushed Alice even more quickly into a mental abyss once again. At this point, she contacted Dr. T. and beseeched him to accept her back into intensive treatment; she felt an earthquake in her psyche and as though her mind had come apart along a huge mental fault line. It appeared as though the threatened loss of her special niece shattered Alice's wish not to know about her own secret sexual relationship with the same woman. In her rage, despair, and helplessness, Alice declared, "It was bad enough she did it to me, but to hurt my niece and drive her to kill herself was the last straw!" Whether or not Alice had an unconscious jealousy and feelings of betrayal were issues that were much too volatile to address initially because she first needed to come clean about the secret of her flight into health. This, however, ushered in an extended period of suicidality that required periodic hospitalizations during the most desperate times.

Alice described, in a jigsaw-puzzle fashion over a period of many months, how she got seduced back into an almost daily sexual relationship with her mother during this time. After her therapy sessions, she would meet her mother for dinner as her husband often worked late, and she would then be invited back home under some pretense. Alice could not say no and hesitantly would go over. Inevitably, she would need to use the toilet before she left, and her mother would casually walk in on her and continue their conversation. She would then inquire about the patient's bowel movements and urine output, much the way the mother of a 3-year-old might. Alice recalled feeling uneasy and then her mind would get hazy. The next thing she knew, she would be in bed with her mother with her face silently being held to her mother's genitals in order to bring on a climax. Alice would then blank out again from the horror of it, having vague memories of her mounting excitement from her mother's manipulation of her genitals. Years later, Alice revealed that her most stimulating masturbation fantasy was of abruptly stopping cunnilingus on her mother just before her orgasm in order to frustrate her and put her into a rage. Alice's sadistic gratification over withholding her tongue just at the last moment gave her a triumphant feeling of omnipotent control over her mother that then easily aroused Alice to her own orgasm.

Alice's hopeless rage at her mother was related to feeling unloved and even hated no matter what she did to try to please her insatiable mother. She felt used, expendable, and caught in a primitive relationship between her parents where she was sought after by her mother as revenge against her absent and alcoholic father. Alice was always accused of lying and was threatened with being locked up for being crazy if she were to misbehave (or reveal family secrets). She lived in terror. She eventually retrieved memories from childhood of nightly visits by mother who inspected her genitals with a flashlight looking for infestations and who then applied ointment to her labia under that pretense. When she resisted, her hands and feet were tied to the bed and she was spanked with a paddle or had to endure procedures that consisted of insertion of painful objects into her vagina. Occasionally her mother would blurt out angry epithets, but usually it was done in eerie silence or with an inappropriate medicalized comment. When Alice reached puberty, she was subjected to nightly breast examinations so mother could monitor their growth. Because this ritual was as routine as goodnight kiss, Alice did not even realize that it was a violation of her body. She never felt that her body was truly her own nor did she feel entitled to any modesty or privacy. She felt like her mother's sexual slave, trained to respond to every subtle, unspoken demand in her desperate attempt to feel needed, recognized, and loved.

When she moved out of the house and got married at

an early age, she hoped to break free, but her mother would visit and invite her over frequently. She lived a double life as a married woman and as her mother's secret sexual partner. Treatment offered her first real hope for emancipation, but her separation anxiety and lack of object constancy overwhelmed her as the transference developed. Weekends and vacations became predictable crises of abandonment and loss of her connection to Dr. T. In addition, as her mother sensed the threat to Alice's lifelong obedience to her will, she told her that Dr. T. was poisoning her mind and trying to dominate her. Alice's only hope for salvation would therefore be to quit treatment immediately before she became indoctrinated into the doctor's "cult" while her mother could still help her. The daily routine prescribed for Alice was a strict diet, a vigorous exercise program, extensive daily talks about the evils of the mental health profession, and daily oral sex. Alice was adhering to this program when she abruptly broke off treatment and had her mysterious flight into health. Once Alice broke her oath of silence about the ongoing incest, she had already reached a point of no return, having decided that she must make the break. It took years to work through this conflict and to go through an analytically facilitated individuation. Throughout this process many of her children personifications begged to return to the way it used to be. Attempts were made to reestablish contact with mother, but Alice refused to comply with mother's conditions that she recant her story. Instead, Alice chose to move forward. In Alice's words, "I want to live now because I am free!"

DISCUSSION

The silence surrounding ongoing mother–adult daughter incest was so profound that when words were finally found, there were crises in treatment and potential danger to both the patient and the analyst. Indeed, the apparent absence of the capacity to verbalize it and the preservation of the conspiracy of secrecy posed a most formidable resistance to any meaningful treatment. In case 1, Grace, a suicidal patient, broke off treatment and menaced her female therapist by stalking her. In case 2, Mary became overtly suicidal and threatening in the transference as she in a defensive, altered state "became" a man who instilled fear in the analyst as well. In case 3, Alice became suicidal following the suicide attempt of her niece, which brought the occult incest to the fore. The regressive potential of such patients should not be underestimated, and having access to an inpatient facility was necessary to allow continuity of treatment in the hospital. Such clinical work is a bit beyond the average, expectable caseload in an analytic practice, and I suspect that the possibility that an adult could be involved in an incestuous relationship while in treatment may seem unbelievable, even after reading this material. Indeed, the question of severe, early sexual trauma and its pathological affects still raises some eyebrows in scholarly discussion of the subject despite a century of clarifying that Freud's discarding of the seduction theory did not mean that he did not recognize that sexual abuse occurred and that it could be toxic.

The lack of acceptance of the scope of this problem may have contributed to Ferenczi's break with Freud and the other members of the inner circle at the end of his career. Like an enactment of the parent's effort to deny or the child's revelations of incest, the historical events surrounding his landmark "Confusion of Tongues" paper is worth reviewing here. He had been dissuaded from reading it at the International Psychoanalytic Congress in Wiesbaden in 1932 because many colleagues felt that it was focused on trauma to the exclusion of psychic reality and the oedipus complex. Freud, moreover, was disappointed in it and offhandedly called it "harmless and dumb." Furthermore, the anxiety and controversy over the paper was exploited by Ernest Jones, Ferenczi's long-time rival, who blocked its publication in English until 1949 (Blum 1994). Amazingly, it was not even published in his native Hungarian until 1971 (Rachman 1997)! Ferenczi, who was dying of pernicious anemia, gave this paper as his farewell address, but his words were denounced as coming from a psychotic man with a diseased brain (Rachman 1997). But even if there is evidence of his regression and lapses in his technical judgment during this time, there appear to be personal and political reasons for how the paper was treated. His opinion about the magnitude of the problem of incest was not to be take seriously and efforts were made to silence him through strong-armed persuasion, suppression and censoring.

A contemporary reading of this exposition, however, demonstrates how Ferenczi brilliantly "presaged a widened interest in the analyst's analyzing functions, unconscious communication, countertransference, and the interplay of reality and fantasy inside and outside the analytic situation" (Blum 1994, p. 871). Specifically with regard to sexual abuse, he emphasized the importance of (1) domination by the parent, resulting in becoming an "automaton"; (2) the correlation between defensive operations, that is, dissociation, to cope with the trauma and later characterological problems; (3) the child's disturbance in reality testing in order to satisfy the needs of the parents; (4) the presence of confusion as an overriding state such that the child comes to believe that the molestation is an act of love rather than the adult's narcissistic exploitation for his/her own sexual gratification; and (5) identification with the aggressor resulting in the shared false belief that parent and child are in a mutually beneficial relationship (Rachman 1989, 1997). Not only were all of these features evident in the three cases as Ferenczi described, but they resulted in major life crises and the unleashing of tremendous aggression in those who were threatened by their coming forth and breaking the silence.

Because of the particular bond between mothers and their daughters even under normative conditions, the problem of separation-individuation (Mahler et al. 1975) and the internalization of psychic function were magnified. In addition, there were disturbances in attachment (Bowlby 1973) and failure to mirror (Winnicott 1967) and reflect (Dennett 1987, Fonagy et al. 1991) the child's experience, which was especially absent during the incest. The conspiracy of silence seemed to have its roots in a developmental failure that was not addressed until the crises in treatment. All of these patients were obedient "automatons" to their overwhelmingly oppressive mothers, who summoned them back or greatly intensified their sexual exploitation when therapy started to progress. Then in their transferences, this identification with the aggressor was expressed by violence, stalking, urges to stab, and litigiousness. Paradoxically, there were temporary improvements in outward symptoms and a flight into health during the upsurges of incestuous activity. It was as though the original adaptation to the perverse reality of childhood resurrected the veneer of normality needed to protect the secret.

These patients' symptoms were all consistent with a diagnosis of multiple personality, now known as dissociative identity disorder (DID). As Ferenczi (1933) formulated it, "If the shocks increase in number during the development of the child, the number and the various kinds of splits in the personality increase too, and soon it becomes extremely difficult to maintain contact without confusion with all the fragments, each of which behaves as a separate personality yet does not know of even the existence of the others. . . . I hope even here to be able to find threads that can link up the various parts" (p. 165). Thus, Ferenczi's expressed interest in a psychoanalytically informed treatment of multiple personality was perhaps even more revolutionary than he realized, and, had he lived to continue this work, he may have caused even more chaos in the psychoanalytic movement than was feared. After all, Anna O., Breuer's case of hysteria treated with the talking cure, was described by Jones as a case of multiple personality! And today, almost seventy years later, with all the advances in theory, technique, and pharmacology, this condition remains the most controversial psychiatric disorder and probably one of the most difficult to treat. My own research and analytic work has been greatly illuminated by Ferenczi's insights, which have enabled me to appreciate the characterological basis of dissociative psychopathology (Brenner 1994a, 1996a,b, 1999a) and, I hope, shed a little more light on the problem. In the cases described above, the "confusion of tongues" was especially poignant because these women held their tongues in silence and used them instead to sexually gratify their mothers.

CONCLUSION

The conspiracy of silence evident in victims of incest was an especially crucial theme in the three women described above, who apparently had continued sexual contact with their mothers well into adulthood. When treatment offered a glimmer of hope for liberation of their mental and physical enslavement, they regressed and their suicidal symptoms intensified. There was evidence of a negative therapeutic reaction associated with a crisis in treatment. The crisis included aggression toward the analyst followed by a flight into health with an intensification or resumption of the incest, which was kept secret. Their symptoms were consistent with multiple personality or dissociative identity disorder and their "confusion of tongues" was very accurately described by Ferenczi. Like the abused child who is crushed after making a death-bed visit to her perpetrator father because he refuses to validate her memories, so, too, was Ferenczi denied his due. His remarkably lucid and far-reaching views about incest and dissociative psychopathology were suppressed and censored by the dying Freud and his loyal followers, who could not tolerate the challenge to the established party line. Ferenczi's own fatal illness and the conspiracy of silence kept his work from being too influential for many years. Perhaps like the patient who needs a very long time in treatment before she acquires the trust and psychological tools necessary to deal with her dreadful secret, so, too, has the analytic movement needed to wait until it was ready to confront the importance of such profound early trauma and its vicissitudes in many of those who ask for our help.

3

The Elusive Defense of Dissociation

The diagnostic criteria for dissociative identity disorder (DID) as set forth in DSM-IV are:

(A) the presence of two or more distinct identities or personality states (each with its own relatively enduring pattern of perceiving, relating to and thinking about the environment and self);
(B) at least two of these identities or personality states recurrently take control of the person's behavior;
(C) inability to recall important personal information that is too extensive to be explained by ordinary forgetfulness; and
(D) the disturbance is not due to direct physiological effects of a substance (e.g., blackouts or chaotic behavior during alcohol intoxication) or a general medical condition (e.g., complex partial seizures). [APA 1994, p. 230]

Of particular diagnostic and therapeutic importance is the phenomenon described in item B, which in DID jargon is commonly known as switching. This emergence of another so-called alter personality is the hallmark of the condition and at times may be florid and dramatic, taking the clinician by surprise, or it may be so subtle and imperceptible that it could be easily missed. As a result, doubts about the legitimacy of the diagnosis, the role of the therapist's undue influence, and the notion of a shared construction as the underlying cause of these psychomotor changes have been advanced. The general psychiatric literature is consistent in its descriptions and observations as major writers have noted changes in voice; patterns of speech; facial expression, especially around the eyes and mouth; body posture; coordination; strength and mannerisms. Regarding speech, for example, changes in pitch, rate, accent, and language use, and speech defects, such as stuttering, have been observed. Studying this phenomenon on videotape, where the time it takes may be less than a second or up to several minutes, Putnam (1989) observed, "The initiation of the switch is signaled by a blink or upward roll of the eyes. There may be rapid fluttering of the eyelids, . . . transient facial twitching or grimacing, . . . bodily twitches, shudders or abrupt change in posture. If the switching takes several minutes to complete, the individual may go into an unresponsive, trancelike state with blank, unseeing eyes" (pp. 120–121).

Sudden changes in affect may occur also, which may be confused with mood fluctuations in bipolar disorder or the inappropriate affect of schizophrenia. In addition, changes in cognitive functioning, such as in the capacity for abstract thinking, comprehension of ideas, or memory, may be noted also. Psychophysiological changes, such as a variability in the response to medication or alcohol, have been widely reported, and more bizarre changes, such as in eye color, have also been observed. One such patient, whom I treated in the hospital, initially refused to meet in a well-lit room, knowing that her irises would change from brown to blue when her angry, malevolent self would emerge and that that would betray her secret. As I got to know her better, the nursing staff and I witnessed these changes numerous times, which made her feel exposed, very vulnerable, and as though she had lost the upper hand in a constant power struggle with the dangerous outside world.

It has been typically described that such patients get "triggered," and that stimuli may bring on a switch. Both internal conflicts and external stimuli have been noted to be possible triggers, for example, "a color, touch, sexual arousal, the need to perform a specific function, the company of certain people, a specific emotion such as fear or anger, looking in the mirror, hearing a baby cry, a phone call from a past abuser, physical pain, having a bath, and a psychotherapy appointment" (Ross 1989, p. 136). By implication, anxiety may be considered as a common denominator and in corroboration of this finding, Ross also has pointed out that high doses of benzodiazepines (anxiolytic medications) can be helpful in the control of the switching.

In my analytically informed work with this patient population, it became imperative to understand the significance of this elusive phenomenon in the therapeutic situation. But as Fenichel (1942) observed, alterations in consciousness occurring during treatment are difficult to study because they are so fleeting. I, too, have been impressed that switching, that most dramatic manifestation of dissociation, can serve a defensive function in that the patient often experiences amnesia not only for this mental event but also for what preceded it.

> I first became aware of this aspect shortly after starting to work on an inpatient dissociative disorders unit when a patient had a violent episode after a community meeting. She had been

> vigorously campaigning to rally support for her election as the new president of the community. Unfortunately for her, she lost the election in a humiliating landslide and she was subject to criticism by several other patients who openly expressed doubts about her maturity and reliability for this position. Her cocky smile and facade of indifference belied her underlying distress, which suddenly erupted as she experienced a switch and began to scream, run wild into a wall, and appear to fight off a hallucinated gang attack. Having apparently lost contact with reality as one would in a sleepwalk or fugue, she enacted a scenario where she was outnumbered, humiliated, and abused, forcing the staff to restrain her for her own protection. Her episode drew others into participating in her repetition compulsion, making it more real and blurring the boundary between the past and the present, as well as between hallucination, memory, fantasy, dream, and external reality. When she eventually snapped out of it and came back to her usual self, she had no idea why the staff were holding her down and could not recall what she had been doing prior to this dissociated self state's emergence.

Since such dramatic and potentially dangerous, agitated behavior was the symptom that needed acute attention, this component of this episode also drew the most attention, as it does in most cases. As a compromise formation, however (Brenner 1982), it also enabled partial expression of her contained impotent rage in response to feeling attacked in the meeting through the dramatization of an attack presumably from her past. As a result, the defensive component, often the most subtle facet of this complex, has generally been underemphasized or overlooked by clinicians. Though clinicians acknowledge internal issues as a possible precipitant, the focus on environmental cues and the aftermath understandably has received much more attention.

As I got more psychotherapeutic experience with this population, I became more convinced that addressing the defensive aspect of this manifestation of dissociation held the most promise for understanding how to work with these patients psychoanalytically. Though quite disruptive and requiring much patience and a very good memory as well as the need for clinical flexibility, I found it helpful to focus on the dual defensive aspect of dissociation in the session. By considering that the activation of altered states from past trauma could be used in the service of warding off anxiety in the present, this became a paradigm that enabled me to listen with a psychoanalytic ear to the seemingly bizarre and quasi-delusional behavior that often obfuscated the immediate issue at hand. My working definition of a dissociation was:

> a defensive altered state of consciousness due to autohypnosis, augmenting repression or splitting. It develops as a primitive, adaptive response of the ego to the overstimulation and pain of external trauma which, depending on its degree of integration, may result in a broad range of disturbances of alertness, awareness, memory and identity. Dissociation may apparently change in its function and be employed later on as a defense against the perceived internal danger of intolerable affects and instinctual strivings. Thus, it may be a transient neurotic defense or become characterological and may even be the predominant defense. The content of associations in dissociation is as important as the defensive purpose it serves and may be accessible through hypnosis but very resistant to psychoanalysis unless the analyst is aware of its presence. [Brenner 1994a, p. 841]

It is significant to point out here that the change of function of dissociation also may result in relative (secondary) autonomy (Hartmann 1939) of the switching process and may account for the fact that many patients at times can will on a switch. As a result, this capacity is easily misunderstood and may be misperceived by certain clinicians as a willful fabrication of this phenomenon. Although the latter deception may occur also in some patients in search of a diagnosis who have been dubbed "multiple personality disorder (MPD) wannabes," the bona fide alter personalities may be both accessed by therapists and willed by the patient at times in the treatment setting.

In an effort to study this phenomenon more rigorously, the research of Lester Luborsky (1964, 1967) has offered a valuable direction. Especially with regard to his early study of momentary forgetting during psychotherapy and psychoanalysis, his approach to studying the dynamic significance of forgetting by examining the context in which it occurred has been a useful model. After studying nineteen patients for a total of 2,079 hours after two years, he came to the following conclusions: "A conscious thought associatively makes contact with a series of potentially threatening thoughts clustered around a repressed drive organized complex of thoughts. . . . The most common quality determining momentary loss of a thought seemed to be potential anxiety about letting oneself and/or the therapist become aware of a thought. The transference meaning of the lost thoughts made them potentially anxiety arousing at the moment" (Luborsky 1967, p. 215). Furthermore, in those moments of microscopic amnesia, he noted,

> The context of thought surrounding the momentarily forgotten thoughts were found to have certain consistent characteristics. By far, the most differentiating characteristic of a context as compared to its control was that the patient was on the verge of a new attitude or behavior that he had not been able to express before, as though he were pushing hard against old, established repressions. The next most differentiating category was difficulties in attention; next in order was the tendency for the recovered thought to be expressed on an abstract level and for the context to contain indications of guilt, shame or embarrassment. (However, contexts in which the forgotten thought was recovered

could not be differentiated from contexts in which the thought was not recovered.)

He concluded, "The analysis of momentary forgetting is offered as a contribution to the 'psychopathology of everyday therapy' as relative methods for systematic naturalistic observation of a type of forgetting which has not been studied before" (Luborsky 1967, p. 216).

As Luborsky's research (Schachter and Luborsky 1998) evolved over the years into the symptom-context method (Luborsky 1996), he applied his methodology to seven different types of symptoms, including forgetting, mood changes, onset of phobic symptoms, migraine headaches, premature ventricular contractions of the heart, stomach and ulcer pain, and petit mal seizures. It was determined by analyzing the recorded transcripts of all seven of these patients that even a unit as small as the patients' fifty words prior to the onset of symptoms were strikingly similar in each episode, in that there was activation of recurrent relational themes that were unique to their psychology that were associated with the affects of helplessness, hopelessness, fears of loss of control, dependency, and anxiety. Regardless of the symptom, be it psychological or psychophysiological, these findings were evident and confirmed by independent raters.

With the help of a small grant from the '76 Fund of Pennsylvania Hospital, I adapted some of this methodology to a pilot study of switching in DID patients. After obtaining informed consent, two suitable patients in my practice volunteered to allow their sessions to be recorded and transcribed for this purpose. Over a six-month period, twenty-six random sessions of the two patients were taped and transcribed. Overall, it was determined that eighteen spontaneous switches were observed. I omitted those switches where, for various clinical reasons, certain personifications were clearly accessed by me or specifically willed forward by the patients. Mrs. A., whose clinical history is described in great detail in Chapter 1, switched to ward off shame, anxiety, and impotent rage, especially over her rape, her body image, longings for women, and transferential feelings. In the second patient, Mary, who is described in detail in Chapter 2 and Chapter 9, intolerable affects related to anxiety, fear, shame, and impotent rage were predominant antecedents to her switching, also. The following examples of their transcripts will illustrate these findings.

CASE 1: MRS. A.

Mrs. A., a middle-aged woman with DID, was in her third year of a five-day-per-week treatment. She struggled with profound self-destructive urges as she felt utterly contaminated and worthless after a childhood of severe sexual exploitation and a vicious gang rape in her late teens. She felt unable to say no to sexual advances and was quite anxious about a male patient at her residential program who had taken an inappropriate interest in her. She entered the office, walked over to the couch, picked up a blanket, sat on the floor in front of her chair, and covered herself up from the neck down. She had been feeling very self-destructive lately and we had been discussing the possibility of rehospitalization.

Mrs. A.: I guess when I'm in the hospital I feel more secure. I don't feel like I have to protect myself. Because I have somebody watching me. When I get out I feel like I can pick up glass and my urges go up higher. I feel like I need to hurt myself to protect me.

Doctor: Protect you from what?

Mrs. A.: It makes me feel safe.

Doctor: How does that work? I never quite could understand that.

Mrs. A.: Well, it's like if you get scared and you go in and cut yourself, you're not scared anymore because you cut yourself and you survived and you cut yourself and you did something and you're not scared anymore. There's a lot of different reasons why I cut myself. That's one.

Doctor: How are you feeling today?

Mrs. A.: About the same as yesterday. About a 7 or a $7^1/2$. [1–10 scale, subjective units of distress]

Doctor: Yesterday you had said Jack would be leaving today? Tell me about it. [The man living at her residential program who had taken a sexual interest in her.]

Mrs. A.: He's leaving this morning. Sometime in the morning.

Doctor: So you think that by the time you get back there . . .

Mrs. A.: He'll be gone.

Doctor: He'll be gone.

Mrs. A.: Because my mentor is taking me out. We have a time-out for five hours to play tennis. [The patient starts to drift off and looks unfocused for about a minute.]

Doctor: What's going on with you right now? Hm? You seem far away. Can you describe what you are experiencing right now?

Mrs. A.: [Drawn back from her reverie, she struggles to speak] Do you know why I wear this blanket all the time?

Doctor: Why?

Mrs. A.: With you and nobody else. Because you know my inner core. And I feel so filthy and dirty around you. And nobody else knows me like you. So I have to cover up my inner dirty self. Nobody else knows what you know.

Doctor: But I don't see you the way that you see you. The way that you feel about yourself, I think, is the way you feel about yourself in my presence. Because you trusted me with certain things about you. [The patient starts to drift off again and cannot keep her eyes fully open.] What's going on?

Mrs. A.: Nothing.

Doctor: You seem very quiet and distant right now after revealing these powerful things about how you feel. You look like you can hardly stay awake right now.

Mrs. A.: I'm not tired.

Doctor: Your eyes are mostly closed. What's going on?

Mrs. A.: They're just heavy. It's hard to keep . . . it's hard to keep . . . it's hard to keep them up. What should we talk about?

Doctor: [Sensing a dissociative defensive regression and possible switch, I encourage her to narrate her inner experience.] I would like to talk more about what's going on inside you right now. Inside the mind.

Mrs. A.: It's all messed up.

Doctor: Can you narrate what it is?

Mrs. A.: Were you going to say something just now? Billy is causing a rumpus. [Her self-destructive alter personality is "activated" and about to emerge.]

Doctor: Billy is causing a rumpus? What do you mean? I'm not quite sure what you mean. You look so sleepy there when you say that Billy is causing a rumpus. Hello? Are you going to talk to me? [The patient becomes unresponsive again.]

Mrs. A.: Billy is causing a rumpus.

Doctor: How is Billy causing a rumpus? What do you mean? Can you put it into words?

Mrs. A.: Do you want to see? [It is unusual for the patient to maintain this degree of observing ego during such a transition and I continue to engage her quite actively.]

Doctor: Do I want to see? I'd like you to communicate it to me. [The patient does not respond.] What is it that you want me to see? Feel free to communicate in any way that you can.

Mrs. A.: He's in here swearing. He never swears. He never swears. I don't know why he's so upset.

Doctor: Why is he so upset?

Mrs. A.: I don't know why he's so upset.

Doctor: The way you describe it, that part of your mind that we know as Billy must be very near, right now.

Mrs. A.: He's right here.

Doctor: He is? How do you know?

Mrs. A.: He's right here, right here.

Doctor: What do you hear him saying?

Mrs. A.: He's mad because he couldn't find any glass.

Doctor: Why would he want to find glass?

Mrs. A.: Just to hold it.

Doctor: For what reason?

Mrs. A.: Just to hold it.

Doctor: He doesn't just hold it. He holds and then he cuts. From what we know, he cuts the skin, he cuts your fingers off. You know that.

Mrs. A.: He just holds it . . .

Doctor: For starters. What got Billy so riled up? Hm?

Mrs. A.: He told me he couldn't get any glass, no more to hurt me, and he got all mad.

Doctor: Where did he want to get the glass?

Mrs. A.: He was looking around this morning.

Doctor: This morning? Why?

Mrs. A.: To see . . .

Doctor: We know from the past that something triggers it. I wonder if you wake up that way, like from having bad dreams.

Mrs. A.: I don't remember bad dreams.

Doctor: You look very, very sleepy right now.
Mrs. A.: I'm not sleepy. I just have heavy eyelids.
Doctor: Yeah, very heavy eyelids. Do you know why?
Mrs. A.: Yeah.
Doctor: It must have something to do with your feeling that Billy is very nearby, don't you think?
Mrs. A.: He's taking my energy from me. [The patient becomes silent, shuts her eyes, and is completely still for about a minute.]
Doctor: Yeah.

[SWITCH] [The patient stands up, throws off the blanket, starts to angrily pace back and forth the length of the office, speaking in a lower, guttural tone with a stutter.]
Billy: G-G-G-Goddamn son of a bitches!!
Doctor: What's the matter, Billy? [The manner of speech and motoric behavior is recognizable and unique to this personification.]
Billy: They dooooon't let me pick up any glass. They take everything away from me. They don't let me take anything a-a-a-anymore. It makes me so sick and tired. I'm so fucking mad at everybody.
Doctor: Why is it, Billy, that . . .
Billy: I am so m-m-m-m-mad at everybody! I just want to go and kill myself.
Doctor: Why is it . . . you don't need the blanket over you? Mrs. A. is huddled in the corner on the ground with a blanket on her. You get up and start pacing, you take the blanket off and you're in a rage? What's going on?
Billy: I'm so fucking scared [muttering].
Doctor: I think we may need to call the hospital and arrange for a readmission. This is no way to start a weekend.

It looks like you are in bad shape right now, don't you think? Hm?

Billy: No.

Doctor: Billy, I noticed today when Mrs. A. was talking to me, that after she had got done telling me why she has to stay covered in my presence because of this horrible inner core that she has exposed to me, that she started to get very sleepy. Can you help me out with that?

Billy: T-T-T-T-That's because you know a-a-a-all about all the terrible things . . . all those things that her [male relative] did to her and things that the g-g-g-guys did to her at work and she feels very dirty and she doesn't like that somebody knows all that about her.

Doctor: How do you feel about that?

Billy: Me? I don't care one way or another . . .

Discussion

The fifty words preceding Mrs. A.'s switch pertained to her urges to cut and her response to my reminding her of the theme from the day before about Jack's departure from the program. Because I had become able to keep her engaged in the dialogue during this self-induced hypnotic evasion (Fliess 1953) she was able to narrate her inner experience. By struggling to stay in contact with me, it also prolonged the time it took her to switch into her Billy personification. Since we had been working extensively to maintain the therapeutic alliance no matter who was out, that is, throughout her defensive alterations of consciousness, she was at a point in treatment whereby this was possible. In the past, she would become silent and unable to articulate what was happening during the switch, and when her alter personality would take over she (or he) would usually be disoriented, bewildered, and amnestic for what had just taken place in the session. Because of the coalescence slowly taking place as a result of the therapeutic process, some co-consciousness had developed, and, as Billy, the patient could continue to observe and comment on her subjective experience.

As a result of this significant advance in the treatment process, Billy became able to essentially verify the defensive flight from Mrs. A.'s intolerable shame, disgust, and anxiety over her body, over a man's sexual interest in her, and over her helplessness to resist. What Billy could not acknowledge, however, needed to be expressed by yet another personification, "Sissey," who apparently owned Mrs. A.'s renounced sexual urges. While Sissey also expressed such dissociated wishes in the transference, and one can see the transference implications in this vignette, this work needed to be addressed with the utmost delicacy and caution. Billy's multiply determined impulses to mutilate the breasts and genitals as well as any other body part that was deemed "bad" would often become too overwhelming and gratifying to be safely managed on an outpatient basis even while Mrs. A. was living in her supervised residential program. As a result, the intensity of her dissociated libidinal wishes in the transference would have to be closely monitored and such interpretative work was frequently deferred, as much as possible, for when she would be hospitalized. During nineteen sessions that were transcribed over the six-month period, eight spontaneous switches were identified. Variations of the paradigm of Mrs. A.'s profound shame, helplessness, anxiety, and impotent rage as illustrated above appeared to be present in each of these instances. Because other personifications might emerge instead of Billy, such as a terrified child or a reassuring parentified teenager babysitter type, Mrs. A.'s affect and thought content could be quite different after the switch and obscure the underlying similarities. The question of the unconscious choice of alter personality to emerge after any given switch was also an intriguing issue subject to analytic exploration in our sessions.

CASE 2: MARY

Mary, a middle-aged woman who was in her fifteenth year of treatment, never expected to live to see her thirtieth birthday. Following a tumultuous course of life-threatening overdoses and severe alcoholism, the patient ultimately revealed her secret, which she feared, if divulged, would have condemned her to eternal damnation: maternal incest persisting into adulthood.

Session 1

[Long silence. The patient is sitting very tentatively, as she is fidgeting and avoiding eye contact. She looks anxious and distressed.]

Doctor: What are you nervous about?

Mary: Just being here and the fact that I have written in the journal a whole lot, actually not at all. [We had discussed the potential value of keeping a journal between sessions in light of her amnesia, as a way of chronicling her thoughts and feelings about what comes up between our meetings.]

Doctor: You have not journaled? How come?

Mary: Too hard. I don't know why I have this aversion to it. I know I can't remember everything.

[SWITCH 1] [After a very brief silence, the patient's facial expression brightens, her posture straightens, and she speaks in a higher tone with flamboyant hand gestures. I recognize this switch to a male alter, Frank, who is reportedly homosexual and has a stereotypical effeminate manner.]

Doctor: And there's a lot you don't want to know.

Frank: There is lots, and I try to encourage *her* to write because I think *she* writes well.

Doctor: Frank, you sort of suddenly emerged here.

Frank: [Very animated, histrionic, and humorous] Hm hm, well, someone has to speak up or she'll . . .

Doctor: Can we go back just a moment, not that I'm not happy to see you, but this sort of happened suddenly. What was going on with Mary to make it so that you came out? Why are you smiling?

Frank: Because she needs me.

Doctor: It's clear she needs you, but I'm wondering how the decision was made.

Frank: She was feeling pressured.

Doctor: Can you tell me what she was feeling?

Frank: I think she was feeling pressured about the journal. You tell her over and over to journal; she doesn't journal. Here we go again!

Doctor: Was there anything I said or conveyed to her, in my silence, that made her feel . . .

Frank: I think the silence was heavy.

Doctor: You mean like in the past when she would give me that phony excuse that she couldn't push the pencil! We all thought that was pretty lame, don't you think?

Frank: It is lame! [Chuckling]

Doctor: Of course, and she knew it, didn't she, because she started to giggle herself, I think. I wonder if she was afraid of being reprimanded.

Frank: I think so. I do. I think she's feeling that more strongly around this time of the year because she fears that her parents are going to get in contact with her and reprimand her for not being around for three years.

Doctor: She was pretty worked up about that Novena card. Why are you laughing?

Frank: It's so silly the things the Catholics do for money.

Doctor: I'm not sure it is just limited to the Catholics.

Frank: That's all she knows.

Doctor: What do you think your mother had to pay for those novenas?

Frank: I have no idea, probably a lot. They're worth a lot of guilt.

Doctor: Yeah, it worked on her conscience a little bit. You're immune to it?

Frank: What? The guilt?

Doctor: Yeah.

Frank: No.

Doctor: It works on you too.

Frank: Works on Mary.

Doctor: How about you, Frank?

Frank: Um, not to the extent that it works on Mary, which is why I suddenly came out.

Doctor: You could tolerate the depression better, too. So, where is she now?

Frank: Inside.

Doctor: Is she listening?

Frank: I think so. I think she is.

Doctor: Can you find out?

Frank: Can we see if she comes back? Does that matter?

Doctor: No, not necessarily. I'll talk to whomever emerges. I'm just curious about how and why, what it's all about. What the connection is.

Frank: About why I came out?

Doctor: But it's not clear how that decision was made.

Frank: I made that decision.

Doctor: You made it? You mean, you were listening in and you made the decision?

Frank: I was protecting her.

Doctor: So, it was getting too hot for her?

Frank: Yeah.

Doctor: Did she know that you were in the wings?

Frank: She knows that I do that.

Doctor: So you think she expected to be bailed out?

Frank: She doesn't come expecting much of anything. She tries to stay open-minded like we all do. But the writing thing, she has a problem with that.

Doctor: Yeah, and I do maintain that there are a lot of things she just doesn't want to know.

Frank: I know, but *we* have to know.

Doctor: That's why you are all here.

Frank: I know. What does she have to know?

Doctor: I think she has to know everything that you all know for starters. But there has to be an exchange transfusion, so to speak, of knowledge and memory and feelings and emotions.

Frank: Okay. One thing that has gotten through to her more recently is that, as I told you many times before, I wear a sock in my underwear. It makes me feel better, more a part of, and she was not always okay with that. And I also know that there was one time or two that you suggested until things cooled off that we didn't have sex, because of Paul [another male alter, an angry transsexual prone to sadism and self-mutilation] and things. When we felt comfortable enough, we did make love and there was one time a couple weeks ago when the kids did it [a reference to her child personifications].

Doctor: The kids did what?
Frank: The kids had sex with her [with Mary's lesbian lover, Harriet].
Doctor: Is that why Harriet was so upset?
Frank: Yes, because she wouldn't want to do that with the kids.
Doctor: So, she found out about the kids?
Frank: Hm, hm.
Doctor: How did she find out?
Frank: Afterward.
Doctor: Did someone tell her?
Frank: The kids were there and told her.
Doctor: Can you explain how that all came about? [Silence. Changes in facial expression to somberness, then to an angry demeanor as she takes her glasses off, as if to fight somebody.]

[SWITCH 2]
Doctor: You got quiet. I sense there is a change going on here. What's going on here? Usually when you take the glasses off I get a signal that it's you, Paul.
Paul: Yeah.
Doctor: Was Mary just here a moment ago when Frank left? How come?
Paul: She felt too much distress.
Doctor: She came back and left. Why did she come back at all if she felt so much distress?
Paul: I think she thought she would be able to tell you.
Doctor: But I guess she couldn't.
Paul: No. I forced them upon her.
Doctor: You forced the children on Harriet?
Paul: Yeah.
Doctor: How did that work?

Paul: They're afraid and when I tell them to do something, they usually do it.

Doctor: What did you tell them to do?

Paul: I told them to have sex with Harriet.

Doctor: Did you give them specific instructions?

Paul: Yes.

Doctor: What did you tell them to do?

Paul: I told them to kiss her and I told them to touch her.

Doctor: Did you tell them where to kiss her?

Paul: I told them to kiss her on the mouth and genitals.

Doctor: Did they listen?

Paul: They were scared and they did everything I told them to do.

Doctor: I can see why Mary wouldn't be able to talk about that because it must have felt to the children that your instructions to them were similar to what Mary went through with her own mother. So, you essentially became like her mother with the inside children.

Discussion

In this session, two spontaneous switches were identified. The first one, occurring very early on, appeared to be a defensive response to the building of pressure to perform in the transference by producing her journal. Mary experienced anxiety and guilt over wanting to be a disobedient daughter to her sexually demanding, callous, and sadistic mother. Her flamboyant male alter, Frank, a caricature of the stereotypical effeminate gay man, replaces her somberness with his exaggerated gaiety. He appears to be unaffected by these pressures, as though he were immune because he is only interested in other men. Here, too, as in Case 1, the alliance had extended and a certain amount of co-consciousness was possible at this point, enabling the patient to analyze the dynamic context of his emergence in the session. Frank continues to appear blasé as he discusses the patient's agonizing sexual identity conflict, a transsexual belief of being a male trapped in a woman's body. However, he, too, seems to become anxious talking about the patient's lesbian practices.

To paraphrase Frank's description, Mary would dissociate and switch into a scared young child while having sex with her lover, Harriet, a very troubled woman herself who had been living monogamously with Mary for several years. Though deeply attached and lovingly dedicated to each other, the two women quite frequently triggered self-destructive regressions in each other, raising the question of whether they were at risk of a double suicide. Their respective traumatic histories and psychopathology joined them in complex ways. Mary would have difficulty differentiating her lover from her mother, experiencing flashbacks, lost time, and terrifying inhibitions, as though she were the helpless child at her mother's mercy. During sexual arousal, this altered ego state would fluctuate with her angry, sadistic, transsexual self, Paul, who personified an identification with the aggressor. Paul could terrorize "the system," Mary's internal world, as well as threaten those on the outside. On more than one occasion, the hair on the back of my neck would stand on end as I listened to Paul's bloody and sexually sadistic revenge fantasies toward the mother in the transference.

The second switch in the session appeared to be in response to the anxiety and intolerance of such sadistic fantasies as Frank began to describe how Paul would sacrifice the children to the cruel mother during Mary's sexual intimacy with Harriet. Then by deceiving Harriet, she, too, became identified with the victim, thus leaving Paul victorious and in control, which aroused him (i.e., Mary in a dissociated state) to orgasm. Of the ten spontaneous switches identified in seven sessions, a recurrent paradigm of shame, guilt, fear, anxiety, and frustrated longing for the maternal object was the dynamic matrix.

The next session to be discussed, which occurred a number of weeks later, is quite remarkable in that Mary had become able to speak quite openly and thoughtfully about the maternal incest, her sexual identity confusion, and her dissociative disorder. At one point, however, she begins to lapse into an autohypnotic state, but as I had become even more acutely aware of the antecedents to her switching as a result of this study, I anticipated it with her and tried something different. I talked her through the anticipated switch and I talked through her to her other personifications. This technical approach appeared to have diminished her anxiety, supporting her observing ego and promoting more coalescence of her psyche. As a result, Mary felt more continuity of the self during this pivotal hour.

Session 2

[Long silence, after Mary revealed she had seen a very significant movie.]

Doctor: Well, I find it hard to believe that if you saw a movie like *Boys Don't Cry* that you don't have much to say about it.

Mary: Well, I do. It brings up rape and just the way she hid from the world like that and convinced other people that she was a boy. Sometimes I find myself in the same situation, only I see myself as a boy. You know, I don't hide my breasts, but . . .

Doctor: You have said you wear certain clothing that obscures your breasts? How?

Mary: Baggy clothes, minimizer bra, and . . .

Doctor: She was very small-breasted. She could bind her breasts.

Mary: Hm, hm. And it's a true story. At the end of the movie it tells you what happened. One guy's on death row. There was one part when she went in somewhere and said she had a sexual identity crisis.

Doctor: She made it sound like it was a specific condition. I am sure if we were to look it up we might come up with a label. Would that be useful?

Mary: No, it doesn't really matter to me. It is not going to change me.

Doctor: I guess one of the questions that I have that may not seem very important to you either is, What is the connection between your sexual identity crisis and your dissociative disorder? Is one more basic than the other? Are they connected or not connected?

Mary: Um, I think they're connected. Frank is fine with it yet Paul is, like, freaked out about it [having a female body]. So different people think different things about the same thing all in line with the symptoms. And myself, Mary, I consciously do it [cross-dress]. I am part of the system, too. Does that answer your question?

Doctor: Sort of. I know we've talked about it in a variety of ways.

Mary: I was just going to say that when I do that consciously as Mary I want to be a boy and I act like it except I do go into the ladies room. I do it consciously by my clothing, boobs, hair, but it is simple to fool people. My hair is cut short.

Doctor: I wonder if you always know that you are getting your hair cut short when you go and cut it.

Mary: Hm, hm. I think I interrupted something you were going to say.

Doctor: That's okay. I want to hear more from you.

Mary: When I pass people I wonder if they think if I am a boy or a girl, although it always surprises me when someone calls me sir. It always surprises me that I set myself up like that. Why wouldn't they? Then I think to myself, good, it's working.

Doctor: You're surprised and then happy?

Mary: Yeah.

Doctor: Never upset?

Mary: I guess a little shocked, but the clues are from me. I guess to be able to wear my hair as short as I have gotten it cut before in order to have the courage to get my hair cut that short, it . . . so that if anything would come up about my hair being so short I think he [Paul] would be the one to step in and defend the haircut.

Doctor: There's a conflict around it, to put it mildly. We know it's a life-and-death war at times. So, what is the connection between the sexual conflict and your dissociative disorder?

Mary: I think that's it.

Doctor: What's it?

Mary: A sexual conflict along with things that my mother did to me. From the minute I first walked into the hospital it was a homosexual crisis because I realized that I was gay or playing gay, I don't know.

Doctor: I don't know, either. It looks like you are just a human being wanting to be loved and love and not get hurt.

Mary: I look at my relationship with Harriet that way.

Doctor: Yeah.

Mary: I think right before Brian split at age 8, I, Mary, thought I was Brian, the boy.

Doctor: So, you grew up for the first eight years of your life thinking or wishing or believing that you were a boy?

Mary: Right.

Doctor: How did you reconcile your anatomy?

Mary: I tried to kill myself at 12 years old.

Doctor: What about the first eight years? Did you pretend that you didn't have a vagina? What did you see?

Mary: I don't know. I don't think I was educated enough to know about my body.

Doctor: You didn't know that boys had a different anatomy than girls?

Mary: I didn't know till I got my little brother; there were all girls in the house.

Doctor: When you were how old?

Mary: Eight.

Doctor: I thought you were younger than that when he was born.

Mary: I think I was 6 when he was born.

Doctor: Six, okay. That's the first time you remember seeing a penis?

Mary: Huh, huh. I don't know. I watched my Dad.

Doctor: Watched him what?

Mary: In his bedroom or in the bathroom.

Doctor: You followed him in? Before you were 6?

Mary: I think so.

Doctor: So you must have seen something different from what you had between your legs.

Mary: Yeah, it was really different but it didn't make sense to me because in my mind I don't think I reconciled that. Maybe that's my problem now. Maybe I haven't reconciled that. I obviously never reconciled.

Doctor: Reconciled what?

Mary: That I have a vagina instead of a penis.

Doctor: And what you're telling me is that you think this goes back to confusion from your early childhood?

Mary: Definitely. Not to mention that I had heard my parents having sex.

Doctor: You did?

Mary: So when my Mom would have sex with me, I was the boy.

Doctor: How old were you when you heard your parents having sex? How did you know it was sex? What did it sound like?

Mary: I don't know the first time. I was younger than 10. Then again in my teens. I could hear the bed moving and them making sounds.

Doctor: What kind of sounds?

Mary: Panting sounds. That blows my mind.

Doctor: What does?

Mary: That I haven't reconciled that.

Doctor: Reconciled that boys have one set of genital anatomy?

Mary: No, that I don't. That I never had a penis.

Doctor: You make it sound like it's a new realization for you.

Mary: It's a new realization.

Doctor: What's new about it?

Mary: I don't know. I feel bowled over by it.

Doctor: I'm delighted to hear that you are really taking it in today and feeling it [and tolerating it without switching]. I am curious, though. What it is about today?

Mary: I don't know. I think it's all in my control and it's not in my control. Thinking that just putting a sock in between my legs is going to make me feel like I am a man, wear men's clothing and all the things I talked about before . . .

Doctor: Like in the movie.

Mary: . . . so my mind changes when I do that.
Doctor: How does your mind change?
Mary: I become a boy or a man and when I don't do that and still wear the same clothes and people know I'm a woman, I don't know if I deal with that right.
Doctor: What do you mean?
Mary: I mean, I've had to have come to some point in the conflict where I can survive either way or I would've been successful in killing myself.
Doctor: How have you successfully dealt with conflict?
Mary: Well, I don't think I have, now that I think about it. That's what I'm finding out today. I can feel it today. When we talk about it . . . all the time we've talked about it, it was just like over there somewhere, but I can feel it today.
Doctor: Because?
Mary: I think the movie has had something to do with it.
Doctor: I think so too. What kind of catalytic effect did that movie have?
Mary: First of all, that there are other people that do that, too.
Doctor: So, you did not feel like such an oddity.
Mary: Right. Um, second of all, it can be dangerous. Gay bashing, being raped, murdered. I'm in my own little world with it.
Doctor: You're in your own little world, but even in your own little world you have almost been killed over it, too, because of the war inside. What was it in the movie do you think that made people want to kill another individual?
Mary: Um, I can give you the stock answer about how people have both sides to themselves, male and female, and people who have homosexual tendencies are people who tend to gang-bash gay people and

that, um, those guys were like that but I'm not sure they were. Maybe they weren't.

Doctor: So it made them angry with themselves about their homosexual . . .

Mary: I don't think it's conscious.

Doctor: Unconscious?

Mary: Unconscious.

Doctor: So an unconscious homosexual trend in them upset them.

Mary: Upset them and they take it out on a gay person. But I think it was because they were fooled. They were tricked.

Doctor: They were tricked and they felt betrayed.

Mary: Uh-huh. I think there's more to that because I think being tricked or betrayed is not enough to murder someone.

Doctor: Unless it resulted in a profound sense of humiliation that is so intolerable, so intolerable that unless a person gets it out of her system with such force and violence that perhaps she'll be afraid she will die of shame. Perhaps.

Mary: Then perhaps I've been there myself also.

Doctor: Perhaps.

Mary: I definitely think that's part of my sexual conflict.

Doctor: Can you put it in your own words?

Mary: Um, the confusion is one thing. Paul wanting to kill everyone so he can have the body [and get a sex change procedure]. A very rageful, intolerable situation that he thinks he's in.

Doctor: So he feels stuck with a vagina and breasts and menstruation.

Mary: That's going away. [She is experiencing menopausal changes.]

Doctor: I know, but I am speaking over time, such as with too much hair on the wrong parts of the body or not enough hair on certain other parts of the body. We know all of these things have driven him wild.

Mary: It's the humiliation that makes him so rageful. But I give in as much as I can. I do. Like, not shaving my legs or underarms.

Doctor: That's a compromise that you negotiated.

Mary: I don't know if I truly negotiated it because Harriet hates it. I think that when there is someone I love and who loves me enough to say I don't like that but I keep it anyway, it gives him satisfaction.

Doctor: Like it gives him a victory.

Mary: But she understands, she says. I want to get back to that, not reconciling within myself.

Doctor: That's a biggie.

Mary: That's where I split.

Doctor: Tell me more.

Mary: That's coming from Brian. That's why I split.

Doctor: When you say split . . . ?

Mary: I guess dissociate and then there are different people's minds and bodies within me.

Doctor: Because you couldn't . . .

Mary: Tolerate.

Doctor: Tolerate what?

Mary: Not being like my father and brother. That was the biggest shock of my life.

Doctor: Why was it so important to be like them?

Mary: I'm not so sure that is the question. I think the question is, Why weren't they like me? Growing up with a vagina. I don't even think I realized what was going on down there with my Mom really.

Doctor: It started so early.

Mary: Yeah, and why weren't they like me with a vagina? But I know that for some reason it was okay that my Dad was like that, but then when my little brother came along and he was like that that's when it got messed up. Because when I was a kid my Mom let me run outside with—a certain age, of course, in the summertime—without a shirt on just like the boys were and then it came a day when I had to cover up and do things the way girls do.

Doctor: And you haven't been right since?

Mary: Uh-huh. Even supposedly being a woman and supposedly knowing my body, I didn't know my body very well. It wasn't until I met Meg [a friend] that I realized that I did not urinate from my clitoris, that there was another opening there! So I always thought I had a little penis.

Doctor: Your clitoris was your penis. How did Meg educate you?

Mary: She had a book on lesbian sex and it had to do with women having only one organ just for pleasure.

Doctor: How did you feel about that?

Mary: What was what feeling?

Doctor: About what women have?

Mary: I'm not sure I really think about it; maybe I think about it too much. Isn't this amazing? I never thought I would get around to telling you that.

Doctor: Telling me what?

Mary: Telling you what Meg said.

Doctor: About the clitoris.

Mary: That I wasn't peeing out of my clitoris.

Doctor: She told you that . . .

Mary: I didn't know.

Doctor: What does that tell you that you finally got around to talk about this?

Mary: That I'm more mature. I can come in and talk all the time.

Doctor: You didn't meet Meg till your late 20s, early 30s?

Mary: Yeah. All that time I thought that I was a boy. If I stood up to pee, that's the hole.

Doctor: Do you usually stand up to go to the bathroom?

Mary: Not usually anymore.

Doctor: When did that stop?

Mary: It happens off and on during different stages.

Doctor: Do you hold your clitoris the way a boy would hold his penis?

Mary: Hm, hm. So there is a big example of not having reconciled myself about that.

Doctor: You look lost in thought. [Patient appears to withdraw into a trance-like state, as though she were in the process of a switch.]

Mary: There's a lot going on inside.

Doctor: There's a lot going on inside and you're working hard, *all of you*. You were ready to see things. [I sense the internal cooperation and acknowledge the presence of the other personifications, in the hope of averting a disruption of consciousness in order to continue this unusually productive dialogue.]

Mary: I guess I was.

Doctor: After you get to talk about things for a decade and a half, you finally see it because I think if you saw it a whole lot sooner, you may have had a different reaction to it.

Mary: I would've been freaked out.

Doctor: Yeah, so . . .

Mary: Just in telling me that I do that.

Doctor: Do what?

Mary: That I put a sock inside.

Doctor: But you made me aware of that a long time ago.

Mary: I know, but that's what I'm saying. That stayed in this room but when I saw it in the movie, it was a true story.

Doctor: I see, because you might have thought that you were the only person who did that.

Mary: Maybe not the only person but not too many people. It's getting a little chaotic inside. [Patient is alerting me again that she is sensing a loss of control to the autohypnotic forces and is asking for assistance.]

Doctor: Why? Who is getting riled up?

Mary: Paul is getting riled up and Brian, too.

Doctor: [I am very aware of her intolerance of the accompanying affects to this material. In an effort to mitigate her shame and humiliation and in order to prevent a switch, I make an empathic comment and once again acknowledge her personified defenses.] Well, I hope Paul and Brian realize that what we're talking about is not intended to hurt, humiliate, or denigrate you in any way. But, in fact, Mary has probably been wanting to tell me about this stuff for fifteen years. I think it's a tribute to your maturity that you allowed her to. I'm sure you're protesting but you allowed her to talk about it today, you allowed her to sit through the movie. Maybe you're all learning something also. I want to emphasize that no one is trying to get rid of anybody here. I think the idea is for peaceful coexistence. [She appears a bit calmer.]

Mary: I think that's part of the idea—that I've never reconciled that with myself, it is affecting Paul and those. [She is acknowledging and describing how she experiences her intrapsychic conflict as a pseudo-externalized interpersonal conflict]

Doctor: What is it about that that is affecting them so much?

Mary: Um, they're threatened.

Doctor: Why is Paul feeling most threatened by the idea?

Mary: The recognition of not having a penis because that's his main thing, that's what he's so angry at. So he wants to kill the body so he gets what he wants and then he will get a penis.

Doctor: Create a new body. But I think Paul is finally realizing that without the body he's dead too. He's fighting against that inside, but I think he knows . . . [The patient is recognizing how her transsexual conflict is related to her suicidality.]

Mary: He knows.

Doctor: . . . he knows it more than ever and I think that's why he's allowing this discussion to take place because Paul doesn't really want to die anymore. So we appreciate that, Paul, and we are more aware that you are suffering but I am hopeful that some sort of compromise, some sort of arrangement, something can be worked out, so don't panic. [By my talking to Paul through Mary, her observing ego is retained and there is no discernible switch.]

Mary: I'm not panicking but I'm really suffering.

CONCLUSION

It is possible to examine the dynamic context in which patients with DID spontaneously "switch" during the course of a psychotherapy hour. In so doing, one can begin to understand the defensive structures and their functions in this complex and perplexing condition. This recognition can aid in therapeutic process that promotes integration of the psyche. The methodology developed by Luborsky to analyze the context in which symptoms become manifest during sessions appears to be applicable to this multiply determined symptom/defense (Waelder 1936), dissociation, where easily observed motivated forgetting is one component. By means of transcribed sessions, these patterns can be discerned by reviewing the preceding utterances of the patient, with units as small as fifty words. In this population, repetitive central themes related to prior trauma and instinctual urges linked with transference implications appeared to induce intolerable amounts of shame, guilt, helplessness, fear, and anxiety. In response, the patients were prone to lapse into personified defensive altered states of consciousness. Over time, with expansion of the therapeutic alliance throughout those autohypnotic states, hypnotic evasion may give way to hypnotic facilitation (Shengold 1989), allowing a continuous narrative of the patient's subjective experience. Then, with the therapist's awareness, anticipation, and recognition of such impending shifts, it may be possible to intervene to promote strengthening of the observing ego and mitigate the disruptive effects of switching, which promotes coalescence of the psyche.

More rigorous research is needed, using blind raters, a larger sample size, and perhaps videotaping to better understand this phenomenon. Concomitant neuroimaging techniques, were they not so disruptive, might also offer an important perspective in furthering our understanding about this seemingly bizarre form of negation (Freud 1925b).

II

SYMPTOMS

4

The Lifelong Persistence of Symptoms

The shock of being forcibly pulled from one's home, eliminated from one's community, and ousted from one's homeland has lasting effects on both the body and the soul. It is a massive trauma that viciously assaults one's identity and all the basic assumptions one has about one's place in the world (Elsass 1997, Kestenberg and Brenner 1996, Krystal 1968). The murder of loved ones, the confiscation of property, the violent atrocities, the starvation, disease, beatings, torture, and slave labor, along with the lost hope for rescue due to feeling utterly forgotten by the world, further the decimation of one's psyche (Federn 1990, Wiesel 1961). And for ethnic or religious groups with a long history of repeated attempts to annihilate them, we find elements of their pasts incorporated into their cultural identity and philosophy of life. These groups, in order to maintain their cohesiveness, tend to memorialize a "chosen trauma" (Volkan 1997) that then becomes a rallying cry to differentiate one nationality from another. These differences may have potentially lethal implications as unacceptable images of one group get projected onto the other, illustrating how psychoanalytic knowledge of the individual may be applied to groups. Such major advances in our understanding of that "second skin" known as ethnic identity may help us comprehend a bit more about how some of the darkest moments of the twentieth century were, in retrospect, predictable outcomes of the melding of modern technological advances with the ancient passions of fear, hatred, envy, and greed.

DARKEST MOMENTS OF THE TWENTIETH CENTURY

The Holocaust, or Shoah, refers to the destruction of the European Jewish population in World War II by the Third Reich of Nazi Germany (Yahil 1990). An ancient people with a long history of persecution, the Jews continue to mourn their ancient exile following the destruction of their temple in Jerusalem 2,000 years ago (Josephus 1984). This lament has been incorporated into their liturgy with prayers for a return to their homeland, and generations of unresolved mourning became institutionalized into the fabric of Jewish culture (Falk 1996). Following their exile into the Diaspora, they were scattered across the continents, and the "wandering Jew" became a legendary stereotype. A homeless people without borders or an army is especially vulnerable to threats to its existence.

It has been estimated that of the 55 million deaths during World War II, about eighteen million were European civilians. Of this group, about one in three of these noncombatant deaths was a Jew (Marrus 1987), known as the "six million." Roughly two thirds of European Jews were exterminated. In what was hideously transformed into genocide from the highly improbable plan of deporting them to the island of Madagascar off the east coast of Africa, the "final solution" of the Jewish question was mass extermination or being worked to death to support the war effort. This solution was secretly planned long before the now infamous Wannsee Conference in January 1942 (Davidowicz 1975, Hilberg 1971). Despite the deadly campaigns against the Gypsies, or Roma, the Jehovah's Witnesses, and homosexuals, the fate of the Jews was especially bleak and unique because Nazi ideology demanded their total elimination. Even as late as the spring of 1944, when the tide had already turned against the German war effort, the official party line put forth by Joseph Goebbels and the Ministry of Propaganda was still being broadcast: "'In the case of the Jews, there are not merely a few criminals (as in other people), but all the Jewry rose from criminal roots and in its very nature it is criminal. The Jews are no people like any other people, but a pseudo people welded together by heredity criminality. . . . The annihilation of Jewry is no loss to humanity but just as useful as capital punishment or protective custody against other criminals'" (Hilberg 1985, p. 1021).

Although survivors of the Holocaust are proof that Hitler did not fully succeed, more than half a century later the Jewish population has yet to recover and it has not kept up with global population growth. Worldwide estimates today are less than the 18 million estimated in the late 1930s, and the Jews have migrated once again. Approximately 5 million Jews live in Israel, comprising about 80% of the population there. The former Soviet Union has been the largest source of recent immigrants, accounting for almost 850,000 people since the great influx started in 1989. North and South America contain about half of the entire Jewish population, while Europe's population still bears most of the scars of Hitler's genocidal intent. Interestingly, Germany has become a very popular new home for Jewish immigrants from behind the former Iron Curtain.

What does it mean to a Holocaust survivor to want to

go home, and how does it feel? And where is home? Is it the ancestral home of Biblical times? Is it the homeland from which one was branded an enemy and condemned to death? Or is it one's adopted homeland? Clearly, there are no simple answers, as it is complex and multiply determined. To illustrate the issues I will describe a man who emigrated to the United States (Grinberg and Grinberg 1989), had gone back to Europe twice in search of his home, and in the last months of his life was planning to go back again.

A MAN WHO SURVIVED

I was asked to see Mr. R., a Holocaust survivor, in consultation, a man in his seventies who was dying in the hospital (Eissler 1955). I was familiar with his history from prior interviews (Kestenberg and Brenner 1996) and it was thought that I could play a useful liaison role. Heroic medical efforts to keep him alive did not seem to hold. The family was agonized over the prospect of inflicting additional pain and equally anguished over the prospect of not making available every possible chance for his continued survival. After all, he was a bit unusual because he had defied the odds by surviving not only almost six years in concentration camps but also the infamous death march from Auschwitz in January 1945. Despite his grave prognosis, to give up now seemed totally out of character with the essence of his life. The family implored the staff to do everything they could to save the man's life. Quite significantly, he told them prior to being intubated and put on a ventilator that all he wanted to do was to just be able to go "home." So how could they live with themselves if they did not support every effort to honor his last request to go home? Amazingly, he did rebound and lived another five weeks, getting off all life support and actually making plans to, indeed, go home. Even the medical staff was in awe at his extraordinary will and almost miraculous turnaround, but this time he did not make it.

During his roller coaster of a hospitalization, after he was removed from the ventilator, he experienced vivid flashbacks of Auschwitz, begging that someone "open the door" to let him get free (i.e., so he could go back home). Another time, in a delirious state, he called out for his dead mother in his mother tongue, begging for her help so he could go back home. And, eerily, by the time his body finally did give out, he had lost so much weight that his weakness and wasting away must have contributed to his feeling that he was back in the camps.

Born in Germany, and the oldest of three children, he was a teenager when Hitler's Nuremberg laws began to tighten the noose around the necks of German Jewry. Seeing the dangers that lay ahead, he had wanted to go to Palestine with a youth group in the mid-1930s to escape the growing persecution, but his father forbade it believing the Nazi scare would blow over and little harm would befall the family. "If only" . . . (Akhtar 1996) he had defied his father, but instead he stayed home. The family business was subsequently destroyed during the national pogrom on November 9, 1938, known as Kristallnacht (night of the broken glass), and less than a year later, in September 1939, he and his father were arrested by the Gestapo. They were taken to the Sachsenhausen concentration camp for what was to be the beginning of an almost six-year ordeal of starvation, slave labor, systematic sadistic degradation, beatings, and the daily threat of death. At the time of their deportation, his mother and siblings were in hiding (Gross 1988), using what little resources they had to barter for their lives.

Three very long years later, in October 1942, Mr. R., his father, and a cohort of about 400 other prisoners (Czech 1990) were transported by cattle car to Auschwitz. A veteran slave laborer by then, he was selected to continue to work himself to death. During his processing, in an ironic moment of Nazi imperfection, there was not enough ink to darken the last digit of his tattoo, triumphantly foreshadowing for Mr. R. that there might also not be enough poison in the death camp to finish him off. After a period of time at the main camp, he was sent to the adjacent Monowitz Camp operated by the giant industrial conglomerate, I. G. Farben (Borkin 1978), where he and the other senior male laborers were forced to build the huge synthetic rubber manufacturing complex simply known as Buna. From the time he arrived, the camp grew from 3,000 to about 12,000 prisoners at its peak prior to its sudden evacuation in January 1945 (Czech 1990, Ferencz 1979, Levi 1986, Michel 1993). Despite risking his life in ongoing efforts to acquire extra food for his ailing father, the man died of starvation, disease, and exhaustion in 1943. In camp slang, he was *eingegangen* (i.e., wilted like a flower).

In the summer of 1944, as the news of the approaching Allies was beginning to filter down to the inmates, two of Mr. R.'s boyhood friends sought his help in their plan to escape the camp (Gutman and Berenbaum 1994). Knowing the plan allowed only the two to leave, he still willingly helped them. He risked his life by going into the infirmary and pretending to be sick. In this way, one of his friends was then able to be assigned to lead the work detail that day, replacing Mr. R. as foreman, or kapo. Therefore, when they snuck away, he would not be held responsible for their escape. However, this plan was very dangerous because sick prisoners who could not work and were no longer useful were simply exterminated. If the SS had the slightest suspicion about his complicity, he would have been hanged or shot on the spot or worse. (This punishment had been recently carried out on three of their friends who were caught trying to escape in order to fight with Russian partisans. On October 9, 1944, the three men were hanged in front of the entire prison population who were assembled for this purpose [Mark 1985]. Mr. R. remembered this horror very clearly, especially because he helped save the brother of one of the condemned men by restraining him as he tried to break formation and stop the hanging. This man most certainly would have been killed also.) In a sense, he stayed "home" in order to help them become free. Incredibly, the escape was successful, and after the war the three men caught up with each other and resumed their lifelong friendship until Mr. R.'s death.

While in hiding, the two men watched the prisoners trudge along in their death march from Auschwitz just ahead of the advancing Russian troops. Mr. R. was among those on this march to Gliwice where he and thousands more were then transported by open rail cars for days, completely exposed to the freezing winter elements. He arrived at the Buchenwald concentration camp back in Germany and was then sent to a satellite munitions factory, Altenberg, where he was liberated by American troops in April 1945. An emaciated living skeleton of about 80 pounds, he was then taken to a hastily built field hospital where he was treated for a number of weeks. There he was so debilitated that he reported that he had to be fed by a medicine dropper in order to get nourishment. He regained his strength enough to then consider his next step, a taste of freedom in the chaotic post-liberation period in Germany. During this time he met an attractive Hungarian woman who had also been recently liberated. A brief romance ensued and she wanted him to join her to see if any of her family had survived. Once again he felt torn in his loyalties, this time between his desire for this woman and his own pull back home to search for his mother. Just as his filial responsibilities had kept him from leaving his family for the relative safety of Palestine before the war, his wish to return home after the war prevailed. He and the woman parted company, never to meet again as they began the uncertain journey to reclaim whatever was left of their former lives. Upon his return, he reunited with his mother and one of his siblings through the help of the local Jewish agencies. Approximately a year later, after liberation, arrangements were made for the family's passage to the United States. Having lost their home, which was to be under Russian jurisdiction, there was nothing keeping them in Germany, so they left as soon as possible.

Mr. R. was eager to forget about his past and make a new life. He married an American woman, started a family, and took whatever work he could get. He was completely oblivious until his archival interviews that an industrial complex visible from his front door was chillingly reminiscent of the I. G. Farben complex back in the concentration camp. Trying to get as far as possible from conscious reminders of the Holocaust, he did not surround himself with other immigrants, refugees, or fellow survivors. However, his periodic reunions with his two friends were enormously important to him. He was determined to assimilate, and prided himself on being able to relate to people from many walks of life. Although he could not concentrate well enough to resume his formal schooling, he educated himself in politics, current events, and the world situation, especially as it pertained to violence, persecution, war, and technology. He voraciously read newspapers, magazines, and other publications that, combined with his horrendous work experience as a slave laborer in a quarry, a brick factory, chopping down trees, building factories, constructing barracks, etc., gave him an extensive breadth of knowledge. Despite certain gaps in his knowledge due to his self-education, Mr. R. exuded a cultured European air that was not snuffed out by the camps and was acquired from his affluent prewar life in a major city. But in the United States, he did manual labor and would idealize certain aspects of his childhood "before Hitler." In his rare moments of nostalgia, he usually would conjure up sensory memories of his favorite food (Kestenberg and Brenner 1996, Werman 1977). Much to the confusion of his children, he would delight in taking them to German restaurants and German-style festivals where, conversing in German, he tried to regain some version of the good times from long ago. His eyes would light up recalling the tasty delicacies from his childhood, a time when he freely played games with his friends and looked forward to a good life. He apparently could revel at such times, being transported back and bypassing his lost teenage and young adult years. He could safely regress with his grandchildren more easily than with his own children, as though the passage of time and generative life experiences had a fortifying healing effect. In addition, he would sing silly songs from childhood, play games from that period, and recall humorous incidents from grammar school. He would even imitate certain memorable teachers, showing a rather intact memory of this idealized time when he was living side by side and equally with his German neighbors.

To preserve memories of the earlier "good Germans" who were uncontaminated by the Nazis ("bad Germans"), he seemed to keep them quite separate in his mind. Interestingly, his attitude toward Jews and his own Jewish identity did not appear as dissociated but rather quite ambivalent and conflicted. Although he was raised in a very traditional and observant family, his belief in God was shattered by what he witnessed and experienced as a member of the so-called Chosen People. He was especially anguished over memories of his pious grandfather being defiled and over having seen grotesque, sadistic torture of very religious rabbis who helplessly prayed until they lapsed into unconsciousness before their deaths. Afterward, Mr. R. felt disillusionment, contempt, and cynicism toward the passively faithful who did little to help themselves except to pray for deliverance. Furthermore, he would experience claustrophobic anxiety and irritability whenever he was in a crowded synagogue, as though being in an enclosed space with large numbers of Jewish people revived memories of the camps.

Throughout the first years of his new life in the United States, he denied having any wish to return to or visit his homeland. His only connection with Germany was through his monthly restitution checks for the years of slave labor, which he ambivalently accepted. A landmark lawsuit filed by one of his comrades from Buna forced I. G. Farben to supplement this pension (Ferencz 1979). The formation of a national organization of these survivors and a historic reunion in New York in 1960 (Michel 1993) was empowering and uplifting.

Then, in 1961, another major event focused Mr. R.'s attention on the past. The trial of one of the most wanted Nazi war criminals, Adolf Eichmann, made worldwide headlines, bringing forth gruesome and painful testimony from the witnesses. His conviction and execution had an impact on survivors like Mr. R., who felt somewhat vindicated and avenged, as though the world was finally beginning to listen to what they had to say. In effect, it validated their traumatic history (Novey 1985) and raised their self-esteem. In the years that followed, numerous oral history projects provided opportunities to give testimonies (Kestenberg and Brenner 1996), culminating in the most comprehensive effort by film director Steven Spielberg's Shoah Foundation. Mr. R. volunteered his narrative on several occasions and felt very strongly that "the world must know." In his later years, after returning to Germany and reviewing his life, he lectured to schools and youth groups about his experience.

Significantly, Mr. R. had gotten fed up with working for "slave wages," and after the I. G. Farben lawsuit and the Eichmann trial decided to go into business for himself so as not to take orders from anyone ever again. He worked long hours and preferred to stay very busy so as not to think too much, a hypomanic defense that under the circumstances seemed quite adaptive (Winnicott 1935). Nevertheless, his children grew up with an awareness of his past, and they felt compelled to travel to Europe, where they met their only surviving relative there. One of his daughters even visited the concentration camp at Dachau, outside of Munich. A depressing and unforgettable part of her trip, it felt to her like a pilgrimage (Poland 1977), as though Dachau were a huge cemetery where she could pay homage to all of her murdered relatives. Seeing with her own eyes what kind of place her own father was forced to live in and being free to walk out whenever she wanted was a triumphant moment of mastery. In a sense, going back to her father's homeland was a mission carried out for him.

Several years later, Mr. R. himself made arrangements to go back, first with his family and then as a special guest of the city with other survivors in order to come to terms with the past. At this time in the late 1970s there was a new spirit of rapprochement, and a series of historic worldwide gatherings of survivors were being planned (Michel 1993). Mr. R. was quite ambivalent about going back, but with the encouragement of his children and several of his survivor friends he proceeded. He was able to locate the house he lived in for a year after liberation and lingered outside for a while preferring only to take it in quietly from a distance. After his trip, his mother, a bitter woman who never recovered from her trauma and losses, died. Having ambivalently regarded his mother, Mr. R. was not able to adequately grieve for her; his long-standing unresolved mourning for his father and sister became even more complicated. Following his mother's death, he had a life-threatening medical emergency, the beginning of a condition that eventually led to his demise.

After his recovery, he took a second trip to Germany, entering Russian-controlled East Germany in search of his original home. All physical evidence of his earlier life was long gone and there were no friends or relatives to contact. The street was renamed and his home had been demolished years before. After these trips back to Germany he felt he had seen enough to satisfy his curiosity and was pleased with the treatment by the officials of his hometown but had no desire to go back again. It was "enough." In the last twenty years of his life, he never returned. However, in 1995, the fiftieth anniversary of the liberation of the camp, he was invited to attend a special dedication at his first concentration camp. It seemed that his family was actually more interested in attending that he was. Ever the stoic, bigger-than-life man that he was, he could not admit any trepidation in front of them, and planned to attend even though his health had seriously declined. As another of his fraternity brothers succinctly quipped, "I never liked it the first time, so why would I want to go back the second time?" Mr. R. did have reservations, and at the last minute, a setback in his health prompted the unspoken fear of his dying on German soil. It was too cruel of an irony to consider, so the trip was canceled, much to his relief and disappointment. Several months later, he died.

TOWARD AN UNDERSTANDING OF THE SUFFERING

An understanding of Holocaust survivors' motives and feelings about returning home requires an appreciation of the interplay of three main influences: (1) historical, (2) ethnic or cultural, and (3) psychological (i.e., intrapsychic, developmental, as well as the effects of massive psychic trauma and its transmission to the next generation). From a historical perspective, the major ideological goals of the Third Reich were to purify Europe and make room for Aryan population growth. The belief in world domination by the superior race of Aryans led to psychotic logic that justified extermination of inferiors, like a surgical procedure to remove a malignant growth from the human body (Lifton 1986). Therefore, cleansing Europe of the Jews (i.e., to make it *Judenrein*) became a top priority even at the expense of sound military decisions (Marrus 1987). It became a capital crime to be a Jew, and after liberation the terror and mistrust of governments could not just disappear overnight. The historical facts of the enormity of the destruction were an undeniable reality that pervaded all aspects of the survivors' views of the world and themselves. Many have had no desire to stay or ever return. Those who stayed or those who returned after the war were clearly in the minority, using a counterphobic stance to prove to themselves that they could go back or stay there and not get killed (Kestenberg and Brenner 1996). Also, some survivors were simply too depleted physically and narcissistically (Freud 1914, Kestenberg and Brenner 1988) as well as too frightened to make any more changes in their lives, settling wherever they could. Following the war, the victorious Allied forces divided up Europe, leading to the Cold War, and prior to the reunification of Germany and the collapse of the Soviet Union, it was estimated that approximately 2 million Jews were still trapped behind the Iron Curtain. In contrast, only 1.25 million Jews voluntarily lived throughout Western Europe (Johnson 1987), and of these only about 35,000 Jews were living in West Germany (Sichrovsky 1986). Travel was restricted or impossible between East and West, interfering with those who wanted to emigrate to freedom as well as those wanting to look for their roots in forbidden places. All that has changed now, providing more opportunities for those who have waited over fifty years desiring to return. Mr. R.'s original home came under Soviet rule, and he was almost shot by wild, drunken Russian soldiers after liberation, so he had no illusions about his safety in Russian hands. He wanted to leave Europe as quickly as possible, trusting only the Americans.

To consider the ethnic or cultural influences on wanting to return, one might hypothesize that different groups experiencing similar persecution might have dealt with the aftermath differently. Such a comparative study would be almost impossible given the enormous number of variables, the passage of time, and the sheer horror of it all. While the Jewish people certainly have had no corner on the market of suffering during World

War II, many historians do agree that the Nazi policy and treatment was singularly unique in its goal of absolute extinction.

The most identifiable group whose suffering closely paralleled that of the Jews was the Gypsy or Roma population. Reviled and feared outsiders to mainstream Christendom since the Middle Ages, both groups were accused of poisoning the wells and bringing on the Plague. Though not a cohesive people but more resembling loosely connected nomadic clans, the "Gypsies have no myths about the beginning of the world or about their origins; they have no sense of a great historical past. The Second World War and its trauma are certainly within memory; there is no tradition of commemoration or even of discussion" (Fonseca 1995, p. 243). Though the Gypsies even have their own word for the Holocaust, *Porraimos*, which means "the devouring," it took fifty years for the first gathering of European Gypsy survivors to honor their approximate half million dead.[1] In great contrast, "the Jews have responded to persecution and dispersal with a monumental industry of remembrance. The Gypsies with their peculiar mixture of fatalism and the spirit, or wit, to seize the day have made an art of forgetting" (Fonseca 1995, p. 276). Indeed, Judaism is all about remembering. There are major holidays marking, for example, the great exodus from Egypt, the receiving of the Ten Commandments, and the destruction of the two temples in Jerusalem. Furthermore, there are special memorial services for the dead during major holidays and annual commemorations with special prayers remembering one's parents.

With a heritage based on thousands of years of remembrances, it was therefore a rather natural Jewish response to create a new holiday, Yom Hashoah, to build museums, to create

[1]In an analogous situation, it has taken centuries for American blacks to get back to their African roots, which was enormously complicated by the legacy of slavery (Apprey 1993).

organizations for survivor-related issues, to start archives, and to learn as much as possible from the past. In the process, a number of long-standing issues that many would just as soon have forgotten were stirred up. Some of these unresolved issues related to the confiscation and theft of the victims' property (e.g., the fate of Nazi gold, the return of stolen artwork, frozen bank accounts in Switzerland, and denied life insurance claims of those killed in the camps). Such painful shame- and guilt-inducing reminders of the past have revived long-standing prejudices and hostilities that fuel cynicism about the Holocaust and denigrate the enormous suffering with many accusations of Jewish greed and preoccupation with money. Mr. R., despite his disillusionment about God, remained firm in his Jewish identity. Psychologically, however, he tended more toward the Gypsy philosophy of living for the day and forgetting the past, a conflict with the cultural values of remembering imbued in him since childhood. His involvement in oral history projects, his teaching young people about the Holocaust, his going to reunions, his attending memorial programs, his visiting Holocaust museums, and even his wish to go home may have been influenced by these factors.

The psychological dimension encompasses the intrapsychic, the developmental, including the age when the persecution started, and the far-reaching effects of trauma, such as intergenerational transmission. Primo Levi (1986), whose personal accounts of survival in Auschwitz-Buna are world-renowned, described two types of survivors:

> Those who refuse to go back or even discuss the matter belong to the first category as do those who would like to forget but do not succeed in doing so and are tormented by nightmares, and the second group who have instead, forgotten, have dismissed everything and have begun to live, starting from zero. . . . [This] second category is composed . . . of those

> who possessed at least a measure of political preparedness, or religious conviction, or strong moral conscience. For those survivors, remembering is a duty . . . and above all they do not want the world to forget. . . . I know many ex-prisoners who understand very well what a terrible lesson this experience contains and who return every year to "their" camp, guiding pilgrimages of young people. [p. 387]

Although Levi seems to contradict himself about the second group's need to forget in order to live again while needing to remember for a higher purpose, I think this type of forgetting is not global repression or dissociation, but a more sublime capacity to set the past aside and transcend it. To do so would require the ego strength to neutralize enough aggression both to stay cognizant of the past and to care about the future. Mr. R. went home twice but was unable to return to one of his camps for the dedication. His two special friends did. Consistent with Levi's observation, the most meaningful part of their trip was the opportunity to talk to numerous classes of Catholic students who were visiting the site. The men felt respected, believed, and honored by the students who listened to their eyewitness accounts in awestruck silence.

OTHER VOICES

Another survivor of Buna, who covered the Nuremberg Trials as a prisoner turned reporter, had this to say about his homecoming in 1960:

> I was curious. . . . I wanted to find my two closest friends . . . who became members of the Hitler youth and who never spoke to me again after I was thrown out of school. I wanted them to know what happened to my parents (who died in

> Auschwitz) and it gave me a perverse feeling of satisfaction to be staying in the same room (in the local hotel) that the fallen dictator (Hitler) occupied 25 years ago. [Michel 1993, p. 205]

But after his triumphant, albeit counterphobic return, he admitted, "I was ambivalent when I left Mannheim. I felt empty, cheated" (p. 207). "There were only tiny traces of the past. The Germans succeeded in Mannheim. It certainly was Judenrein. I had no business being there and I was sorry I'd come back" (pp. 208–209). Yet when he went to Auschwitz in 1983, he rose above his earlier defiant position: "I was physical and psychological proof, living proof that despite what happened here 40 years ago, I was back, on my 60th birthday, to celebrate my survival in the place that tried to kill me" (p. 266). "I had chosen to build a Jewish future because I had been an inmate in Auschwitz. I was who I was because of what happened to me here, in this place" (p. 269). "I had survived to see Israel reborn out of the ashes of Auschwitz" (p. 270). This survivor devoted his life to the rebuilding of the Jewish people through fund-raising and did not cry until he saw the Star of David on the Israeli airliner that took him safely out of the death camp and back home to the United States. It is notable that Auschwitz, one of the most hated and revered sites on earth, is Poland's greatest tourist attraction. It draws millions of visitors each year, which attests to the extraordinary pull it has on the psyche.

Mr. R., like the fund-raiser, was able enough to forget in order to build a life, yet he was one whose duty it was to remember also. However, the indelible, unspeakable nature of massive psychic trauma does not lend itself to be fully integrated, and he had symptoms that are prevalent among survivors (Krystal 1968). Mr. R. lived with reminders of the camps and unconsciously repeated elements of his experience on a regular basis. His house was in direct view of a huge industrial complex resembling the I. G. Farben works and he never made the connection. He worked very long hours doing manual labor six days a week and in his precious little spare time read about all the dangers in the world. He was always preoccupied with not having enough food. His affects were constricted and encapsulated into claustrophobic symptoms as well as a variety of psychosomatic ailments. He was preoccupied that his ears would "close up" on him during colds or nasal congestion, causing great anxiety. His losses were incalculable and adequate mourning was not possible (Pollack 1961). He could not speak more than a sentence or two at a time about his father or sister, and when his mother died many years later, his inability to express himself perhaps contributed to the onset of his life-threatening medical condition. Under the influence of the repetition compulsion, aspects of his trauma were enacted throughout his life even up to his last hospitalization, where he experienced a florid episode of flashbacks when he was unable to eat, had lost considerable weight, and had become so weak that he could hardly move.

Kitty Hart (1981), another survivor of Auschwitz, highlights this persistence of trauma during her irresistible return to the camp: "You see grass. But I don't see any grass. I see mud, just a sea of mud. . . . Don't go too close! The watchtowers still look down. There must still be guns in there trained on you, I belong here. I knew I ought never have come back, because it proved I'd never been away" (p. 163). The past is more real than the here and now in victims of such profound trauma. Another death camp survivor kept punctuating his interview with me by looking around and exclaiming, "I still can't believe I'm really here [safely in the United States]! It's been over fifty years and I still can't believe it!" The urge to return to the "scene of the crime" affirms the perceptions of that part of the mind that never left. It is a mental phenomenon that may not really come into awareness until one journeys back home and contrasts one's perceptions with the traumatically etched images of the past.

Returning home is also related to a primordial wish for reunion with the lost object. Observational studies in the second half of the first year of life provide important data about a recurrent motif that may be a template persisting throughout life. Mahler and her associates (1975) noted obliviousness to the mother's absence and an easy attachment to a substitute but a huge upheaval with negativism upon her return. Metapsychologically, the split that exists in the internal part-images of the mother is easily activated, and "the mother of separation must be reintegrated as the 'all good' symbiotic mother so as not to hurt or destroy the good object" (p. 67).

The themes of attachment, loss, reunion, and returning home were present throughout Mr. R.'s life also. Interestingly, his second trip back to Germany occurred after the death of his mother. As though he was searching for his own idealized childhood before the war, he was determined to find his original home in Soviet-controlled territory. He was terrified of subjecting himself to Russian soldiers once again, but became emboldened by other survivors in his group and proceeded. He was dismayed to find that his street was renamed and the building had long since vanished. He recalled looking up and down the street for familiar faces, all the while knowing there would be no one he would recognize. As a teenager who had foreseen the danger, Mr. R. was forbidden to leave his mother and father, so his attachment prevailed over his better judgment. Although he could not admit it, he was furious with his father but did not abandon him. On the contrary, he risked his life to keep him alive as long as possible while nurturing him with his own meager rations. Then, after his father died, a horrendous oedipal victory in Auschwitz, Mr. R. expiated his guilt by staying "home" in the infirmary at Buna, risking his life again to help his boyhood friends escape. In so doing, he symbolically became the heroic mother of their individuation, and their emotional reunions were joyous highlights throughout his life.

Mr. R.'s reunion with his own mother was extraordinarily painful, and neither went into detail about the horrors of their survival ordeal. A tense wall existed between them until her death, though he remained devoted to her and at her side until she died. Even in the last days of his own life, he was preoccupied with going back to the camp, had flashbacks of Auschwitz, and called out for his mother like a young boy in his native tongue. All he wanted to do was just go "home." Consciously, going home meant being free to leave the hospital, but on a deeper level, he also expressed a trauma-induced wish to go home to the camp, to go home to his idealized nostalgic prewar childhood home, to reunite with his all-good symbiotic mother and ultimately to go to his grave, his final home. Fortunately, he was surrounded by his wife and children, so that when his delirium cleared he knew he was still loved and not abandoned (Madow 1997), and that every effort was being made to keep him as comfortable as possible. When it was time for him to finally go home for good, he died quietly in his sleep. In keeping with Jewish burial law, a small amount of soil from Israel was thrown into the grave, to symbolize the return of his soul to the Holy Land and his reunion with God.

THE SECOND GENERATION

Like many other survivors, Mr. R. derived enormous strength from his children, whose very existence gave his life meaning. The role reversal seen in children of immigrants who quickly assimilate the new culture and language enables them to lead the way for their parents and is especially evident in the children of these survivors. Their legacy is one of making up for the irreplaceable losses, of doing the work of mourning that was not possible, and at times even feeling that they too were there. Described as a psychological time tunnel, this unusual phenomenon of transposition occurs when a member of the second generation lives a quasi-double reality of the Holocaust and of his or her own in present-day life (Bergmann and Jucovy 1982, Brenner 2000a, 2000b, Kestenberg and Brenner 1996, Kogan 1995). Attributed to the intergenerational transmission of trauma and not psychosis, this may occur when a survivor parent deposits his or her traumatized self into offspring (Volkan 1997). Parallel to that of the survivors, there was a proliferation in the 1970s and 1980s of local, national, and international organizations to provide support and education for these coming-of-age children who felt a powerful connection to their parents' Holocaust past. Much to the dismay of many of their aging parents, who never spoke of it and tried to shelter their children from any knowledge of it, the second-generation movement became a catalytic force in helping both generations come to terms with the past. This involved making pilgrimages to their parents' towns and villages in Europe, visiting old Jewish cemeteries, searching local records, and, of course, visiting the concentration camps. A woman describes her first trip:

> I grew up . . . surrounded by secrets. By the time I was five years old, I was eavesdropping in twice as many languages as I was able to speak. . . . Secrets always came cloaked in either German or Yiddish with a quiet ritual that demanded attention even from a child. My memories are of half said things, the almost palpable feeling of words implied but never uttered. . . . When I was young enough to only listen, I fell in love with Krakow. My mother was vibrant when she spoke of life in Krakow before the war. Sharing her happy times

> made me feel closer to a mother who was otherwise difficult to understand. With stories of wonder and excitement . . . before the war . . . I'm not sure if I expected Poland to be intact. In fact, the countryside was lovely. I found myself trying to see it through my mother's eyes then in its innocence before the slaughter and burial of millions of Jews. Most of my parents' families had never left Poland alive. How could I go? [Her parents never did go back.] Both of my parents had died, secrets intact, leaving a large hole in my history. I remember how scared I felt about going and how unthinkable it is now not to have had the experience of feeling and smelling Poland. The plane was packed with people speaking Polish. I somehow expected to know them and have them recognize me as the daughter of my mother. I felt a combination of excitement and guilt as if I was being unfaithful to the memories of my parents. I wondered whether they would have understood and supported this trip. My gut feeling was that my father would have and that my mother would have been scared. There was a sense of familiarity although it was my first time in Poland. [Muller-Paisner 1998]

Mr. R.'s children also made pilgrimages to his homeland, preceding and catalyzing his own return. One even visited concentration camps long before such visits were, in the Jewish cultural way of mastery, incorporated into new traditions, such as "The March of the Living." This program, which started in 1988, has already taken thousands of young Jewish people to Auschwitz, Treblinka, and other sites of great importance in Poland. In this way, future generations are provided an institutionalized way of remembering, returning, and trying to work through what their parents and grandparents were unable to.

CONCLUSION

Returning to one's former home and to the hallowed graveyards of Europe is part of the legacy of the Holocaust that appears to be transmitted to the next generation and beyond. The weaving together of historical, political, cultural, religious, and psychological issues may create such an overwhelming tapestry in the minds of survivors that it cannot be fully taken in within one lifetime. Intrapsychic, developmental, and traumatic contributions to this phenomenon may persist and converge in the terminal phases of life, as illustrated in the case of Mr. R. Ongoing study of the pilgrimages of Holocaust survivors, their descendants, and their contemporaries may further our understanding of the interdigitation of culturally specific traditions and psychodynamics. At the bottom of it all is the triumph of survival, such as it was voiced by the man who went back to his home town and stayed in the same hotel room Hitler slept in 25 years before: "He was dead. I was alive!" (Michel 1993, p. 205).

5

Intergenerational Transmission of Symptoms

An article in *The New York Times* (May 24, 1998) described the German government's plan to return the capital to Berlin after four decades. Fifty years after the West Berlin airlift and after the reunification of both Berlin and the country itself, the return of the capital was to put the head back on the giant that lives in the center of Europe. And the upcoming elections were to be fateful. Once reassembled, what would it look like? How would it behave? What would it remember? As *The Times* puts it, "Nothing intrudes into Berliners' contemplation of their future so painfully than the angst laden debate over the diagram of a new Holocaust memorial that is supposed to be built in the heart of the new city, literally atop the crumbled foundation of Hitler's Third Reich . . . symbolizing modern Germany's central dilemma: whether to reaffirm a history predating the Holocaust or to be defined by 12 genocidal years." These societal issues seem to represent a large-scale enactment of the dilemma of the individual because memories of the destruction and loss are buried just beneath the surface in everyone affected. But there was disagreement and conflict over how to deal with it. Left alone, buried and not talked about? Dredged up and memorialized so that it would stare everyone in the face, stirring up collective shame and the powerful defenses against it? Or could there be some sort of compromise without compromising the truth?

But such decisions cannot be made simply because unconscious forces exert their influence, especially when there has been severe psychological trauma. And one of the most unappreciated aspects of such trauma is how it is transmitted to the next generation.

The daily absorption of the parent's traumatic past taken in by the developing psyche of the child as a function of routine mothering and/or fathering may be easily overlooked (Bergmann and Jucovy 1982, Jucovy 1986, Kestenberg 1972, 1980, 1982). While it may be considered strain trauma (Kris 1956) or cumulative trauma (Khan 1963), there are several reasons why it may not even be recognized. An oversight is likely to occur if overt, gross abuse, deprivation, or shock trauma (Furst 1967) overshadows it, or if the parent's trauma history is not clear. In addition, countertransference issues may induce the analyst to unconsciously collude with the patient's silence to avoid painful affects such as grief, anxiety, shame, and guilt, which may accompany the parent's past (Danieli 1981, Klein 1973, Moses 1978).

Nevertheless, it has been possible to examine transmission in cases where the history of parental trauma is not in doubt, when it was time-limited prior to the child's birth and where the child himself was not directly affected. Children of Holocaust survivors have provided most of these data.

SURVIVORS AND THEIR CHILDREN

In genocidal persecution, the shock of being physically ejected from one's home, excluded from one's community, and exiled from one's homeland has a permanent effect on one's psyche. It is a massive trauma that brutally attacks one's identity, sense of security, and all the basic assumptions about the future (Elsass 1997, Kestenberg and Brenner 1996, Krystal 1968). The murder of family members, loss of property, sadistic atrocities, starvation, disease, beatings, torture and slave labor, and the loss of hope because of feeling completely forgotten about can destroy one's humanity. It is estimated that there are fewer than 300,000 Holocaust survivors still alive today. Their number is dwindling quickly but they have produced a second, a third, and even a (very) young fourth generation. The lessons to be learned about politics, religion, and human nature are endless. Our understanding of the long-term effects of massive psychic trauma (Grubrich-Simitis 1981, Krystal 1968, Ornstein 1986) on adults and on developing children (Kestenberg and Brenner 1996) has also greatly increased, and the passage of time has allowed us to examine the mechanism of intergenerational transmission.

CASE 1

Simon, a man in his late twenties, had an aversion to all things German. He refused to buy or even ride in German-made vehicles and would get nauseated hearing the language. He often dreamed of being chased or imprisoned, trying in vain to escape and rescue his family. He recoiled at the thought of trains, showers, and, especially, barbed wire. Simon also had contempt for policemen, mistrusting any authority figure wearing a uniform. His parents were the sole survivors of each of their families, having endured ghetto life, slave labor, and concentration camps. As the oldest of three children, Simon was named for his maternal grandfather who was gassed and cremated at Auschwitz. Simon's mother was chronically depressed, passive, and mute about her past, whereas his father could not stop talking about it, although he actually disclosed very little. All of his father's friends, social activities, intellectual pursuits, and spare time had some connection to the Holocaust. Simon grew up feeling left out of this secretive and all-consuming past life of his parents, especially when his father would get lost in thought. He felt that his father was more interested in his private world than in his son. As he got older, Simon tried to join in on the father's obsession, and they even developed a sardonic special greeting for each other: "Heil, Hitler!"

Simon sensed that he had a huge burden in that he somehow was to make up for all of his parents' losses. His problems were seen as insignificant to their suffering, and he felt that he had no right to complain or to experience pleasure. He also felt that he could never measure up to some idealized image of stoicism and imperviousness. Despite his adolescent rebellion, Simon was quite enmeshed with his parents, whose unresolved grief was unspoken but always present. His mother needed to know his whereabouts at all times, and Simon complied. The most striking feature of all, however, was the sense he had at times that he was actually "there," living through the Holocaust. Without realizing it, he aspired to be a criminal, but it was out of an unconscious sense of guilt (Freud 1916). He almost went to jail several times for a series of minor infractions that could easily have been remedied. He derived a perverse sense of victory each time he escaped incarceration. He seemed to unwittingly bring on these sanctions and punishments through neglect, passivity, and a curious confusion over rules and laws.

This confusion created a near catastrophe when he gave into an overwhelming urge to help a very ill friend escape from the hospital intensive care unit. The friend was in a semi-delirious, postoperative state and was feeling trapped, scared, and helpless. Instead of rescuing a victim, Simon found himself participating in a destructive enactment. The friend urged Simon to take him to a woman's apartment for one last sexual experience just in case he were to die. Simon had doubts about this request but could not say no, feeling too guilty about leaving his friend behind and not granting possibly his last wish. In fact, it almost did become his last wish when the friend collapsed from the exertion, as a horrified Simon heard him crash to the floor during a violent sexual episode with the woman. It created a true life-and-death situation. Simon then experienced a constant panic as the failed rescue mission ended in disaster. Instead of becoming a hero, he felt like a perpetrator, a helpless bystander, and a guilt-ridden survivor as his parents' traumatic past suddenly became superimposed on his own reality. Analytic exploration was necessary to help him eventually see his unconscious participation in re-creating both a Holocaust scenario and a dangerous primal scene from his childhood. Interestingly, he later learned that his father's wartime experience included resistance activity and a series of near-captures by the Gestapo. When Simon's father was finally caught and sent to a concentration camp, he was in the midst of trying to secure safe passage and escape for his family through his underground connections. Simon's father was perpetually tortured by guilt over not having been able to save his family.

Discussion

The phenomenon of living in two worlds simultaneously, borne of trauma and not of psychosis, was described by Kestenberg (1982) as a "time tunnel." There appeared to be a profound communication of the survivors' traumatic experience to their children, resulting in the feeling that they were living a Holocaust reality as well. The developing ego of the second-generation child was confronted not only with the usual tasks of adaptation but also with the integration of his parents' traumatic reliving of the Holocaust. Consequently, there could be an intensification of developmental dangers, for example, annihilation, loss of mother, castration, loss of love, and fear of superego, along with a characteristic preoccupation with survival, loss, persecution, and Jewish identity. The resulting feeling of almost "being there" could have a surreal, uncanny, or dissociative quality to it, which raised important questions about the specificity of Holocaust trauma and the transmission of trauma in general.

At a most basic level, it may be that certain conditions merely accentuate and fixate the tendency in young children to assume they have always been part of their parents' earlier lives. For them to ask a question such as "Where was I before I was born?" is not only a function of the separation-individuation process (Mahler et al. 1975) but also a cognitive milestone, for it requires a comprehension that there was a time in the world before their existence. As with other universal, anxiety-laden issues, this theme is depicted in popular literature and films and it is often in the form of time travel. Interestingly, the hero is frequently a child who goes back in time and gets caught up in the dilemma of changing the past in order to avenge a crime, correct an injustice, or prevent a tragedy. In transposition, there is an ambiguity between the past and the present, which in severe cases may even progress to confusion and defensive altered states associated with a blurring of fantasy and reality (Brenner 1994a, 1996a, 2001).

Simon, however, was quite aware of his hypersensitivity and repugnance toward German and Nazi symbolism. He intellectually knew it was related to his parents' past, but the deeper aspects of his living as though he were in the Holocaust was unconscious. Specifically, he was oblivious to the meaning of his bizarre rescue of his hospitalized friend, which was a repetition or concretization of the father's Holocaust trauma (Bergmann and Jucovy 1982). He enacted an unconscious reparative fantasy of wanting to rescue a family member like his own father, which, importantly, was also a feat that his father was unable to do. So there was both a competition and an identification with his father in addition to the wish to rescue both him and his mother.

An organizing fantasy that incorporated these themes is one of the "selection" (Brenner 1988b). Woven into this Holocaust scenario of going left or right, both oedipal and preoedipal conflicts, for example, the elimination of rivals, being separated, and so on, may be played out with sickeningly real imagery from the parents' past.

> I described this frequently seen phenomenon years ago when a woman consulted me asking me if she should have a baby. She was the only child of two concentration camp survivors. Her lover was German, and their sex life involved the use of Nazi uniforms and regalia. She unconsciously put me in the role of a doctor at the selection, deciding if any product of her union with her German boyfriend was worthy of life.

Here, too, this motif has emerged in popular literature with *Sophie's Choice* by William Styron. Ilany Kogan (1995) described such a woman who found psychological refuge in a perverse solution characterized by sadomasochism and a phallic woman fantasy (Bak 1968) in which she became a female Dr. Mengele in an SS uniform wielding her deadly phallic baton. In her mind she made the selections on the entry ramp to Auschwitz, deciding who would live or die by a casual wave of her powerful stick. To maintain total control over her object world, she became the omnipotent Nazi angel of death (Abraham 1986).

This Holocaust culture (Kestenberg and Gampel 1983) may completely saturate the mental life of children of survivors as though they are transported back to a time when reality was worse than fantasy. Almost eerily, some would unconsciously re-create and repeat elements of the past when they reached the age their parents were during their ordeals. Such an internalization of the parents' past seems to extend beyond the symbolic or metaphorical world, suggesting a very deep, preverbal communication between parent and child (Herzog 1982). Other writers have seen the same thing. Volkan (1981, 1995, 1996), in his work on pathological grief and ethnic conflict, described a depositing of the parents' traumatized self-representation into the child. Faimberg (1988) has conceptualized a type of identification with a "telescoping of generations." She postulates an intergenerational narcissistic problem in which the parent appropriates the capacity for experiencing pleasure from the child and is internalized as a dominating and intruding object. It is similar to Bollas's (1987) notion of extractive introjection. In this formulation, a condensation of three generations may occur in which elements of a secret history not belonging to the patient gets incorporated. These identifications are unconscious and timeless and may be uncovered in the transference. In such cases a pervasive anhedonia with a feeling of inner deadness is reported. As the child becomes the "container" (Kogan 1995) for the parents to deposit their losses, fears, and hopes, the role of projective identification is considered to be a central mechanism here. Continuing the work of the parents' unresolved grief is a crucial part of this legacy and is evident by pilgrimages to their parents' hometowns and ancestral cemeteries and to the concentration camps (see Chapter 4).

In addition, Anna Freud (1936) had long since concluded that "identification with the aggressor" was often seen in trauma, recognizing that projection of guilt was at the core of it. Consequently, the projection of what was later to be coined as "survivor guilt" (Niederland 1961) would be an essential part of the intolerable burden transmitted to the second generation. Blum (1986, 1987), however, reminds us that identification with the rescuer and identification with the victim are other important outcomes in the resolution of trauma, which we see in Simon's case also.

An unusual manifestation of survivor guilt (linked to the Holocaust) is evident in the following case.

CASE 2

Sarah, a middle-aged woman, experienced an uncontrollable panic following the death of her aged cousin, a woman she had been caring for and for whom she felt totally responsible. The old woman's health had been steadily declining, and a hospice medical team was involved in helping ease the pain of the dying at home. As planned by the old woman, she was to be made "comfortable" with pain medication and sedatives during her final hours, but when Sarah called the medical team, no one was available to make a house call. They instructed her to give a certain dose of medicine, but in her anguish and confusion she gave the cousin almost double the dose. The cousin then drifted off to sleep, dying in Sarah's arms. By all accounts, it was a peaceful, planned, expected, and humane death, but Sarah was devastated.

She became obsessed with having accidentally overdosed her cousin, thus bringing on her death as in euthanasia or an assisted suicide. The ambiguity haunted her. Overwhelming self-condemnation, guilt, and dread consumed her for weeks. She could not stop sobbing, crying out to God and to the world, "Why me? Why does this always happen to me?" Her conviction of being both the victim and the perpetrator was unshakable. Indeed, she felt a sense of déjà vu, but this time she blamed herself for the death, whereas in the past she had been accused of killing someone else. This is her story:

Sarah was the child of Holocaust survivors, who was essentially given away by her parents to be raised by her grandmother, as a replacement child for an aunt who was killed in a concentration camp. Named for her immortalized but rarely spoke about dead aunt, Sarah grew up under confusing circumstances, which greatly affected her identity formation. Her grandmother, after years of hiding from the Gestapo, was massively traumatized and relived the past on a daily basis. She would confuse Sarah, the granddaughter, with her daughter, Sasha, whose Hebrew and Yiddish names were identical. Any loud noise sent the grandmother scurrying under the bed or behind furniture, fearing the Nazis had finally caught up to her. Sarah was not allowed out of her sight and essentially grew up as a prisoner of her grandmother's persecuted and guilt-stricken past.

On the surface, to a casual observer, Sarah lived a privileged life of material comfort, extensive travel, and access to the world of adults from an early age. However, psychologically, Sarah felt suffocated, tortured, and totally engulfed. Living essentially two realities, she was the reincarnation of her dead aunt in hiding from the Nazis. She was not allowed to talk to anyone or to be apart or separated from her grandmother, whose watchful eye, suspicious nature, and intrusive protection overwhelmed Sarah's capacity to individuate. Any violation of these rules would risk betraying their identities as Jews in hiding and could cost them their lives, according to the grandmother. A car backfiring in the street became a machine gun or a bomb, and any man in uniform was the enemy. Sarah was instructed on how to take essential items and food from stores in order to help them survive. Of course, as she got older, she realized that in reality she was being taught to shoplift and would get into trouble if she got caught. This conflict between Sarah's own developing superego and reality testing versus that of her grandmother's traumatically fixed wartime reality left her feeling like a confused, helpless captive forced to commit crimes. Superimposed upon her deep sense of inner badness for whatever unknowable misbehavior caused her parents to send her away as a little girl, Sarah's sense of guilt was indelibly etched into her psyche. It felt like her soul was trapped behind barbed wire in the concentration camp with her dead aunt.

After a chaotic adolescence, intermittent depression, and a general sense of alienation, she entered into abusive relationships with men who were happy to mistreat her in the way she thought she deserved. Ambivalently bound to her grandmother, Sarah panicked when the old woman became ill and deteriorated. Staying at her side until her death, Sarah, then a free woman in her twenties, felt utterly abandoned and lost. When Sarah attended the funeral, she was confronted by a bitter, jealous, and equally traumatized relative. This woman glared at her and shouted in front of everyone, "You killed her!" Mortified and utterly terrified, this condemnation proved to Sarah that she was indeed a murderous criminal and she ran away. Her self-imposed exile lasted over twenty years until she contacted the remnants of her family and was accepted by the cousin.

Discussion

The nightmare of Sarah's being accused of killing her grandmother was repeated when she unconsciously gave her cousin a greater than recommended dose of medicine. She experienced crushing guilt over her mistake and became her own accuser this time. Transmitted survivor guilt from the grandmother over the loss of her daughter and Sarah's inability to be the perfect replacement were crucial underlying factors in Sarah's psychic development. She grew up with an impossible burden, feeling neither loved nor accepted for who she was. Sarah's internalized aggression suffused her relationships, resulting in sadomasochism and profound ambivalence that was expressed in the unconscious medication error. Intolerance of her affects contributed to a life of action and repetition rather than reflection until this event brought Sarah into therapy.

Like many others, Sarah's treatment was supplemented by a second-generation support group, an outgrowth of the second-generation movement that flourished in the late 1970s and 1980s (Fogelman and Savran 1979). Since then, there has been a coming of age for this surprisingly resilient population in which many defied the rather pessimistic prognosis for their mental health (Krystal 1968). Indeed, those who were better able to integrate the dual realities, transform the unresolved mourning into creativity, and sublimate their aggression became leaders in the second-generation movement, the arts, the helping professions, and in various social causes.

In examining transmission from the survivor's perspective (Kestenberg and Brenner 1996), our data suggest a continuum of behavior, from traumatic repetition to mastery and regeneration. On the maladaptive end, those survivor parents who were primarily under the influence of the repetition compulsion endlessly repeated scenarios of survival and included their children.

> One adolescent, for example, survived in hiding with a series of lonely German women whose husbands were off to war. He exchanged sex for protection, living in fear of certain death if he were to displease them and be turned over to the Gestapo. After the war, he continued this pattern, living a marginal life with a series of Gentile wives and sending his own children to be raised by others on the outskirts of town. Then his teenage son joined a motorcycle gang that sported Nazi helmets and insignias and terrorized his father. As a result, the man felt persecuted by his antisocial son, a little Hitler, as he perpetuated and legitimized his life in hiding. He had no idea how such a seemingly cruel twist of fate could have been visited upon him after all his suffering. After a number of years, the two reconciled their differences. Interestingly, the son eventually sustained a number of work-related injuries, making a career living off workmen's compensation and lawsuits. The survivor father apparently then felt a bit of pride in his son, who stopped being a perpetrator and became a successful victim. Interestingly, the father was envious of older survivors who received a monthly restitution check from the German government and felt that his son had pulled a fast one on the authorities. Beating the system by outsmarting the one in charge had survival value in a world where one was being hunted down like a rabid animal, when being a Jew was a capital crime.

This type of superego seems to reflect a lack of cohesion or a split (Kestenberg and Brenner 1986), which developed in some young survivors who were caught between obeying their parents' precepts and following their own instincts for survival.

In case 1, Simon's disregard for certain rules, laws, and standards of behavior, although multidetermined, may have also been an example of this survivor superego transmitted to the second generation. A similar phenomenon has been observed in other persecuted minorities, too, such as the African-American population (Apprey 1993).

TRANSMISSION OF TRAUMA AND DISSOCIATION

Transmission takes on a more pathogenic quality when it is associated with disturbances of memory, awareness, consciousness, and identity. While most of the reported cases (pertaining to the Holocaust) emphasize transposition associated with repression or splitting, one report does describe dissociative symptoms. Even though the etiology of dissociation itself remains somewhat of a debate, many authorities share the view put forth by van der Kolk and Kadish (1987) that, barring organicity, it is caused by psychic trauma.

> In this case (Gampel 1982), a young girl presented with amnesia, disorientation, and "absences." Her father survived the Warsaw Ghetto and a concentration camp. Although he supposedly never spoke of his past, his daughter was secretly obsessed with the fear of a fence that could electrocute children who were placed against it. While it is unclear what, if any, other traumatogenic influences may have existed in this silent family, it does appear that she identified with her father as a child victim.

I treated a woman who, after several years of analysis, drifted into amnestic altered states before she could reveal her father's experience as a child survivor.

CHILDREN OF NAZIS

In 1985, Kestenberg and I had the privilege of presenting a paper on the superego to the International Psychoanalytic Congress in Hamburg. Being the first meeting of its kind since before World War II, it was highly charged, and many young Germans wanted to talk to us about our work. One young man developed an instant transference to Kestenberg and followed her around for several days. He was very pleasant and engaging but so overly polite that he kept apologizing for the simplest things that needed no apology. In fact, it became a bit annoying. He would bow when he saw her, sit at her feet, and bring her coffee and snacks even though she did not want them. He kept trying to tell her stories of his childhood but would abruptly stop talking. He hinted that he wanted to tell her something important about his father's involvement in the Nazi Party but was not able to find the words. Instead he kept apologizing until Kestenberg, in a moment of exasperation, said to him, "Why do you keep asking me for forgiveness? I cannot give it to you!" In her typical forthright manner, Kestenberg then turned to me in frustration and said, "They may want to, but they are still not talking!" This man desperately wanted to confront his father's Nazi past but he became inhibited and mute as though he, too, were bound to the oath of silence, the blood cement, *bludkitt*, of the SS (Alexander 1948). As in other criminal organizations throughout history, they were required to commit crimes to prove their loyalty and to ensure their own silence. The young man knew he was troubled and burdened by what belonged to his father's generation but had no words.

As Bergmann and Jucovy (1982) pointed out, "No social experience known is comparable to surviving a concentration camp but the destructive effect of Nazi ideology on German children was nevertheless profound. Children of Nazis are also victims" (p. 29). Simenauer (1982) and Rosenkotter (1982) recognized superego disturbances in their analytic patients and concluded that Nazi mothers seemed to have a greater pathogenic impact than Nazi fathers. In particular, those mothers who instilled a shared sense of omnipotence in their children provided fertile ground for the indoctrination of Nazi beliefs. Gertrude Hardtmann (1982) theorized that German women who were especially damaged narcissistically, that is, those with very low self-esteem and a tendency to devalue themselves but idealize others, basked in the glory of Hitler's grandiosity. These women were eager to bear children to be given over to the Fuhrer to fulfill his glorious dream of the Third Reich. This act gave them such a sense of exaltation, pride, and purpose that they felt undying loyalty for even the most destructive causes so as not to lose their euphoria and cohesion of the self. To do otherwise would result in massive disillusionment, shame, despair, and disintegration of their very fragile sense of identity.

Children of these mothers who grew up with the utter humiliation of defeat as well as the clash of their parents' Aryan values with those of postwar Germany were likely to have disturbances of superego integration and regulation of self-esteem. Furthermore, the repetition of the parents' callous, arrogant, aggressive, and inhumane behavior by these children toward their German analysts resulted in enormous stress for both parties in treatment. The German analysts who came from similar backgrounds were susceptible to the sadistic assaults by their patients, which warranted second analyses and extensive supervision as they went through a soul-searching once again. Confronting history in themselves and their families posed enormous challenges to their neutrality and the risks of countertransference problems were and are great. As Kestenberg (1982) described it, "Patients treat their analysts as they have been treated by their parents. It stands to reason that an analyst who grew up under Nazi rule would be vulnerable when faced by an individual behaving with the grandiosity and inhumanity of a Nazi" (p. 163). A shared conspiracy of silence or a relentless pursuit of the truth in an unempathic manner are at either end of the spectrum of technical problems.

In comparing and contrasting the two second generations, Kestenberg (1982) observed: "Both children of persecuted and of persecutors live in a double reality; both may have a mission to rehabilitate their parents and undo the past. However, their missions are different. Nazi children must solve the problem of their parents' moral degradation; [whereas] survivors' children's concerns about their parents' guilt is in great part an illusion" (p. 165). She concluded that children of Nazis may have more difficulties because the transmitted Nazi ego ideal is based on grandiosity and Aryan superiority that valued power, justified aggression, conquest, victory, and elimination of inferior races. As a result, a persistent narcissistic vulnerability may manifest itself as insensitivity to the suffering of others or as pseudo-compassion that masks an underlying sense of emptiness, shame, and despair. What may appear as sadness and concern for others is self-pity and the continued mourning over the loss of the Aryan dream. Interestingly, the ego ideal of the Jewish victim is also built upon grandiosity and a notion of superiority but for very different reasons. With the Jews, it is based on their premium on intellectualism, achievement, ethical behavior, and their special relationship with God as the "chosen people."

The taming of drives, the consolidation of identity, and the mending of the rifts in the superego are therapeutic goals with both generations.

> This challenge was very clear in a man I met several years ago after giving a talk on the Holocaust. After we chatted for quite a while, he revealed that a former SS officer and a Jewish camp survivor got married and he was the child of that union. But he was so embarrassed and ashamed he deliberately covered his name

> tag. Perhaps his wish to hide his identity betrayed a wish to hide both his yellow star and his lightning bolts from me. Now an isolated, tormented man, he lived a solitary life spending most of his free time endlessly writing his memoirs. Trying on his own unsuccessfully to integrate the internalized perpetrator and the victim, this man left Germany to study abroad and never returned. He seemed to be living in secrecy, like both a fugitive war criminal and a Jew in hiding from the Gestapo. Conflicted over his aspiration to be in a helping profession, he stayed in a low-level job and could not complete his education. And though he never did give me his name, I learned that we had a mutual friend and we corresponded through this intermediary.

I felt I could not push for direct contact. I was also reminded of two patients I had previously treated.

> One was a German woman who played in the bombed-out ruins of her city as a child. She grew up with her Nazi father who never came back from the war. She secretly idealized him but could not talk about it. She came to the United States as a nanny, and when the woman of the house died suddenly, she stayed on and eventually married the grieving widower. Miserably trapped in a loveless marriage and feeling imprisoned for unspoken crimes, she developed a variety of bizarre hysterical symptoms. She confessed that she was essentially waiting for the old man to die in order to inherit his money and be free. She felt both entitled and very guilty about these wishes. When transference issues emerged in the treatment, she became terrified of her repressed longings for her father and launched into a defensive anti-Semitic tirade: "You are Jew, aren't you? And what is a Jew like you doing with a German name?" Appalled and embarrassed by this outburst of her concealed contempt, she felt caught and too ashamed to work it through. She broke treatment shortly afterward and helplessly returned to her life sentence.

> The second patient, also a German woman, had come to the United States to complete her graduate education. She had recurrent manic-like symptoms that disturbed her neighbors, and she was repeatedly visited by the police. She would then become suicidal. She refused medication, suspicious of anything she perceived as domination or mind control. Her anxiety would escalate and then suddenly disappear whenever she tried to describe the discovery of documents pertaining to her father's Nazi past, which were locked in a forbidden closet at home. She grew up in an emotional void where the unspoken secret dare not be breached for fear of her father's brutality and her mother's complicity. She had hoped to find her freedom in the United States, but a series of sadomasochistic relationships replicated her childhood. She fled treatment rather than "open the closet," and two years later was found dead of an apparent suicide.

So I knew I should not and could not push the man without a name. He had offered to let me read excerpts of his memoirs but never sent them. He gave up his professional aspirations, confronting the realities of middle age. He then turned to organic gardening where he became enthralled with the idea of growing food without using insecticides, thereby not having to kill any living organism. His effort to purge himself of any murderous identifications then took an ironic twist when he started a grandiose project to revolutionize farming. His idea was to breed a superior form of earthworm that would prepare the soil for new growth and rid the land of undesirable pests, an ingenious derivative of the Aryan dream of a Judenrein Europe. When last heard from, the plan was a complete failure and he was despairing.

Though limited, such an experience is consistent with the findings described by Dori Laub (1998) of Yale, who stated, "I am not aware of, although there might exist, a single case report of a successful analysis of a child of a Nazi" (p. 5). He offers a challenge to us all to further our dialogue on these issues.

CONCLUSION

It is a lifelong endeavor for members of the second generation on both sides of the barbed wire to integrate the past and the present. There may be identity conflicts and intensification of the developmental dangers of childhood, for example, abandonment, fears of punishment through bodily injury, and retaliation or aberrations of the superego, as one has to grow up in two psychic realities where the Holocaust past was worse than fantasy. In a world of victims, perpetrators, rescuers, and helpless bystanders, simple decisions could have life-and-death implications that may saturate all aspects of the person's inner life. Secrecy, silence, and denial of the painful realities of that time are likely to perpetuate the transmission of pathological trends such as unresolved grief, irrational guilt, and the avoidance of responsibility. Through therapy and other life-affirming activities that promote a reconciliation with unmetabolized introjects from the Holocaust, one may then achieve growth, healing, creativity, and the opportunity to pass on a new legacy to future generations. This is the legacy of wisdom, understanding, and humanity.

6

Unresolved Grief

The Nazi reign of terror during the 1930s and 1940s plunged Europe into a totalitarian nightmare, where anyone could become an enemy of the Reich (Shirer 1984). However, certain groups were obligatory enemies, as their vilification was central to Nazi ideology. Most notably, the Jews and everything attributed to them were seen as the greatest danger to the glorified Aryan dream of world domination. Therefore, our own field of psychoanalysis, which was condemned as the "Jewish science," became a threat to Hitler. Those analysts who escaped the persecution became refugees in strange new countries such as the United States, but interestingly, the impact of their plight on the evolution of theory and technique has yet to be fully appreciated (Akhtar 1999).

No less a figure than Sigmund Freud himself nearly became a victim of the murderous hatred that was unleashed at that time. He arrived in London on June 6, 1938, less than three months after the Anschluss, or the Austrian annexation by Germany. It was an uncontested occupation that ushered in unprecedented barbarism to Freud's beloved Vienna. Even Freud, the world's greatest expert on mankind's dark side, was surprised at the vicious enthusiasm with which the Austrians embraced the Nazi cause. Still, he was hesitant to leave. It was not until his daughter Anna was called to Gestapo headquarters for interrogation that Freud decided to let his influential friends like Princess Marie Bonaparte and Ernest Jones help him escape. The uncertainty over Anna's fate that day was underscored by the fact that Max Schur, Freud's physician, supplied her with a lethal dose of medication to be taken were she to be detained, tortured, imprisoned, or worse. Eventually, only those in Freud's immediate family were permitted to leave. As a result, four of his aging sisters were left behind to suffer the deadly fate that befell two-thirds of European Jewry.

It has been thought that Freud's survivor guilt commingled with his relief over the prospects of escape and motivated his most risky statement prior to his celebrated departure. Because of his international fame and because of the facade of propriety still being maintained by the Third Reich, Freud was required to sign a document stating that he was not harmed or unfairly treated by the Gestapo. After so doing, he, in his inimitable style, sarcastically added, "I can most highly recommend the Gestapo to everyone [!]" (Gay 1988, p. 628). This provocative statement by an 82-year-old man, now a persecuted Jew weakened by old age and a cancer that he had been battling for fifteen years, could have jeopardized the entire Freud family's exodus, but Freud could not leave without some form of protest. Perhaps it was this defiance that he romanticized in a letter written over fifty years before to his wife-to-be Martha: "I have often felt as though I had inherited all the defiance and all the passion with which our ancestors defended their temple and could gladly sacrifice my life for one great moment in history" (Freud 1886, p. 165). Though Freud relished his being a "godless Jew" and rejected organized religion, he never renounced his ethnic identity or his Jewish ancestry. He, too, was a member of a persecuted minority that was threatened with extinction. But who exactly is this minority group? Who were Freud's ancestors and how have they retained their group identity over the millennia?

A VERY BRIEF HISTORY OF THE JEWS AND THEIR PERSECUTORS

Modern science has provided an answer to a question that at various times in history has had deadly consequences: Who is a Jew? Genetic testing of the subtle variants of the DNA in the Y chromosome has supported historical and biblical accounts about a group of families that inhabited the Middle East about 4,000 years ago. They were the ancestors of today's Jewish people. Since the Y chromosome is known to be transmitted essentially unchanged from father to son, this finding has enabled scientists to determine that these people and, in fact, all men, have descended from a single Adam who lived about 140,000 years ago. However, the persistence of an identifiable group for over four millennia is most unusual, and the occasional genetic errors in transcription are used as markers to recognize such groups. The Jews, known as the "chosen people" in the Old Testament, were promised that they would be the "eternal people" if they kept their covenant with God and followed the laws that were set down. Indeed, their longevity has been remarkable and a source of great ethnic pride. It has also been rather vexing for many other groups.

Because of the religious ban against intermarriage and other factors reinforcing the Jews' separateness, such as social isolation and persecution, scientists have been able to trace their dispersal and worldwide migration, which began about 600 B.C.

For example, the Jews of Eastern Europe, known as the Ashkenazim, have apparently descended from the Roman Jews who had been captured and enslaved there following the destruction of Jerusalem, about 2,000 years ago. Advanced genetic techniques have also concluded that in the approximately 80 succeeding generations of this Eastern European contingent, intermingling with the local population was remarkably small, reportedly less than 0.5 percent per generation (Hammer, Redd, Wood, et al. 2000). As a result, the Jews were a rather "pure culture" in genetic terms, retaining many of the physical and facial features of their Mediterranean ancestors and brethren, the Palestinians, the Syrians, and the Lebanese. (This fact has significant implications for the current problems in the Middle East, which is beyond the scope of this chapter.)

Combined with the separatism and characteristic dress of the very religious, the Jews of Eastern Europe were easily stereotyped after centuries of persecution. Accused of everything from killing Christ to being in league with the devil, poisoning the wells and spreading the Black Plague, as well as kidnapping innocent Christian children and using their blood as a secret ingredient for matzah on Passover, Jews were, and are, often viewed with suspicion, fear, and hatred. In a sense, because they did not become extinct through conversion 2,000 years ago, their mere presence could evoke doubts about the legitimacy of Christ and threaten the predominant belief system in Europe. Indeed, it has been argued that the major issue influencing the history of the Church has been its relationship to the Jews (Carroll 2000), an ancient problem ominously referred to as "the Jewish question" by the Nazi leadership who tried to solve this problem with the "final solution."

As the ideal repository for the projection of disowned attributes of the Christian majority, the Jews incurred even more contempt when, after given rights and freedom, they would become overrepresented in the arts, sciences, and business. If they were not "kept in their place," it was feared that the Jewish menace would infiltrate and contaminate the civilized world. The descendants of those who refused to accept Christ as Lord and who were accused of putting him to death were also seen as having the arrogance to want to take over the world. Indeed, fears of world domination by the Jews and fears of the spread of Bolshevism, whose main architects were of Jewish ancestry, provided the political rationalizations in the 1920s and 1930s for the development of the most lethal form of anti-Semitism in history to be cultivated in Germany.

Devastated by its humiliating defeat in World War I and punished by the enormous reparations demanded by the Versailles Treaty, the need for the Germans to have a recognizable, vulnerable enemy was essential for their tenuous group identity (Volkan 1987). It became crystallized through the rise of National Socialism and the meteoric success of an anonymous eccentric corporal who galvanized the country with his hypnotic rhetoric, offering a grandiose dream of an Aryan super-race and promising the ruthless destruction of his enemies. Adolf Hitler, the Führer, with his uncanny ability to sense the moral decay in others and his appeal to the working-class masses, incorporated his idiosyncratic views pertaining to the Jews, which were capitalized upon to his political advantage. For example, his belief that they were the carriers of syphilis who would infect the world and bring about wholesale degeneration of the human race was legitimized by the Nuremberg laws pertaining to racial purity which set the stage for genocide (Redlich 1998).

Genocide is the ultimate narcissistic injury. It is intended to obliterate the individual and his kind of all traces of his past, present, and future immediate and extended family. The term for this "crime without a name" was coined in 1943 by the jurist Raphael Lemkin when he learned what was happening to the Jews of Europe (Marrus 1987). It occurs when a human being is progressively deprived of his rights, his possessions, his home, his loved ones, his dignity, and ultimately his right to live, simply because he is a member of an identifiable group. The resulting assault on the ego is utterly overwhelming, and when flight to safety is not possible, regression in the service of survival may be necessary in order to avoid the depletion and total despair that may lead to suicide. On an individual level, Ferenczi (1929), in his essay, "The Unwelcome Child and His Death Instinct," described how maternal aggression intensifies the internalized aggression of the unwanted child, who is more prone to get sick and die. When this familial paradigm gets enacted on a large scale in a society, the helplessness and impotent rage may contribute to the demise, or near demise, of a whole people. Although other groups, such as Gypsies, homosexuals, and Jehovah's Witnesses, were mercilessly treated also, the German government's final solution to the "Jewish problem" did not allow any exceptions for the Jews. By the end of World War II and the liberation of the concentration camps, it has been estimated that two-thirds of the Jewish population of Europe and about one-third of the worldwide Jewish population was murdered. Of the 18 million civilian deaths in Europe, one out of every three, or 6 million, were Jewish. More than 1.5 million children were included in this incomprehensible number.

What started as a rather farfetched idea to exile European Jewry to a remote island off the coast of Africa, the Madagascar Plan was replaced by the monstrous reality of genocide. It began with mobile killing units (*Einzatsgruppen*) in the Soviet Union and mass unmarked graves. But because of the inefficiency of the shooting squads and the concern about the murderers themselves becoming traumatized by the heinousness of their assignment, their task became industrialized. It has been estimated by historians that at its peak of efficiency in late 1942, the gas chambers and crematoria at Auschwitz-Birkenau were "processing" about 17,000 ill-fated prisoners per day (Marrus 1987, Yahil 1990). This marriage from hell between technology and bureaucracy to dispose of "life unworthy of life" began in an idealistic manner to rid Germany of medical and psychiatric incurables who were a drain on the *Volk* and its very precious resources. The medically supervised eugenics program of forced sterilization and quiet extermination through lethal injection became the prototype of a much more ambitious project following the infamous conference of Wansee in 1941. With the help of industrial giants such as Degesch, that manufactured the lethal cyanide gas pellets known as Zyklon B, and Topf & Sons, that manufactured the ovens for the crematoria, the infrastructure of the killing centers took a huge leap forward (Pressac 1989). The planned extermination of Jews, Gypsies, homosexuals, Jehovah's Witnesses, and political prisoners required the cooperation of all levels of society across occupied Europe along with the ignorance, indifference, or even tacit approval of the Allies and even the Vatican (Cornwell 1999). Through criminal legislation and progressive terror, the condemned were robbed of their wealth, ghettoized, starved, tortured, enslaved, and turned into dehumanized beings, making it easier for their captors to lead them like sheep to the slaughter.

A JUNGIAN THOUGHT

Those who worship Adolf Hitler celebrate his birthday, April 20, with what the rational world would call terrorist activities. The fireworks of exploding buildings (Oklahoma City, April 1996), the bombing of aircraft, and the shooting of helpless children in schools by their own classmates (Columbine, April 20, 1999) have commemorated this infamous day. Carl Jung might have attributed this coincidence to his cosmic theory of synchronicity, but, as Freud would have said, we psychoanalysts really know nothing about such things, and after his break with Freud, Jung's own preoccupation with Aryan mythology led many to conclude that he too had become a Nazi. One of his closest disciples, Jolande Jacobi, who was Jewish, reported Jung's comments on the subject: "You know, I would never like to have children from a person who has Jewish blood." Forever ambivalent, his admiration and envy were expressed in this way: "You know, your ancestors were already doctors and rabbis and scientific persons for six thousand years and my ancestors were still running around naked with the skins of animals a thousand years ago in the German woods" (Noll 1997, p. 275). With regard to Jung's theory of archetypes, which is outside the realm of analysis, it is noteworthy that both Jung's and Hitler's most important mythological character was Wotan, the Germanic god of creation and destruction. Both had identified with this terrible, omnipotent deity, who was hauntingly depicted by the artist Franz von Stuck as a demonic-looking creature with a cape riding a huge horse and wielding a sword. Von Stuck's painting, *The Wild Chase*, was painted in 1889, which, ironically, was the year of Hitler's birth. Hitler's identification with this god is evidenced by his love of ravens and wolves, Wotan's pet creature totems. According to the legend, Wotan demands that a horrific, apocalyptic battle occur during the time of Ragnarok.[1] During this lustful destruction full of incest and murder, Wotan's great wolf Fennin is to mercilessly devour both the gods and men (Waite 1977). In Hitler's depraved mind, the flames of the crematoria at Auschwitz may have been the fulfillment of this

[1]It is theorized that the crash of a meteor into the island of Saremaa off the coast of Estonia about 600 B.C. inspired this ancient myth. This Kaali meteorite, thought to have had the power of the atomic bomb dropped on Hiroshima, would have been seen and felt in Scandinavia, according to experts and historians (Meri 1984). A catastrophe of this magnitude occurring as relatively recently as this may have seemed like the end of the world as the "sun" set in the east and wreaked havoc from the explosion.

ancient myth. But his mission ultimately failed and my mere presence here attests to that fact.

In my work with survivors and their families (Kestenberg and Brenner 1996), I have focused on three major areas:

1. The persistence and repetition of trauma throughout life (see Chapter 4);
2. The intergenerational transmission of the trauma (see Chapter 5); and
3. The effects of life-threatening trauma on the developing psyche.

A case report of an adolescent survivor with an unresolved mourning and manic defense illustrates these points.

CASE REPORT

A woman consulted me for advice on how to cope with her slowly dying husband. A hint of a European accent suggested why this mysterious Jewish woman might have been referred to me. Mrs. D., as I eventually discovered, was an unusually gifted woman who had built a business empire, but had always let her husband, an insecure but well-intentioned man, be in charge of it and take the credit. She had always propped him up, but now found herself in a hopeless situation. She was terrified but unable to confront him about his declining function. As decisive and ruthless as she had to be in the business world, her meekness in this situation was all the more startling.

At times, her husband was too weak to walk. He could not remember the route to their headquarters but insisted on driving them to work nonetheless. Mrs. D. perpetuated the illusion of his health, navigating each way as though he were a puppet. She would tell him when to apply the brakes, remind him that red lights meant stop and green lights meant go, and even told him that he needed to turn the wheel to stay on the road. When she became depressed over the implications of this problem, she agreed to a psychiatric consultation under certain conditions. She feared that her husband would become paranoid, jealous, and possibly violent, and insisted on a mediator to schedule all of her appointments and to relay any messages to me. She also insisted on paying cash and refused any receipts or documentation of our visits, fearing that such evidence would betray her. She carefully prepared her alibi each time she escaped the isolation with her incurable husband. I was struck by the elaborate secrecy of our meetings, wondering about her own paranoia. It seemed as though she were in a prison and taking great risks to come see me. Starved for intellectual companionship but feeling intensely guilty and disloyal over her secret forays to see me, Mrs. D. cried out for help but kept me at bay. We met for several years in intensive psychotherapy before she became afraid to be away from her husband even for an hour at a time, getting pulled back into her personal abyss.

As we came to understand her plight in light of her survival in Nazi-occupied Europe, it became clear why she could not tolerate any painful affects and would become extremely uncomfortable, changing the subject at every opportunity. Insisting her past had little or nothing to do with the present despite her associations, she retreated to a position of denial and made frantic efforts to undo her connections. An appreciation of her history put her eventual escape from treatment into perspective, as she ultimately resorted to her lifelong defensive adaptation and took flight from the transference.

Mrs. D. was the older of two daughters from a very prominent family in an Eastern European town. Given the finest of material comforts and private education, young Mrs. D.'s charm and grasp of foreign languages, music, and mathematics earned her the position as the father's favorite. Her gifts were recognized at an early age and her education became a family priority. Traveling with her father as a young child on his business trips and spending time at his offices, this precocious little girl became fascinated by the world and how everything worked. As a prodigy, she excelled in everything while her younger sister, because of the two-year age difference and a lesser endowment, was essentially eclipsed. Her mother was less demonstrative than her father as she tended to ally with the younger daughter in their more mundane domestic activities.

When the patient was 11, the German occupation of her town changed her life forever. She was not permitted to attend school, the father's business was confiscated, the family was forced into a ghetto, and they experienced constant terror. About a year later, the father was arrested and driven off in a truck without saying good-bye to anyone. His whereabouts and fate were unknown, but the rumors about executions were widespread, although too awful to believe. At that point, the mother and her daughters went into hiding, hoping every day for the father's return. Conditions deteriorated as little food, disease, unsanitary living conditions, harsh weather, and the regular disappearances of familiar faces weakened their resolve. When they, too, were eventually rounded up, the younger sister was removed from the line and sent away on one truck with the elderly, the sick, and the children while Mrs. D. and her mother were transported to a nearby labor camp. In those moments of stark panic, neither reacted.

Conditions were primitive and barbaric. Prisoners were starved, beaten, and humiliated, and many froze to death in the winters. When there was not enough construction work to do, they were given meaningless tasks like digging ditches and refilling them to keep busy and satisfy the sadism of their guards. Mrs. D., the ever-resourceful optimist, convinced herself that she would somehow survive and kept the flame of hope alive for both her and her mother. Her mother, who was about 35 at the time, never adjusted to the rigors of the camp and steadily deteriorated. Living on half rations and working double-time, Mrs. D. shared her watery soup and crust of bread with her mother, did some of her mother's work detail and huddled with her mother every night in the harsh winter to keep her warm. Despite the life-threatening conditions, Mrs. D., who was in her early adolescence, went through menarche at this time. She was horrified at the blood and struggled to stop the monthly flow of her menses with whatever rags or scraps of paper were available. Her mother meekly informed her about the reasons for menstruation, which were so incongruous to the situation that nothing more was ever said about it. Secretly, she was sustained by the hope of reuniting with her beloved father. Through her strength, defiance, intelligence, and, as always in such cases, luck, both mother and daughter survived this man-made hell for over two years until they were liberated by Russian troops in the spring of 1945.

Mrs. D. spoke numbly about the frozen corpses stacked like firewood and the cruel work details that depleted the prisoners' strength and the strange but distant fondness that she thought her overseers had for her. Being one of the youngest, she felt she was somewhat special and shined against the gray background of the bleak, daily existence at the camp. She later reveled in telling stories of how she occasionally snuck through the fence and foraged in nearby farms for vegetables and anything edible to feed her half-dead mother. Mrs. D. apparently emerged from this experience a cunning and defiant teenager of 15, convinced that she was able to do anything and could get out of any situation. Feeling energized after a period of physical recuperation, she returned to her hometown, searching in vain for her father and her sister. It all seemed unreal, as Mrs. D. never accepted their deaths. There was no proof. Her affects were sealed off and were never expressed. Loss and death remained an untouchable subject surrounded by emptiness.

Following the reestablishment of peace, mother and daughter tried to assume some semblance of a life in a bleak, displaced-persons camp. As a remedy, the mother remarried a widower she had met who promised her a more secure life. Young Mrs. D. was confused and outraged by this decision as she was still searching for her father. Furthermore, she could not stand this new man, whom she felt looked at her in a strange way when her mother was not around.

Mrs. D. resumed her education, trying to get back on track developmentally. Her outgoing personality and good looks drew a lot of attention from both men and boys of all ages. Meanwhile, her resentment toward her mother grew. Her stepfather, she realized in retrospect, given her sexual naïveté and lifelong inhibition, often tried to fondle her. But at the time, only fear and great annoyance registered. By this point in her life, she was an expert in survival and became convinced that she must escape her intolerable situation at home. The easiest solution for her was to get married also.

So, with the impulsivity of an adolescent, the canniness of a war veteran, and the desperation of a devastated child, she vowed that she would marry the next man who proposed to her and she did! I was struck by the twinkle in her eye and her mischievous smile as she reported an improbable account of her abbreviated courtship. A flash of her youth broke through as she let herself reminisce about some of the absurdities of life after surviving the Nazis. Mr. D., a serious but very anxious and diffident man 10 years older than Mrs. D., casually proposed to her during a movie on their first date. Though she had just met him, she promptly accepted without thinking about it but was neither attracted nor particularly interested in getting to know him better. All she knew was that he survived in hiding, that all of his family was murdered, and that he wanted to come to the

United States. They had a similar past and shared the same dream for the future—America. Over her mother's strenuous objections, Mr. and Mrs. D. married shortly thereafter and eked out a meager existence while they made plans to emigrate with the help of his distant relatives who escaped before the war. Mrs. D. mastered the English language and tirelessly imagined a new life and a new beginning.

Following their arrival in the United States, they took menial jobs and saved their money to buy a small business, which, through Mrs. D.'s ingenuity and brilliance, was to grow into an international success. Both husband and wife worked 18-hour days, numbing their pain from the past and rarely taking time off to live or think too deeply. Mrs. D. barely slowed down enough to give birth to her two children. She hired caregivers to raise her son and daughter, convincing herself that building financial security was the most loving thing she could do. On reflection many years later in treatment, she ruefully acknowledged that she simply could not sit still at home without becoming profoundly sad about her father, her sister, and the destruction of all that she had known as a young child. Unconsciously reliving her childhood through the growth of her children was intolerable, and she had to be busy. She was always on the lookout for danger and was single-mindedly driven to acquiring enough wealth so that she and her family could leave the country on a moment's notice and live comfortably anywhere in the world. Passports, jewelry, and cash were packed at all times.

She spent her life building her business and traveling abroad to set up complicated financial and living arrangements in various countries and entrusted her children to a baby-sitter and her very kind boyfriend who over time acted like an adopted uncle. Oblivious to the possibilities that anyone so trusted could betray them, Mrs. D. became profoundly depressed years later about the revelation from her then-adult daughter about long-standing sexual abuse by the boyfriend. Shortly thereafter, she had consulted me, as her world seemed to collapse underneath the weight of her guilt. The tragic irony of her life was that while she was slaving away as an adult to create a life of privilege, security, and safety for her children so that the Holocaust would "never happen again," both her children were being molested regularly right under her nose. She also did not realize that she, too, had been molested and that her children relived a greatly magnified version of this aspect of her childhood. Though spared the horrors of the Holocaust, her children were nonetheless subject to very serious victimization in their own private Holocaust (Shengold 1999).

Mrs. D. could not explore her guilt about being a failure as a mother for not protecting her children. Instead, her guilt intensified her wish not to fail or abandon her deteriorating husband. In addition, she could not easily differentiate him from her father who disappeared without saying good-bye and she redoubled her efforts on his behalf. It then became clear to her that she would soon be unable to take care of him and would need to rely on outside help once again for a loved one, or, worse yet, send him to a nursing home. It was virtually impossible for her to ask for help, and in therapy she feared her deepening involvement in the transference. She adamantly refused to consider medication for herself, as it represented a crutch and a sign of weakness at the very least; it more deeply terrified her at the thought of having her mind controlled by a drug, that made her feel like a human experiment in a camp. Although she intellectually knew better, her projected aggression into the transference would have transformed me into a Nazi and she would never let herself become enslaved to someone outside her family ever again. Her husband was prone to violence, and his driving was nightmarish. Mrs. D. was risking her life to save him, and in the process was becoming more and more isolated from the world. She was unconsciously reliving her isolation of the Nazi slave labor camp but was unable to see it and work it through at this point in her life. Even though she feared she might die trying to save her husband, she could see no other way out and refused to consider any other possibilities, being the super-survivor that she indeed was. She would figure out a way once again, on her own, or die trying.

Discussion

One of the most remarkable aspects of aging child and adolescent survivors is the persistence of both their ego strengths and their vulnerabilities throughout the life cycle. This phenomenon is also seen in Armenians who survived genocidal persecution in Turkey early in the twentieth century. Although not studied as extensively, their accounts and their memories of atrocities reflect a similar indelible impact. Like resilient sapling trees that have had to grow at unusual angles to bypass obstructions to sunlight, those who at a young age endured genocidal persecution have followed their own twisting and turning paths in order to grow. From chronic psychosomatic disturbances in the very young to characterological disturbances in the older ones, many have bypassed certain developmental tasks, but have nevertheless functioned well until illness, loss, or old age set in (Kestenberg and Brenner 1996). In addition, their survival ordeals are indelibly imprinted in their psyches and may repeat themselves in symbolic or in actual scenarios until they die.

> A very successful professional man in his late 70s who survived by repeatedly escaping his captors became profoundly depressed when he was sent to a nursing home because he could not figure out how to break free from this new form of incarceration. His failing cognitive capacities and the traumatic repetition of his

past conspired to create an insoluble trap that prevented him from appreciating his current circumstances, and he was inconsolable for many months.

Another survivor, a 70-year-old woman who was a child when her mother died in her arms from shrapnel wounds, decompensated when she heard that her neighbor's house had been burglarized. Her own house had been ransacked by the Nazis shortly before they threw the lethal hand grenade through a window. Nightmares and flashbacks of her childhood, which had more or less been encapsulated for decades flooded her and she became paralyzed by fear and despair.

Another survivor, a man in his late 70s with end-stage cardiac disease, had spent six years in concentration camps and slave labor camps (Mr. R. in Chapter 4). While in the intensive care unit, he became convinced that he was back in Auschwitz after he was intubated, put on a ventilator, and had his arms restrained. He had an unexpected recovery after a daily struggle for survival for almost six weeks, refusing to give up and give in to the inevitable. When plans were finally being made for his discharge, that is, his liberation, he died peacefully in his sleep, knowing that he was going to be a free man.

In the case of Mrs. D., she appeared to be unconsciously reliving the experience of trying to keep her mother alive in the camp and rescue both her father and her sister, as her ailing husband's condition progressively declined. She was afraid of becoming dependent and trapped in the transference, fleeing from one situation back to the helplessness of trying to save her dying husband. She could not tolerate any hint of negativity toward him, and tried to renounce all of her aggression, having witnessed so much death and outright murder in her life. Interestingly, when she would first enter my office she had a habit of rushing over to inspect my plants and vigorously tear off any dying leaves. Her need to prune my plants had a sense of urgency about it, as though she were unconsciously performing a Nazi selection of those leaves that were fit to live and those that had to be eliminated. In this symbolic selection ritual she turned the passivity of the victim into an identification with the aggressor and perhaps also rescued the plant from imagined disease. Finally, when asked about this repetitive invasion of my plants, she smiled briefly, and flatly stated that the dead ones needed to be removed and taken away.

Freud's notion of a repetition compulsion being the agent of the death instinct helped him explain why people have recurrent, unpleasant dreams and repeat painful scenarios. In "Beyond the Pleasure Principle," Freud (1920) further developed his earlier ideas of breaching of the stimulus barrier, a model for psychic trauma that revived the helplessness of the infantile state. Many clinicians continue to feel that this conceptualization, or elaborations of it (Krystal 1968, 1988) are useful, but that the death instinct, which is one of Freud's most controversial theories, is not useful. Indeed, more contemporary-sounding ideas emphasize repetition in the service of mastery, the developmental aspects of aggression (Akhtar 1992), or neuroendocrine theories in which endorphin release during trauma results in addictive-like repetitive behavior in order to elicit more of this endogenous opioid (van der Kolk 1996, van der Kolk and Greenberg 1987). Yet the theory of the death instinct does not seem to be able to totally rest in peace, for both the Kleinians and a number of clinicians working with the severely traumatized continue to find it valuable (Brenner 2001). At the very least, the battle between Eros and Thanatos continuing to the grave and even beyond, by way of intergenerational transmission, has great metaphorical value.

In addition to redirecting psychoanalysts' attention back to the undeniable importance of psychic trauma after more than two decades of relative silence following the end of World War II (Krystal 1968), the study of the Holocaust led to the realization that there may indeed be transmission of trauma to the second generation and beyond (see Chapter 5). Through the daily ministrations of maternal caregiving and the family climate of unconsciously reliving the trauma, children of survivors may be affected through a type of psychogenic osmosis. Terms such as *transposition* (Kestenberg 1982), *telescoping of the generations* (Faimberg 1988), and *deposition of the traumatized self* (Volkan 1996) have been offered to describe this phenomenon. In addition, disorganized-disoriented disturbances of attachment in children of nonabusing traumatized parents have been observed, which then appear to become templates for future relationship problems (Hesse and Main 1999). Likened to experiencing a strain trauma (Kris 1956) or cumulative trauma (Khan 1963), children of survivors have had the developmental challenge of integrating their current reality with the traumatic pasts of their parents, who were unconsciously reliving aspects of it in their daily lives. Interestingly, urinary cortisol levels have also been found to be lower in children of survivors, just as it is seen in their chronically traumatized parents, and they are more at risk throughout their lives to develop posttraumatic stress disorder than their peers, according to research by Yehuda (1999). And, as a result of their double psychological book-keeping, as it were, many second-generation children grew up with an uncanny sense of almost having experienced the Holocaust despite having been born after the liberation of the camps. This phenomenon can have a dissociative quality to it, as it may even become triggered by the well-known symbols of the Third Reich such as crowded shower rooms, trains, men in uniforms, German vehicles, industrial smokestacks, and prisons (Kestenberg and Brenner 1996, Volkan et al. 2002). Consequently, the second generation's developmental conflicts became imbued with

Holocaust themes, which greatly increased the typical dangers of childhood, such as separation, loss of love, castration, and retribution by the superego (Freud 1926).

In a world where reality was worse than fantasy, the Holocaust "culture" (Kestenberg and Gampel 1983) pervaded the child's early life in his or her unconscious attempt to rescue the parents, make up for all of their irreplaceable losses, and justify their own improbable existence. While there is not agreement on the presence of a specific second-generation syndrome, the preoccupation with survival and guilt, conflicts over Jewish identity and belief in God, as well as unresolved mourning over lost relatives one has never met are almost invariably found. In their analyses, it has been observed that a unique phase of treatment may occur in which both analyst and analysand have a profound experience in their joint acceptance of the reality of the Holocaust (Grubrich-Simitis 1984). I suspect Mrs. D.'s children would have been no exception, but their plight was vastly more devastating, as it was complicated by the trauma of their own sexual abuse in addition to the secondary transmission. Shengold (1999), in his comparison of survivors of concentration camps and child abuse, observes, "The victim of soul murder is usually in some despot's charge; every child is so dependent that tyranny and oppression by a sadistic parent are easily possible" (pp. 97–98). In Mrs. D.'s case, the sadism was by proxy, as her children were essentially raised by surrogate caregivers. This situation occurred due to the absence of an unsuspecting mother whose need to keep her own past horrors at a distance resulted in emotional unavailability and a manic-like flight into her work.

The manic defense, distinct from manic-depressive illness, has been described as a characterological way of warding off the affects associated with unresolvable mourning and loss (Akhtar 1992, Klein 1935, 1940, Winnicott 1935). Akhtar, synthesizing Klein's ideas that were elaborated upon by

Winnicott, observed that the manic defense is characterized by denying internal reality, a flight to external reality, the keeping of parental introjects in a state of suspension, and the using of opposites. While the awareness of this response to traumatic loss is not new and certainly not unique to the Holocaust, I have been struck by the presence of this potentially adaptive defense in adolescent survivors more than in infant survivors, latency-age survivors or adult survivors. As many experts have noted (Jacobson 1957, Katan 1961, Krystal 1988, Wolfenstein 1966, Zetzel 1965), adolescence is the time of life for the maturation of affects, which facilitates the capacity for grieving at a higher level. While there is controversy over the extent to which younger children can truly mourn their lost objects, the adolescent is better prepared for a number of reasons. Specifically, there is the opportunity for a second individuation that bolsters object constancy (Blos 1967), the acquisition of abstract thinking promotes a deeper comprehension of death, greater physical strength facilitates alloplastic adaptation in order to alter one's environment (Hartmann 1939) and sexual maturity enhances the capacity for new and enduring object relationships to supplant the loosened ties with one's parents.

Henry Krystal (1968), who developed the concept of massive psychic traumatization in Holocaust survivors, identified the presence of a constellation of symptoms, including anhedonia, inhibited ability for self-care, hypervigilance, depression, masochistic trends, psychophysiological disturbances, and alexythymia. He put an emphasis on posttraumatic disturbances of affects and their expression through resomatization, which led him to focus on the importance of the development of affect tolerance in adolescence. "What is commonly taken as a fear of calamity, disasters or even death can be seen to be the fear of one's own affects. Affect tolerance is the ability to take our reactions off the signal and put it on the meaning, the import, of that signal" (p. 69). Noting the adolescent's "counterphobic and exhibitionistic tendencies" and "narcissistic invulnerability," he concludes that "optimally, as one progresses into young adulthood and maturity, one reaches the point where one can tolerate depression" (p. 68). He extends Anna Freud's (1936) notion of the dread of the instincts in adolescence to the dread of affects in an analogous fashion to the way C. Brenner (1982) elaborates upon Freud's theory of defenses against signal anxiety from instinctual danger to include defenses against dysphoric affects. In so doing, the warding off of unpleasurable or intolerable affects through defensive operations becomes as central to the understanding of psychic functioning as the warding off of anxiety.

Mrs. D. could never tolerate depression or grief, and she appeared to be in a lifelong state of manic denial. She could not grieve for her father and sister and desperately clung to her mother, risking her own life on a regular basis to keep her mother alive during the war. It gave meaning to her desperate hold on life, which in turn increased her sense of mission and self-importance, feelings very much associated with narcissism. Indeed, it has been theorized that under life-threatening conditions such as genocidal persecution of children, there may be a redistribution of narcissistic libido to fortify those psychic functions necessary for survival. As such, this so-called tertiary narcissism could reinforce the primary narcissism associated with healthy development and achievement of milestones, as well as the secondary narcissism associated with feeling loved, valued, and needed by others. It may be, therefore, that such alterations in the psychic economy could become fixed in the developing mind under such overwhelming circumstances (Kestenberg and Brenner 1995).

In her adult life, Mrs. D. focused single-mindedly on the acquisition of wealth, a multiply-determined symbol derived from all stages of development. In addition to the classical psychosexual interpretations, Olsson (1986), who blended Rank's (1936) and Kohut's (1971) ideas in his study of the subject, has observed that the "dynamic of phenomenal wealth lies in the association and linkage at an unconscious level of immortality, power fantasies and the grandiose self" (p. 68). Its meaning is especially important in those who have survived life-threatening ordeals, such as Mrs. D. It was necessary for her to use all of her talents, which enabled her and her mother to survive, and such a triumph of life over death may be suffused with both manic-like excitement (Klein 1935) and narcissistic omnipotence. In the extraordinary memoir of his own survival during the ages of 9 to 15, child psychiatrist Yehuda Nir (1989) described the ideal survival traits as belonging to those adolescents who possess "the combination of their age, intelligence, zest for life, flexibility and strength that allowed . . . [them] to continually mastermind escape strategies that would have made Houdini jealous" (p. 111). Although we certainly know, sadly enough, that even many of these heroic teenagers were not lucky enough to avoid the random events that would have killed even the most clever, it could be argued that the qualities of adolescence, including the propensity for regression, have great survival value. Not surprisingly, therefore, a number of those like Mrs. D. who did survive became quite successful in achieving "the American dream," harnessing their narcissism and manic energy in the direction of these pursuits.

In a rather unusual article in *Fortune Magazine* (Loomis 1998), five Holocaust survivors who became multimillionaire entrepreneurs and philanthropists were profiled. As with Mrs. D., there were a number of common denominators in these men that support this hypothesis:

1. All five went through at least part of adolescence either in hiding, in slave labor, or in concentration camps.

2. All five suffered object losses, including the sudden separation or traumatic loss of their fathers, either before or during the war.
3. All five were described as very bright, precocious, mischievous, defiant, or energetic.
4. During their confinement, all five broke the rules and risked their lives trying to stay alive and to save other people's lives.
5. All five had unshakable confidence, optimism, and a conviction that they would and should somehow survive.
6. All five were either described by loved ones or described themselves as having traits consistent with omnipotence and a manic defense. For example: "This drive, this incredible drive"; "Working six days a week . . . [and having] the attention span of a gnat"; "He was crazy. I didn't have a husband"; "I've been through the war and I'm not going to take any crap from anybody"; "I figured I could handle just about anything"; "Business is war. I don't believe in compromise. I believe in winning."

One of these men, Sigi Ziering, survived from the ages of 11 to 17 with his mother and brother. He did not show any emotion for over fifty years until May 1997, when he, along with 105 other founding members of the U.S. Holocaust Museum in Washington who donated at least $1 million each, were treated to a parade of flags representing the U.S. Army divisions that liberated the camps in 1945. In his speech, Ziering proclaimed, "Today, I cried because the worst memory of the ghetto and the camps was a feeling of total isolation and abandonment by the rest of the world. This feeling of utter despair and hopelessness weighed more heavily on us than the constant hunger, the beatings, and the imminent death facing us every minute." Ziering, whose indefatigability earned him a

Ph.D. in physics and a career working on nuclear reactors and space projects, in which he ultimately became the CEO of a very successful company that developed radioimmunoassay materials, never forgot about the element of luck either. In describing the selection process at a camp he landed in prior to liberation, he mused, "With German precision the guards went at their jobs alphabetically (each week) and never got to Z" (Loomis 1998, p. 82). Yet he did not rely on chance or divine intervention. He was tireless and very productive. Living out the stark motto on the iron gates of the death camps, "*Arbeit Macht Frei*," he bluntly stated his philosophy of life and secret of survival: "Unless you work, you're destined for the gas chambers." He outwitted the Nazis at their own deadly game. And, true to his word, it was noted in his obituary three years after the interview at age 72, "He survived the Nazis but never stopped working until about a year ago when he was diagnosed with brain cancer" (Oliver 2000, p. 20).

CONCLUSION

The unique features of adolescence seem to facilitate survival under the most extreme circumstances of genocidal persecution, which require strength, intelligence, resilience, creativity, and defiance. However, the massive traumatization resulting from the ever-present threats of sudden death or slow deterioration, the helpless witnessing of atrocities, and the loss of loved ones under the most degrading and inhumane conditions greatly interfered with the developmental task of acquiring affect tolerance. As a result, it became very difficult, if not impossible, to learn how to mourn for lost objects. One of the adaptive responses under these circumstances was the development of a manic defense, which could become a characterological trait. It is speculated that alterations in narcissistic libido could occur also. Adolescent survivors who fared well in adulthood by achieving "the American dream" may have acquired great wealth as a multiply determined by-product of their flight from intolerable grief. Such unmastered tasks are likely to have been transmitted to the second generation and beyond. In addition, it appears that the nature of massive psychic trauma is such that it is indelibly etched into the human psyche and is expressed by repetitions or revivals of survival scenarios throughout one's life. The clinician must be wary of unrealistic therapeutic goals that could destabilize these patients, especially if they are untreated until the later stages of life. The clinician must have a healthy respect for the unusual strengths and vulnerabilities of these exceptional people.

III

TREATMENT

7

The Analyst's Own Trauma

This chapter examines the multiply-determined nature of the analyst's anonymity, owing to educational influences, the fate of identificatory processes related to one's training analysis, and the pressures of the intersubjective matrix. These factors may be highlighted if there is a sudden loss of anonymity, such as when a patient inadvertently discovers highly charged information about the analyst. Such a discovery would have an impact on the analytic process, as case material illustrates; there was a significant affective resonance in this analytic dyad, which, when ultimately addressed and analyzed, furthered the process. Anonymity may be used unconsciously by the analyst as a refuge from incompletely resolved issues, which may be worked through while conducting an analysis. While self-analysis and consultation with a colleague are preferable to Ferenczi's "mutual analysis," it may be necessary at times to disclose or confirm certain realities to the patient. In conceptualizing the analyst's state of mind, it is useful to consider the notion of an "analytic membrane." Disturbances in its permeability may result in excessive disclosure or undue abstinence. Maintaining the integrity of this membrane would therefore be an essential part of the analyst's self-monitoring and maintenance of his/her adequate functioning.

Descriptions of the analytic postures and attitudes have run the gamut from Freud's (1912) metaphor of the "surgeon, who puts aside all his feelings, even his human sympathy" (p. 115) to Ferenczi's (1932) experiments in mutual analysis. In the former, the analyst is anonymous, detached and "concentrates his mental forces on the single aim of performing the operation as skillfully as possible" (Freud 1912, p. 115). In the latter, he literally trades places with his analysand, gets on the couch for a period of time, and free-associates about his unresolved conflicts in the hopes of surmounting them for the benefit of the patient's analysis. By today's standards, both of these extremes seem like caricatures, and I suspect that most contemporary analysts adopt a stance somewhere in between. But where and why and under what circumstances they might move along such a continuum is not completely clear, as such topics are being vigorously debated today. The basic technical principles such as neutrality, abstinence, and anonymity (Hoffer 1985, R. Michels 1983, Pine 1997) have been called into question (Balint and Balint 1939, Renik 1993, 1995, Singer 1977) as the realms of disclosure, countertransference analysis, and intersubjectivity (Aron 1991, Cooper 1998, Ehrenberg 1992, Hoffman 1983, Jacobs 1991, Mitchell 1988, Renik 1996, 1999) are continually expanding. Has this old reliable trio of guideposts (Greenberg 1995) finally become shaken by the winds of change?

Ferenczi (1932) concluded that severely traumatized patients may have required more of the person of the analyst, such as honesty, humanity, and openness. Introducing the importance of self-disclosure over seventy years ago, he recommended that "the analyst, like an elastic band, must yield to pull of the patient, but without ceasing to pull in his own direction" (Ferenczi 1928, p. 95). Those who have worked with such traumatized individuals, such as Holocaust survivors and their offspring, rediscovered the same thing. Years before the current reappraisal of analytic technique, it was recognized how difficult it was to maintain neutrality and anonymity while working with those affected by genocidal persecution and profound unresolved grief (Bergmann and Jucovy 1982). It appeared that some patients just needed to know certain things about their analysts, such as whether they were Jewish, in order to trust them enough to proceed. On the other hand, Kestenberg's (1972) questionnaire sent to child analysts in 1969 to 1970 revealed that a conspiracy of silence could also exist between analysts and their young patients in order to avoid the psychic pain. "The analyst acted like the silent survivor parent who does not want to talk about the Holocaust" (Bergmann and Jucovy 1982, p. 363). These findings suggested that analysts might tend to overcorrect and become rigidly abstinent in the face of such a countertransference burden associated with massive psychic trauma and its intergenerational transmission. A case described by Blum (1985) illustrates such a collusion in which both analyst and analysand were European and affected by the Holocaust but never directly addressed the painful issues they both had in common. Indeed, Akhtar (1999) has suggested that many European analysts who escaped or survived the persecution of the Nazi regime in the 1930s and 1940s may have been too traumatized to fully address or even write about their cultural dislocation and difficulties with a new language. Consequently it may have been easier for them to err on the side of silence and anonymity, thus contributing to a too-literal interpretation of Freud's technical principles.

This chapter extends the discussion about technique by reporting on the clinical process between an analyst who was indirectly affected by the Holocaust as a child of survivors and a patient who was sexually abused.

The analysand made a chance discovery about her analyst's family background, which seemed to have had the same type of impact upon her as has been described in cases of extra-analytic contact, that is, the patients were deeply affected but avoided bringing it up (Ganzarain 1991, Strean 1981, Tarnower 1966, Weiss 1975). I will focus on the analyst's reaction and how it affected the clinical process. To put this material in context I will first briefly review some aspects of the effects of the Holocaust.

EFFECTS OF THE HOLOCAUST

The psychoanalytic study of Holocaust trauma has traditionally focused on three areas: (1) the massive psychic trauma of adult survivors (DeWind 1968, 1972, Krystal 1968, Niederland, 1961, 1981), (2) the effects of such trauma on development in child survivors (Kestenberg and Brenner 1996), and (3) the intergenerational transmission to the second generation (Bergmann and Jucovy 1982, Brenner 2000a,b, Grubrich-Simitis 1981, Kestenberg 1972, 1980, 1982, Kogan 1995, Levine 1982, Wangh 1968, Winnik 1968). The persistence of the effects of trauma has also been examined in survivors at the end of the life cycle (Brenner 1999), as well as via transmission to the third generation (Fonagy 1999), but second-generation studies appear to have predominated. They have been the subject of the New York–based study group started in 1974 by Judith Kestenberg, Martin Bergmann, and Milton Jucovy. When these leaders retired in the early 1990s, there was a changing of the guard, which heralded a new generation of younger analysts who started to attend the study group, and in this mix there were a number of children of survivors. With this new core group and the trend toward more open discussion about countertransference and how the analyst's mind works, I began to wonder if the second-generation psychoanalysts' experience of conducting an analysis could provide a new source of data on the vicissitudes of intergenerational transmission of psychic trauma. In particular, I wondered what might be learned about the working through of these issues in light of the demands on the ego necessary to do analytic work. The suffusion of psychic development with the parental transmission of unresolved grief, survivor guilt, and aggression is often seen in clinical practice, but it is especially marked in the analyses of the second generation. In addition, an uncanny feeling of almost having been there was described by Kestenberg (1982) as a psychological time tunnel or transposition. It is associated with the preoccupation with survival and deep feelings about one's Jewish identity which have characterized virtually every analysis of the second generation that has been presented in the Holocaust discussion group (Brenner 2000a,b).

To my knowledge the postanalytic fate of such issues and their impact on the analytic process from the analyst's perspective have not been documented in the literature. The following case comes from a West Coast analyst, who consulted me and was willing to offer excerpts of his personal journal.

CASE REPORT

Margo, a young Gentile woman with an obsessional and masochistic character and no overt connection to the Holocaust, was convinced that her life was doomed to failure. Although very bright and creative, she could not tolerate any success and was prone to a self-imposed, brooding isolation. She felt inferior to other women and undesirable to men, dressing and behaving in such ways as to prove herself correct over and over. She was referred for analysis after several years of once- and twice-a-week psychotherapy when it became abundantly clear to her therapist, Dr. J., that her isolation of affect and entrenchment in a self-defeating lifestyle would require a long-term, intensive approach with a very patient analyst. He referred Margo to one of his fellow psychoanalytic candidate colleagues, Dr. K., whom he knew to be enthusiastic about analysis and willing to take on a difficult, low-fee case. Although there were certain legitimate logistical reasons that prevented Dr. J. from "converting" Margo to a psychoanalytic case in his own practice, he felt that he had not been particularly effective with her. Dr. J. was a warm and interpersonally oriented therapist who was very capable of engaging patients and working with them psychoanalytically. However, he began to feel frustration with Margo, who had a suspicion of early sexual abuse but was unable to take it any further. She seemed to have become more remote over time but was devastated by the referral nevertheless. Instead of seeing it as an unusual opportunity for the most comprehensive treatment available, she experienced it as a crushing rejection from her handsome doctor, a man whom she had secretly come to like a little too much for her own good. She swore it would never happen again. After minimal outward protest she dutifully obeyed Dr. J. and consulted Dr. K., who commenced the analysis five days a week after a brief evaluation. Margo, scared and exiled, resigned herself to the couch of her new analyst, who was undaunted by her pessimism and perhaps mistook her passivity for a spirit of cooperation.

Margo rarely missed appointments but was frequently late and seemed totally blasé about the therapist's vacations or schedule changes of any kind. When she did miss an appointment, she frequently did not give any warning and did not comment upon it afterward unless asked about it. Typically she would silently enter the office with her head hung low, avoiding any eye contact or social pleasantries, and scurried to the couch, letting out a deep sigh. At the end of sessions she often exuded the feeling of someone who had just endured a painful dental procedure. Many of her associations in the first several years centered on lamenting about having to leave Dr. J., the futility of her life, and the bleakness of her childhood. She would bring in leftovers of old dreams, old conversations, and old feelings, avoiding any contact in the here and now. Dr. K. began to realize what Dr. J. had meant about it probably being a long analysis and he patiently settled in trying to maintain empathic listening while Margo tried to ignore his presence. Margo showed flashes of wit, insight, and pleasantness, which, along with periodic reports of disturbing nightmares, punctuated the monotony of the daily sessions. Dr. K. quietly listened and tried to point out the nature of her resistances when Margo was amenable, and over time the therapeutic alliance evolved. He was delighted to have another analytic patient despite her recalcitrance because his training was going well and he was gaining confidence in the analytic method.

Having finished classes at his institute, Dr. K. started this case as an advanced candidate nearing graduation and in the early termination phase of his own analysis. His courses on technique had been essentially classical, although he was familiar with the emerging debate on self-disclosure. In the second year of the analysis, Margo heard startling news about him, but he did not learn of her discovery for over two more years, as she had rationalized that it was unimportant and did not need to be brought up. In fact, she was aware that she was keeping a secret from Dr. K., and it felt quite natural for her to do so. It was only much later that she realized that her feelings about this information were very powerful and deeply woven into an enormous resistance over confronting the trauma of her own past. Margo belatedly informed her analyst that a very close family friend who happened to be a Holocaust survivor attended a special workshop conducted by him. Under the guise of respecting his privacy, and because she doubted the family friend's reliability in such delicate matters, Margo tried to put it out of her mind.

Significantly, Margo disclosed her discovery during the time she was agonizing over whether she could trust her never-forgotten memory of her uncle's fondling her as a child. The uncle served as a surrogate father, as Margo's own father's unusual career kept him away for long periods of time. She was afraid it was the tip of an iceberg of childhood memories of sexual abuse. Margo noted offhandedly that her older sister, who absolutely hated the uncle, imagined that his cruelty, secretiveness, and invasiveness was because he was a Nazi spy. Since he was born in Europe and spoke very little about his own growing up, it provided a kernel of reality for this fantasy. Even though Margo and her sister were born in America many years later and whatever happened in wartime Europe would have had no direct relevance to her, Margo was nevertheless overwhelmed and haunted by the stories of the Holocaust since she first heard about them as preadolescent. Such a preoccupation with imagery of the Nazi era is not unheard of even in those with no connection to it, and the meaning of it is multiply determined. For example, patients with sadomasochistic tendencies may incorporate images of the Third Reich into their fantasy lives (Bergmann and Jucovy 1982, Volkan et al. 2002).

The complete unexpectedness of Margo's announcement surprised Dr. K. and caught him off-guard (Smith 1995). He reported that he felt a jolt of anxiety, followed by a sense of being "found out," as his anonymity, that is, the analytic armor that he was supposed to have, was suddenly stripped away from him. It was as though his "analytic superego" (Bibring, G. 1954) was still a bit harsh and rigid, not allowing him the flexibility of a more seasoned practitioner. A mixture of shame, embarrassment, and confusion over this sudden exposure made it difficult to listen comfortably at that moment, as his analyzing ego was temporarily disabled.

Unable to associate to this affective flood, he felt that he lapsed into a wooden caricature of an analyst, defensively confronting the patient with questions about *her* feelings, as he was uneasy with the poignancy of the moment. He noted that he was troubled by this involuntary reaction, and when he regained the capacity for self-analysis, he associated to a childhood memory of playing "war" with the neighborhood boys, a most popular activity in the 1950s among the latency-age sons of World War II veterans who returned victoriously after defeating "the Krauts and the Japs." Using their fathers' own helmets and other equipment, they created combat scenarios and fantasy battles, and young Dr. K. was the only boy whose father did not bring back military souvenirs. The fact that his father spoke with an accent and had numbers tattooed on his arm further magnified his sense of being different at a time when he only wanted to be accepted as one of the boys. At a later point, he also realized that being "found out" felt like being caught and feeling stupid, an identification with his father who would berate himself for making stupid mistakes. His father condemned himself for not following his own intuition and going to Palestine with a youth group when he had the chance. Instead, he obeyed his *own* father, stayed home, and got caught by the Gestapo.

Having grown up with an attunement to the pain of the family's wartime tragedy and losses, young Dr. K. delicately broached the problem with his father, who took him to an Army-Navy Surplus Store and bought the necessary items so his son could fit in. Dr. K. intuitively knew that the boys would tease him and would never understand the truth about his father, the nature of which filled him with grief and pain. Dr. K. also came to realize that in that unexpected instant when Margo revealed what she had heard, the shock of it revived the pain of trying to hide the truth about his father from the neighborhood Gentile boys. Being in hiding and secretive about one's Jewish identity also had survival value, so Dr. K. may have unconsciously preferred to identify with his relatives who survived in hiding. He might therefore have felt smarter and more clever than his father if he were to be a step ahead of the Gestapo and never get caught. But, at the time, he was unable to utilize his insights and affective experience to further Margo's analysis because of his wish to hide and protect himself from the regression induced by the psychic pain. This experience raised questions about the meaning of his anonymity (Renik 1995) as it provided a legitimization for keeping things inside, a repository for Dr. K.'s incompletely worked through affects. Having recently terminated his training analysis, this experience (A. Freud 1968, Firestein 1978) may have also represented his idealization of his own anonymous analyst, in his effort to be a classical "keeper of the analytic process" (Calef and Weinshel 1980) and carry on the tradition (Cooper 1986). While this childhood memory did come up in his analysis, it lacked the intensity and immediacy of the abreaction induced at this time. Consequently, Dr. K. was too consumed by his own affective regression to address his concordant identification (Racker 1957) with the patient's shame over confronting the secret in her own life—her sexual relationship with her uncle.

Dr. K. wondered if he unconsciously colluded with Margo to avoid the topic of her knowledge about him until he had more sufficiently worked through his own issue. As the analysis proceeded, the patient felt that his abstinence re-created life with her evasive uncle and her absent father. Her renunciation of curiosity in other aspects of the transference was due, she insisted, to her identification with her mother who "looked the other way" and avoided painful realities. Moreover, her uncle never answered any of her questions and neither did her analyst. This time, however, she would not play this game, and the paternal transference merged with Dr. K.'s stiff, technical stance, as the daily enactment of her past may have contributed to the duration of the treatment. Even as Dr. K. became more experienced and more comfortable with his other cases, he still found it difficult to free himself from the projective identification with Margo, who grew up being instructed by her mother not to dwell on the past.

Ultimately he became conscious of his wish to modify his stance and talk to her about himself, after forgetting to turn the volume down on his answering machine before a session. The call that interrupted them was from a woman friend leaving a warm message, and Margo reacted with jealousy and despair. However, she was able to associate to the woman's name, which led to a memory of her murky childhood, where she, at age 3, had drawn a picture of her uncle exposing his genitals. She had given the drawing to her mother, who turned a blind eye until years later, after the man had died. Therefore, the mother felt enormous guilt over subjecting her daughter to years of abuse, and Margo also felt guilt over her displaced oedipal victory. A pact of silence existed between Margo and her mother until the answering machine incident in her analysis, after which Margo started to feel her rage at mother for not protecting her (Escoll 1999). And, in a sense, Dr. K. did not protect Margo either from the intrusions of a third party, thereby enacting the mother's unconscious complicity. As if to illustrate the two very different but intersecting psychological tracks of patient and analyst, this electronic parapraxis seemed to betray Dr. K.'s unconscious wish to open up and tell Margo more about himself. In so doing he would simultaneously compensate for the loss of his analytic functioning during her revelation of the discovery about him and become the open, available father and uncle in the transference whom Margo never had.

Several months later Margo reported a dream in which Dr. K. wished to reveal more of himself to her. In the dream Margo was eavesdropping on his telephone conversation, which he knowingly allowed her to do. He was planning a big party and making the preparations. Margo felt uneasy and guilty about listening but was titillated by the opportunity to get closer to Dr. K. and be allowed to listen in. In the dream she was unsure of her role in his life. Was she to be invited to the party also, or was she an intruder? She also was unsure if he was doing something wrong by letting her in on his private life. Avoiding further exploration of her wishes in the transference, she preferred the pain of reconstructing her traumatic past to the anguish of her present-day frustrations. Consequently she was able to recall a childhood memory of eavesdropping in the hallway outside her sister's door while her uncle was performing a painful sexual act upon her. She was horrified about knowing any further secrets and withdrew for weeks afterward.

But, as fate would have it, Margo would become privy to more information about Dr. K.'s life. About a year after the eavesdropping dream, she was rather late for a session, and Dr. K. decided to answer the phone, thinking it might possibly be her. Instead, the caller notified him that a very close relative had just died. Though the death was not unexpected, the news came as a surprise. Moments later, Margo hurried in and immediately sensed something wrong. Almost before he could finish telling her that he had just received bad news and would not be able to see her that day, Margo turned around and rushed out the door. She had a sickly smile on her face and nodded, but left without a word. Over the succeeding weeks and months, the profundity of this moment was examined in great detail, as it seemed to encapsulate the core of her analytic dilemma. Dr. K. was puzzled by Margo's peculiar smile and the rapidity of her exit, wondering if the heaviness of his sadness and grief had overwhelmed her. In her typical manner, she dutifully obeyed without asking questions, but her leaving so quickly was a bit mysterious.

Margo subsequently revealed that in that moment of seeing how upset Dr. K. had been, she indeed had become overwhelmed, but not with sadness or grief. Instead, she ran out because she became mortified by an overwhelming urge to comfort him sexually to make him feel better. Yet she had the thought that he was tricking her into feeling sorry for him in order to get her to masturbate him. So, to avoid an enactment of her childhood memory, Margo turned on her heels and bolted from the office. Another layer was Margo's underlying sadism and wish for revenge against her uncle. Sensing a moment of vulnerability in Dr. K., Margo also envisioned cutting his penis off and holding up her bloody trophy in a triumphant gesture. This fantasy may have also reflected her rage at Dr. K. over feeling sexually rejected by him, which revived memories of her uncle's losing interest in her after he got married and of her being sent away by her former therapist, Dr. J. But the moment of Dr. K.'s sadness and vulnerability brought her back to the question of his Holocaust background. At this point in the treatment, both the depth of Margo's understanding of herself and Dr. K.'s comfort with his own legacy had increased significantly, so the topic was easily revisited. He was also more experienced as an analyst and had become more resilient in his work. Wanting to handle it as well as possible, Dr. K. consulted me and decided that he would tell her that he would consider answering her question if they both felt that it might further her analysis. They discussed the parallels to her childhood, with Margo not being sure she would trust her judgment regarding what she heard, saw, or remembered, and what went on with her uncle. In lieu of demanding an answer from Dr. K., she then drew on her own strengths, beginning to own her desperate longings for her uncle and her absent father, the anguished secret victory over her mother, her guilt-ridden pleasure, and her rage over feeling exploited as an innocent child.

But it appeared that Margo's curiosity about herself could only go so far without returning to the original question about Dr. K.'s background. Was it true, and if so, what did it mean? How did his parents survive? What were they like as parents? Did Dr. K. have an unhappy childhood, too? Did analysis help him deal with it? Was his becoming an analyst related to the Holocaust? And if so, could he really help her overcome her past and come to feel that her life was worth living? Her wish to be rescued by him through analysis and then marriage were thoroughly explored, as Dr. K. better understood the influence of his own wish to rescue his parents. Dr. K. ultimately acknowledged that what she had heard was true, and Margo had a cathartic experience, crying with relief and sadness. She finally allowed herself to feel just how curious she really was and how incredibly important it was for her to know this. It really was okay for her to know, and Dr. K. trusted her enough to tell her. She became elated over the unlimited possibilities in her life if only she could be free enough to really be able to learn. Then, as a foreshadowing of what would lie ahead before she could terminate and go out on her own, her euphoria was replaced by panic over feeling trapped in the transference once again. For if Dr. K. knew just how insatiably curious she was, that she had hundreds of more questions about him, then he would surely take advantage of her as her uncle had done. The uncle exploited his young niece's natural curiosity for his own sexual pleasure for as long as it suited him, and she learned the lesson of a lifetime: Curiosity killed the cat. Now she felt caught, exposed and vulnerable once again, which, not surprisingly, were the same affects that Dr. K. experienced years before when Margo told him what she knew about him.

DISCUSSION

There appeared to be an affective resonance in the analytic dyad that was communicated unconsciously and required the analyst's comfort in order for the work to proceed optimally (Beres and Arlow 1974). Having come full circle, Dr. K. was then able to help Margo work through this aspect of the transference after she had inadvertently helped him work through his own affect-laden issue, which had been activated as a concordant countertransference (Racker 1957) years before. Through conducting an analysis that began when Dr. K. was terminating his own, Margo may have become unconsciously linked (Volkan 1987) to the impending loss of his own analyst. Perhaps his reported difficulty in handling Margo's projective identification in order to modify his stance and not enact the deprivation of her childhood was also related to unresolved mourning for his own analyst. While he had evolved into a more flexible clinician with his other cases, it seemed as though he were somewhat frozen in time with Margo, that is, back in the time when he was still in analysis. I am reminded of a talented candidate who sought supervision with me during the last days of his analysis. Even though the case was problematic, the sense of urgency to begin the analysis was so great that it suggested that his temporary lapse in judgment, in which he apparently was trying to short-circuit the mourning for his training analyst by an unconscious replacement with a supervisor and a new analysand, was in order to avert the pain of loss. Observations about replacement fantasies in the final hours of an analysis are well known (Blum 1989, Lipton 1961) and may be easily masqueraded in the training situation. In Dr. K.'s case, the transmitted unresolved grief in a child of Holocaust survivors added to the burden of mourning, and he may have had an especially challenging time giving up his analyst because of this factor, too. Through his professional activities, living his life, and the passage of time, further mourning of his own analyst was possible however, enabling him to better sublimate his wish to rescue his survivor parents, and make better use of his self (Jacobs 1991) as an analyzing instrument (Balter et al. 1980).

The eventual confirmation of Margo's chance discovery of his Holocaust background, after exploring her fantasies and curiosity, served to facilitate the analytic process. Dr. K.'s attitude of comfort and openness seemed crucial, but his self-disclosure was limited to only what she had already heard. There were times throughout the analysis when he wanted to tell her about himself, but his training and characterological tendency to be reserved about such matters prevented him from doing so. Noting the differences in analysts' character styles, Renik (1999) nevertheless suggests that his advice about the willingness to self-disclose applies to all, in order to "render his or her experience available to the patient" (p.535). However, he does imply that such an approach may feel more natural to those with more extroverted, flamboyant, or exhibitionistic traits. Even so, the type of disclosure he advocates pertains more to how the analyst's mind works rather than to autobiographical data, an area that is less well studied. Such disclosures seem to be more controversial and when carried to an extreme may approach a mutual analysis. Staying within Renik's metaphor, if what he recommends is "playing one's cards face up," then Ferenczi's experiments (Grubrich-Simitis 1986) might well be considered "strip poker"! Perhaps the best known example of this baring of himself (Hoffer 1990, Masson 1984, Rachman 1998) was his disclosure about his "small penis complex." This entry in his diary entitled "On the Feeling of Shame" was on July 21, 1932, less than a year before his death and a month before his resignation as president of the International Psychoanalytic Association:

> Her next dream concerns a fairly robust man with a minute penis. Details pointed to my person. I was able to satisfy her curiosity and tell her something about my own anxiousness and bashfulness, small penis complex, etc. As she noted that I did not conceal any of my weakness, so that she cannot hurt me any more by alluding to these weaknesses, she ceased to rub my nose in my ineptitude, analytic or otherwise, and began to wonder whether . . . the "trauma" in her case was not created by the withdrawal of love rather than by rape. [Ferenczi 1932, p. 164]

Ferenczi then notes that as a result of this revelation and further related interventions, his patient's shame and guilt over sexual matters were ameliorated.

Despite the vast differences between Ferenczi's provocative revelation about his childhood fantasies of a small penis and Dr. K.'s eventual confirmation of his Holocaust background, there are common affective themes. Ferenczi described his anxiousness and bashfulness, and Hoffer (1990) reported even feeling "embarrassed for him" (p. 724). Similarly, Dr. K. reported feeling a jolt of anxiety followed by shame, embarrassment, and confusion when he was first found out. Furthermore, both patients who were sexually seduced and ultimately rejected by the adults were consumed by shame. Given that the defensive manifestations of shame include an urge to hide, avoid eye contact, and be secretive, are the unconscious residues of this affect susceptible to be woven into the cloak of anonymity that is worn by or thrown off by the analyst? The extent to which the vicissitudes of shame are an issue in both the analyst and analysand may be a factor in where the analyst initially finds himself along that hypothetical continuum between disclosure and anonymity. Therefore, the complexities that belie the technical decision on whether and how to disclose may be influenced by the analyst's own regulatory mechanisms regarding this affect.

Dr. K.'s confirmation of what Margo had heard was a crucial technical decision, which although seemingly catalytic is an arguable point. But it was essential for Margo to learn to trust her judgment and reality sense, a function of giving up her tendency toward negation (Freud 1925b). One might wonder if she could have benefited further by confirming the information on her own through other sources that were available to her. Did the analyst make it too easy for her by telling her? Could his handling it the way he did have led to greater demands for gratification in the transference, thus becoming an enactment of her uncle's showing her too much of his own self (body)? And was Margo's initial shocking revelation a reflection of her identification with the uncle? Undoubtedly, Dr. K.'s initial reaction to Margo's announcement was less than optimum, and he had a wish to repair not only himself but the therapeutic process as well. His "electronic parapraxis" and the patient's eavesdropping dream reflected their combined wishes of wanting to confide in someone and to be privy to personal information. Margo's earlier access to the secrets of her uncle's sexuality made such wishes highly dangerous for her, and her curiosity became profoundly inhibited. Margo's behavior was mechanical and stereotyped, as she avoided eye contact, never looked around the office, and rarely commented on the shared sensory experiences that not infrequently occur during an analysis, such as loud outside noises, blinking of the lights, problems with the heat, and so on. Her marked isolation of affect made it almost impossible for her to experience her self, also, and it took years until a spontaneous interchange became possible. Dr. K. suppressed his own wish to engage in a mutual analysis by writing in his journal, employing self-analysis, and availing himself of a consultation. Nevertheless, the wish itself appears to have been an important signal of a disturbance in the analytic field that needed to be remedied.

Ferenczi's radical solution of a mutual analysis would have been anathema to Dr. K., who in his own analysis had not analyzed the meaning of his use of anonymity in his role as the analyst. In addition, he identified with his analyst, whose anonymity was valued by their training institute, since a special tutorial was arranged when the training analyst was scheduled to teach one of Dr. K.'s classes. Moreover, since the institute was a nonreporting program, the training analyst did not reveal anything about Dr. K., which in turn protected his privacy and perhaps further reinforced the virtue of anonymity (Calef and Weinshel 1980). Not surprisingly, an informal poll of training analysts suggests that candidates rarely examine how their own incompletely worked through conflicts may find a refuge behind the cloak of anonymity as they learn to conduct analysis themselves. And as Rosenblum (1998) observes, "Typically the most rigid practitioners of abstinence and anonymity are those analysts with unresolved conflicts whose conflicts have been activated by a particular patient or by the very process of conducting an analysis" (p. 541). He agrees with Schafer (1983) that the neophyte analyst must resist the temptation to use the analysand for his own purposes. Ferenczi, who has been criticized for doing just that but whose rehabilitation continues as his ideas have gained more credence in the last fifteen years (Bonomi 1999), felt that the analyst's failure to acknowledge his mistakes would retraumatize a vulnerable patient and lead to a stalemate. Therefore he advocated honest interactions which also set an example for how to overcome one's shame, but recognizing the pitfalls in going too far, considered "mutual analysis only (as) a last resort!" (Ferenczi 1932, p. 115).

CONCLUSION

The myth of anonymity notwithstanding, the analyst's striving for it and attitudes about it are multiply determined and may become part of the analytic superego. Educational influences, the fate of identificatory processes with his/her training analyst, and pressures in the intersubjective matrix in the clinical work appear to be major factors. Through maturation and further clinical experience, the analyst's flexibility and openness may increase, which seems to parallel the evolution of psychoanalytic thought on the same technical issue. It seems that certain aspects of the analyst's background exert additional pressure on the analytic dyad, highlighting the challenge to maintain the optimal technical stance. For example, it may be that for some patients the suspicion or knowledge of their analyst's connection to the Holocaust is so affectively charged that it becomes a psychological lightning rod. In the case described above, a patient with a history of early trauma resonated with an analyst who had a history of familial trauma and felt like a kindred spirit. The discovery about the analyst was inadvertent and kept secret for two years, but eventually became a central theme. Unless there is an opportunity to analyze these issues thoroughly and to get some confirmation of reality, certain resistances may develop that are insurmountable. While it is well known that external reality itself may be used as defense (Inderbitzin and Levy 1994), under these circumstances the opposite may also be true. Failure to acknowledge such a reality might be countertherapeutic. Analysts who aspire to an idealized level of anonymity may be unconsciously seeking a refuge for incompletely worked through shame-laden conflicts; if this protection is suddenly and unexpectedly lost, it can interfere with their analyzing capabilities. Since it is quite possible that analysts in training will not examine the meaning of their use of anonymity, analytic supervisors might be alert to this tendency when technical problems arise in the treatment situation.

To expand upon one of Freud's (1920) well-known medical analogies, the living cell has a membrane that controls the flow of chemicals from within and without. This permeability, which is essential for the integrity of the cell, can change if the health of the cell or the surrounding environment is compromised. If the permeability increases, there can be extravasation and leaking of vital contents, whereas, if the permeability decreases, then communication is shut off. So, too, one might envision that the analyst has a permeable membrane, which if too permeable can result in inappropriate disclosures and boundary violations, but if too impermeable can result in undue abstinence, anonymity, and unavailability. An optimum level of responsiveness (Sandler 1976) would seem to require a well-maintained perimeter. Analysts probably develop their own unique analytic membrane owing to variations in character, the influences of psychoanalytic education, and the extent of unfinished business, including termination issues in the training analysis. Disturbances in this membrane may occur for a variety of inner and outer reasons resulting in certain signals. Such signal affects may play an important role in the analytic relationship and warrant further study (Emde 1999, Spezzano 1993). The wish to reveal oneself or enter into a mutual analysis is an example of one of these signals. Ferenczi's (1932) warning, "mutual analysis: only a last resort! Proper analysis by a stranger, without any obligation, would be better" (p. 115), betrays the desperateness of his own circumstances. Deprived of such an opportunity because of his unique place in psychoanalytic history and his complex relationship with Freud (Hoffer and Hoffer 1999), he could imagine what he was missing. Seventy years later, the contemporary analyst fortunately does have the advantage of a "good enough" training analysis, supervision, self-analysis, consultation, and reanalysis when indicated.

8

Falling Asleep as Countertransference Enactment

The fact that the doctor at many interviews pays little heed to the patient's associations and only picks up his ears at certain statements also belongs to the chapter "On Countertransference"; dozing may happen . . . [and] we were reacting unconsciously to the emptiness and worthlessness of the associations. . . . At the first idea of the patient's that in any way concerns treatment we brighten up again. The danger, therefore of the doctor falling asleep and leaving the patient observed is not great. (I owe full confirmation of this observation to a verbal discussion of the subject with Prof. Freud.) [!]

[Ferenczi 1919a, p. 180]

Take for example, falling asleep. Falling asleep is certainly not a defense mechanism but it can be used to defend against aggression, to ward it off.

[Sandler J. and Freud, A., 1983, p. 43]

The first time it happened to me, I was in my first year of practice and swore it would never happen again. I was sitting with a heavily-medicated man late one afternoon when his heavy eyelids, slow speech, and droning, monotone voice lulled me into a very relaxed state. My largely unsuccessful efforts to engage him in intensive therapy and explore the dynamics of his periodic psychosis were met with his usual pseudo-compliance and bewilderment that day. Somewhere in the midst of his soliloquy, I lost consciousness. I abruptly woke up from my siesta, which seemed like hours, when my patient loudly proclaimed, "Hey, doc! You're sleeping!" I felt ashamed, embarrassed, guilty, and quite dazed. The patient, who was struggling with homosexual anxieties and an insoluble engulfment by his youthful, pretty, and oversolicitous mother, was undeterred by my poor manners. Expecting an angry rebuke, which would have corresponded to my own internal reproach, I was stunned when he apologized to me for being so boring. At that moment, his observing ego was more functional than mine and he could see how difficult it could be for anyone to spend time with him and to take his delusional preoccupations seriously. He felt pity for me, and I, in turn, felt sorry for him and his absolute lack of self-worth.

My affective reaction, an admixture of shame, embarrassment, and guilt, was a prototypical reaction to being caught unawares and feeling that I had done something wrong. While it was true that he had a role in my somnolent withdrawal from him, it would have felt disingenuous to ascribe it all to my reaction to "the emptiness and worthlessness of the associations" (Ferenczi 1919a, p. 180). At that time in my career, I was just starting my private practice after working a nearly full-time job, commuting at least two hours a day for analysis and classes, and being up late at night with young children. I was a bit overextended and apparently ripe for a nap when my heavily-medicated patient arrived that day. It therefore seemed reasonable to consider that my sleep-deprived state would have made me more susceptible to this type of patient's soporific influence. However, it was my responsibility as a clinician to recognize that I needed more rest; I was sufficiently chagrined and thought that I could take the appropriate steps to prevent a recurrence. As is often the case in such a reaction, therapists are uncomfortable with these seemingly unprofessional lapses that are thought to be greatly underreported, even in the sophisticated psychoanalytic literature (Alexander 1981, Cohen 1952, Dean 1957, McLaughlin 1975, Scott 1975). Yet, there can be much meaning in the analytically informed situation when we examine "the continuum of vigilance to sleep experienced by the analyst during his working day" (McLaughlin 1975, p. 381). It therefore occurred to me at a later point in my training that I may have experienced unconscious anger over the patient's inability to make progress as well as anxiety over his homoerotic attachment to me which was warded off by my multiply-determined sleepiness (J. Sandler and A. Freud 1983, Waelder 1936). I do suspect, however, that had I not found myself deeply involved in the work with seriously traumatized patients utilizing defensive altered states of consciousness years later, I, too, may have repressed this incident (Alexander 1981).

McLaughlin (1975), who felt that falling frankly into a deep sleep is rare, described three categories of patients who may induce sleepiness in the analyst: (1) passive-aggressive, obsessional, and neurotic characters whose withholding, isolation of affect, and withdrawal leave the analyst bored and susceptible to sedation; (2) borderline and psychotic individuals whose negation of the therapeutic alliance and inability to make progress may induce rage, which gets warded off by tiredness; and (3) those whose conflicts and defenses are too similar to those of the analyst's or his important objects so that countertransference problems arise that defensively dull the mind. I would offer a fourth category of patients: those who regularly utilize defensive altered ego states and manifest autohypnotic, dreamlike phenomena. Such individuals, including those who would fulfill diagnostic criteria for dissociative disorders, may find their way into the unsuspecting analyst's office and present a variety of challenges. Staying awake and alert may be one of those perennial challenges with this patient population. While McLaughlin's description that "the phenomena constitute defensive and expressive compromises literally close to the ways of the dream" (p. 364) apply to all the patient categories described above, it is in my view especially relevant to those who dissociate.

Nevertheless, there is a difference between examining countertransference issues behind the analyst's narcosis and seeing it as a facilitation to a therapeutic process. After all, advancing an argument that falling asleep on the job could actually be beneficial to the patient might, on the surface, be seen as so outrageous and self-serving that I doubt any professions outside of psychoanalysis would have the audacity or theory to put forth such a notion. Perhaps it is an inevitable benefit of being in an "impossible" profession (Greenson 1966) that we would allow ourselves the freedom to consider that such behavior, that under usual circumstances would be boorish, could in fact be therapeutic and perhaps even necessary. For example, Eshel (2001), in a recent report on her work with a traumatized and inaccessible woman, described how she would regularly fall asleep while her patient would stay awake and study her: "After the first ten to fifteen minutes of listening and responding, I would fall into a deep sleep totally devoid of feeling" (p. 549). Sensing that she must have resonated with a split-off and dissociated aspect of the patient's psyche that eventually found its way into treatment, the author concludes, "A sense of total helplessness, of dissociated, unspeakable abuse and longing. . . . Clari increasingly projected these basic central elements of her inner world to me. . . . The experience of being inside a dissociative, blank process was occurring in *me*—a *vicarious* self-state dissociation, thus detaching and distancing itself from her while she observed from without" (p. 557). In such situations, Brown (1977) emphasizes the role of projective identification, in which "the analyst feels depleted or half-alive and, thus, disoriented and out of touch with the basis of what is most alive or would be most alive at this time if the patient were truly there" (p. 480).

The treatment of Eshel's (2001) patient was apparently able to proceed "beyond the dissociation" (p. 558) because she was able to contain and tolerate the patient's fragmented, psychic material within the "symbiotic relatedness between patient and therapist" (Searles 1965, p. 524). The analyst slept and detoxified this deposited material from her traumatic past while the patient looked on for several years and had the opportunity "to identify with the therapist who survives the fullest intensity of this attack to which the patient was exposed in childhood" (p. 536). Lichtenberg and associates (1992) describe the severe mental effects on the developing mind of "especially acute, traumatic abuse [as] cognitive, affective paralysis . . . with . . . a gap of information processing. The person is apt to be left with a vulnerability to dissociative 'self-states'" (pp. 167–168). In treatment, the assault on the analyst's mind results in a comparable but temporary inability to think, a transient thought disorder (Bach in press) described by Bion (1959) as "an attack on linking." This effect on the analyst could thus be seen as a mini-traumatization or resonance (Kelman 1982) induced by the patient, resulting in symptomatology similar to her own.

Shengold (1989), in his extensive work on the subject, cites a vignette about an analyst who, like Eshel, became sedated regularly: "I found myself after about ten minutes or so of each session rapidly losing concentration, becoming sleepy . . . [which] happened persistently and with a shocking (I felt as I realized it) regularity" (p. 153). His severely abused patient, who used to hide in a closet to protect herself from a psychotic mother, reexperienced in the transference "a murderous, extremely dangerous, cunning, psychotic 'analyst mother.' Unconsciously, it was kill or be killed and the hypnotic drone of her voice (coupled with her associations that were a form of defensive–dissociative and isolating–listmaking) protected her from murderous rage towards me . . . and represented an attempt to soothe me. At that time, she effectively 'murdered' my ability to analyze" (pp. 153–154). Considering a shared autohypnotic defense in the dyad, Shengold concludes that "the hypnosis was transmitted to the analyst," and he adds, "I have found in supervising analysts and in my own cases that this kind of 'putting the analyst to sleep' happens much more frequently than has been written about. . . . The analyst too must be aware of how difficult it is to face and own feelings of intense hostility towards the parent and from the parent. Here the pre-oedipal and oedipal terrors merge: the Oedipus complex is about patricide and matricide as well as about incest" (p. 154). Significantly, Shengold differentiates this manifestation of hypnotic evasion

(Fliess 1953) from hypnotic facilitation, in which hypervigilance, improved recall, and other enhanced cognitive functioning might occur while one is entranced, too. This facet of the autohypnotic state could also contribute to some situations where treatment is facilitated, and much more clinical data are needed to clarify this facet of mental functioning.

The notion of the patient's self-hypnosis transmitted to the analyst raises a number of problematic issues for psychoanalysis. As Freud (1923b) reminisced, "It is not easy to overestimate the importance of the part played by hypnotism in the history of the origin of psycho-analysis" (p. 192). Lewin (1954), elaborating on this theme, concluded,

> Since the beginnings of analysis in hypnotism, we got away more and more from the sleeping or partly asleep patient, and we rejected a good deal of the technique that depended on the patient's partial sleep. It is worth examining whether, along with this rational development, we may not have erected an unconscious defense as well so as to live down our suspect history as hypnotists and our mythical prehistory as anesthetists. If we have, we may not be aware of all the traces of hypnotism and anesthesia we have unwittingly carried along with us. [p. 503]

If this is so, then the possibility exists that "the traces of hypnotism" could also influence the analyst, that is, the analyst could become hypnotized by the patient. However, the notion that a patient could unwittingly induce a psychoanalyst into a hypnotic trance out of his or her awareness might sound rather disconcerting to those who prefer to minimize the susceptibility of the analyst's psyche to such influences. In fact, we have no idea about the potential hypnotizability of analysts. After all, it would be anathema for the admissions committees of analytic institutes to assess prospective candidates for hypnotizability as part of the evaluation for their suitability to do analytic work. Such a criteria might seem as outlandish as assessing an applicant's psi capacity, i.e., potential for extra-sensory perception, to determine his or her potential to receive unconscious communication because paranormal events may occur during the analytic work also (Lazar 2001, Mayer 1996, 2001). These phenomena may be considered to be beyond the realm of psychoanalysis or simply not exist at all; part of the problem may be essentially metapsychological owing to a difficulty in satisfactorily explaining them in psychoanalytic terms (Brenner 2001). Perhaps it is for these reasons that the literature on analysts falling asleep seems to describe the same phenomenon in a variety of ways, from being in a hypnoid state (Dickes 1965, Dickes and Papernik 1977) to "as if I had been injected with a sleep-making drug" (Wolfenstein 1985, p. 83) to being "charmed" (Rittenberg 1987). Indeed, Rittenberg suggests that "we analysts must allow ourselves to drift toward sleep" (p. 394) because we "may be especially susceptible to charm with its promise of conflict-free blissful sleep" (p. 395).

Ferenczi (1919a) observed that the analyst's identification with the patient revives his own patienthood on the couch and is a basic form of countertransference. The patient has "evolved" from the hypnotic subject who is induced to sleep in the session into the analysand who free-associates while in a state of mind similar to the hypnogogic state preceding sleep. Therefore, Lewin (1955) reasons, dream psychology may be applied to the analytic hour itself, as the analyst fuels fantasies in the transference in the analogous way that he contributes to the day residue providing raw material for the dream. The manifest content of free associations may be equivalent to the manifest content of the dream. From this perspective, the sleeping analyst also could be seen as belonging to the prehistory of analysis, that is, the era of hypnosis, and thus having experienced both phylogenetic regression and narcissistic withdrawal. In such a state, he or she is unable to listen and analyze but is able to experience dream-like mental processes such as those occurring in hypnogogic states, for example, autosymbolism and the functional phenomenon (Brenner 2001, Silberer 1909). This universal tendency to symbolize one's own alterations of consciousness somatically, metaphysically, and anthropomorphically underlies self-state dreams described by Kohut (1977) and may have implications for the nature of the communication in the dyad if the analyst enacts a dream within a dream (Fodor 1951).

With this latter notion in mind, the sleeping analyst may be thought of as living out a dream within the patient's metaphorical dream during the session. This phenomenon was enacted with a patient, which resulted in a dramatic development in the treatment and led to an important discovery about the pathogenesis of her seemingly bizarre psychic structure. The patient was severely traumatized in childhood and manifested defensive altered states of consciousness in the form of personifications. These so-called alter personalities are the hallmark of dissociative identity disorder (DID), formerly known as multiple personality disorder. In my own study of this condition, I found it helpful to think of it as a lower level disturbance of character formation in which dissociation rather than repression or splitting is the central defensive operation. My working definition of dissociation is as follows:

> A defensive altered state of consciousness due to autohypnosis, augmenting repression or splitting. It develops as a primitive, adaptive response of the ego to the overstimulation and pain of external trauma, which, depending on its degree of integration, may result in a broad range of disturbances of alertness, awareness, memory and identity. Dissociation apparently may change in its function and be employed later on as a defense against the perceived internal danger of internal

> affects and instinctual strivings. Thus, it may be a transient neurotic defense, or become characterological and may be even the predominant defense. The content of associations in dissociation is as important as the defensive purpose it serves and may be accessible through hypnosis but very resistant to psychoanalysis unless the analyst is aware of its presence. [Brenner 2001, p. 36]

Considering the dual nature of dissociation as both a here-and-now neurotic defense and a defense/symptom complex related to early trauma may facilitate the analytically informed treatment of this population.

CASE REPORT

Cindy was an enigmatic woman who presented with suicidal depression and whose history of severe, early sexual abuse was revealed by seemingly separate selves over time during an analytic treatment (Brenner 2001). As the nature of her dissociative psychopathology was unfolding during her second year on the couch, I became very, very tired during a session one afternoon and actually fell asleep toward the latter part of the hour. Around this time, she reported a very disturbing dream in which she was sitting happily with her uncle who was suddenly transformed into a grotesque character and chased her around the house. She ran down the steps outside the front door just in time to save her life. The dream seemed very real to her and she felt the terror for days. Prior to the session in question, she had another nightmare in which her uncle was so drunk and unable to stand that she had to help him get to bed. After she did, the dream shifted suddenly to a bare mattress on the floor in a dingy room with a bare light bulb overhead. The uncle was lying there naked, grabbing a young girl toward him while Cindy looked on from a distance. Once again, the patient awoke in a disoriented panic, which persisted and left her feeling rather depersonalized. Cindy would experience amnestic periods and find herself in places where she did not remember going. She had very few friends for fear they would discover that she was "crazy." She avoided intimacy and divorced her husband before he could discover how odd she thought she was. She had numerous ingenious ways of covering up and compensating for her memory loss, keeping extensive calendars, writing notes to herself, and never volunteering personal information. She would appear to be a good listener to others while she desperately tried to elicit clues from their conversation to piece together the patchwork of her memory. The nature of her career was such that these deficits could be hidden, especially when she was not overly symptomatic. In therapy Cindy would lapse into silences for long periods of time on the couch and when she did speak, she often sounded like a very scared and lost young girl.

During the session, she was very uneasy and anxious about the meaning of her dreams, unable to determine whether they represented actual events related to her or to somebody else or were merely flights of fancy. She recalled her poverty-stricken young life, the rampant alcoholism in her male relatives, and her mother's working two jobs to support the family of nine children. Abandoned by her father at an early age and living with a large, extended family in a rural area, she cryptically alluded to having to do what the women were supposed to do when she was a girl. Several days prior, after a "switch" during a session, a dissociated self-state of a young girl named Tina tentatively introduced herself to me. Her predominant affect was one of fear as she contained memories of incest and torture. As the current hour progressed, the patient became more visibly anxious on the couch, a topic we had discussed quite regularly with the imminence of sexually traumatic material coming to the fore and my growing awareness of her becoming disoriented at such times while she was lying on her back. I anticipated she might "switch" again and tried to intervene. As her passivity and anxiety increased, I reminded her that she was not required to lie down and use the couch. At one point, I said something to the effect that she was free to use any piece of furniture she wished. At the time, I was trying to emphasize my acceptance of her possible need to adjust her body position and sit in a chair once again, but was reluctant to specifically request it. I wanted to maintain as much of an analytic atmosphere as possible and examine her conflict rather than legislate her actions and tell her where to place her body.

Cindy thanked me for the comments and seemed temporarily relieved but insisted that she would be okay where she was. Her perfectionistic superego and her wish to adhere to the "rules," a reflection of years of parochial schooling, made it all the more difficult for her to take any initiative on her behalf, so she suffered through the hours on the couch. She lapsed into periods of silence that were punctuated by clipped responses to my inquiries. As the silence continued, I felt myself becoming extremely tired as she became less responsive to my comments and inquiries about what she was experiencing. Making a bargain with myself that I could not keep, I said to myself that I would rest my heavy eyelids by closing them for just a moment (!) but I lost consciousness for the rest of the hour. I awoke to the sound of my heavy breathing and thought I saw my patient twist around on the couch staring at me blankly. Trying to regain some sense of control, I curiously ended the session on time in my dazed state and silently escorted my patient to the door in my usual fashion. On the way out, she tentatively asked, "Did you fall asleep?" I was struck by the seeming uncertainty of her observation about me as well as my fleeting temptation not to answer her directly, a multiply-determined wish to hide both my lapse and to explore her inability to trust her perception in the transference. However, I simply told her, in what must have been a rather contrite way, that I apparently did fall asleep and that I hoped we could discuss it in more detail the next day. She seemed relieved that I confirmed her suspicion and walked out. I felt surprised and still a bit dazed but, interestingly, it resolved very quickly as soon as she left. For the rest of the day I was quite alert but felt a bit sheepish and rather curious about how Cindy and I would analyze the situation.

The patient arrived late for her next session. Although she mechanically lay down on the couch again, much to her credit she brought up the subject of my somnolence, albeit haltingly and very meekly. Once again, I had a disturbing sense that she was so obsequious and unsure of herself that I might have been able to convince her that she was wrong—that I might have been able to make her believe anything (Calef and Weinshel 1981)—to essentially impose my will and my reality upon her. At this point, I chose not to comment on my subjective sense of this aspect of the enactment, and reaffirmed that in the ensuing silence of the hour I did doze off. I told her that I imagined that she would have had some rather strong feelings about that. Cindy became silent again for many minutes and I wondered if we might be repeating the scenario from the day before, but I felt on guard this time and was more active in my inquiries to her. She eventually told me that she had had a difficult time the day before also, but could not elaborate. Instead, she simply said that when she thought she heard my slow, deep breathing, she became aware of the little girl inside named Tina who felt paralyzed with fear. As a result, she said she felt very strange and could not move until "Jack," another alter personality, got very angry and turned around to see what was going on. As noted earlier, I apparently regained consciousness at that time, so perhaps her moving around and looking at me may have brought me out of my state. The patient "heard" from Tina that she thought she was back in bed with her uncle, terrified to move for fear that he would awaken from his drunken stupor and hurt her again. In a moment of defiant protectiveness, Tina was then replaced by Jack, an angry, elusive male self, who became outraged to discover my condition. He was not afraid of me and was prepared to defend the helpless girl. Cindy experienced incredulousness with the description of her inner experience, which made her sound truly "crazy" to her own ears, and she certainly thought I would share the same dim view of her sanity. Her worst fears about losing her mind and being taken over by unseen forces were being realized and she wanted to flee. I told her that what we learned about how her mind worked might explain a lot about her tendency to get both very quiet and very forgetful at such times. I reassured her that I had some familiarity with what she was telling me and that what she was describing was not random insanity. Rather, it all had meaning and could be potentially understood in the treatment. I then told her I was curious to learn more about Tina and Jack and "anyone else" who might be around, essentially welcoming these personifications into the therapy.

In the subsequent days, the patient was quite remote and guarded as she slowly revealed more about her very troubled childhood in the form of vague stories narrated by Cindy in the first person and apparently as terrified dramatizations in the moment (Laub and Auerhahn 1993) through her child personifications. An older personification, serving a benign babysitter-type function, had revealed that "they" had been hoping for years to find someone they could trust with their secrets, since Cindy was not interested in knowing about them and was quite mentally unstable. Essentially, the patient described her resistance to knowing while in the very dissociated state she employed in order to keep from knowing and remembering. As though in a sleepwalking or fugue state, she would jump off the couch, scream and protest to her hallucinated attackers, run to a corner, curl up in a fetal position, and cry inconsolably. After such regressive episodes, the patient was usually disoriented, amnestic, confused, and quite ashamed.

Following one of these sessions, Cindy was quite late for her next appointment and I stepped out very briefly for a drink of water leaving the door open for her should she arrive. Expecting to see no one waiting for me in those intervening moments, I was rather surprised (Smith 1995) and felt a wave of apprehension when I saw a man in a leather jacket sitting in my chair when I returned! Beneath the angry snarl and the baseball cap, which I later discovered contained her long, dark hair, I approached this person and did a double take as I recognized Cindy's features. Even then, I still was not sure and did not allow myself to recognize what was going on. I had a fleeting thought that perhaps she sent one of her brothers to give me a message until I heard a guttural version of Cindy's voice saying, "Yo, Doc! What took you so long?!" I had an uncanny feeling as the patient's voice sounded both strange and familiar at the same time (Freud 1919b). Then, I realized that I was in the presence of her angry male personification, Jack. Jack was snarling, quick-witted, and very confrontational, the antithesis of Cindy's passive tentativeness. He introduced himself and said that he knew very well who I was. I said I was glad to meet him and gently gestured him to the patient's chair in order to regain my own territory and, I hoped, my composure along with it during this most unusual interchange. Jack laughed mockingly and refused to get up, using my own words against me when he retorted, "Hey, Doc. Didn't you tell *us* the other day we could use *any* piece of furniture we wanted?!" Disarmed by both his ironic humor and the deadly seriousness of the situation during this moment of surprise, I could only say, "You've got a point there" and sat down in the patient's chair across from him, continuing my conversation with him for the remainder of the hour. I was informed by him also that my breathing had scared Cindy, so Tina came out at that time.

Tina, however, was even more scared, so Jack came out to protect Tina. The dissociative defense he described was like a revolving door, in which one self would leave and another would emerge to take over functioning of consciousness and bodily activity in response to anxiety in the transference. Jack was prepared to defend the body if any attempt were to be made on my part to hurt anyone.

I subsequently learned that Jack would typically go out late at night, drink at bars alone, and get into fights with other male patrons if they were observed making unwanted sexual overtures to any of the women there. Cindy's periodic arrival at the office with mysterious bruises, facial injuries, and even fractured ribs were eventually explained by Jack to be the proud battle wounds of his chivalrous but often failed rescue missions. Cindy would have amnesia for these times and be totally at a loss to explain how she had gotten so beaten up. His appearance in the office was clearly meant to scare me and warn me that he was watching me from the inside of Cindy's mind. He had contempt for any efforts to help her and clearly was on alert for any unprofessional behavior that would physically endanger the vulnerable girls. I told Jack that I understood his concern but I had no intentions of hurting anyone and that if I had indeed been under his observation all along, he would have known that I had not done anything threatening to them in the past. I also went on to say that I, too, was concerned about my falling asleep and hoped that I could understand it over time with everyone. He gave me a skeptical, derisive look, begrudgingly agreeing that I had not been dangerous before, but had nevertheless scared everyone by transporting Tina back to the uncle's bed through my sleep. Furthermore, Jack was not the least bit interested in analyzing my enactment and made that very clear. He thought that all my therapy was "bullshit." He was there to issue a stern warning to me. In addition, he was not interested in discussing what to me, an outside observer, was seen as the patient's cross-dressing and a reflection of a deeper dissociated transsexual conflict (Brenner 2001). Jack was convinced that he was a man who was trapped in a woman's body by a quirk of nature. He hid the female body parts and sought out hormone treatments and surgery to change his anatomy. Due to the explosiveness of the affects involved, this aspect of the treatment had to wait for a much later time.

Not surprisingly, Cindy had an autohypnotic, dissociative amnesia for the session with Jack. When she finally expressed curiosity and a wish to know about this hole in her memory, it was after weeks of gentle reminding on my part. Had I not been somewhat active in this inquiry, I think her resistance would have prevailed because she often was not able to remember that she had forgotten anything. When I did give her an accounting of Jack's appearance, she was incredulous at first, but it further opened the doorway to her complex psyche.

Discussion

Jack's dramatic appearance was a critical event that brought Cindy's severe dissociative disorder clearly into the therapeutic situation. On a manifest level, my somnolence induced a tremendous amount of anxiety in Cindy, which was most notably warded off by her amnesia, a defensive component of her dissociative compromise formation (C. Brenner 1982, I. Brenner 2001). Her switch to a child personification, Tina, might be seen as expressing the symptomatic component of this complex as well as reactivating a defense from her disturbed childhood, for as in her Tina state of mind she recalled and recapitulated the terror and pain of being forced to sleep with her alcoholic uncle who had raped or beaten her when he woke up. She tried to be as quiet as possible so as not to wake him up in the transference, an experience made all the more lifelike by my own unconscious compliance with her compulsion to repeat. Cindy experienced this inability to move as a transient paralysis, which to an outside observer might be diagnosed as a conversion reaction.

It did not become clear until much later just how important the dream as a metaphor for the session actually was in understanding some of the pathogenesis of her condition. Cindy's intrapsychic connection to Tina was revealed by certain types of dreams that were reported and often preceded Tina's appearance in the sessions. This phenomenon was later recognized to have occurred in the session described above, also. Several days before Tina's appearance, Cindy reported a dream that presaged this enactment when she described a shift from participant to observer of a young girl being pulled onto the mattress by her uncle. At a later time, Cindy reported a seemingly bizarre and very disturbing recurring dream in which she was watching a young girl who she did not know get taken to a barn and forced to perform certain sexual acts with an animal in front of bright lights. Several days after reporting that dream, Cindy spontaneously switched to Tina during a session following a period of extended silence after an upsurge of anxiety and shame associated with another aspect of her childhood. Significantly, I became quite tired again and this time had a sensation that the top of my head was being lifted off. I came to recognize this sensation as a somatic signal that would become an important indicator to me that Cindy was lapsing into a deep, autohypnotic trance that could be infectious. When she would sit up at such times, it enabled me to see that her eyes would become glassy and unfocused prior to the emergence of another personification. I found that directly looking at her, into her eyes, made me feel even drowsier. This "Svengali" effect in reverse, as it were, appeared to represent the patient's unwitting capacity to hypnotize another as she herself lapsed into her own dissociative world. Instead of the malevolent doctor putting the helpless female subject into a trance in order to exploit her (Pick 2000), here the doctor himself could fall under a spell. The more I became aware of it, the more I could anticipate, self-analyze, and protect myself from becoming analytically disabled by maintaining a modicum of observing ego.

During the session after Cindy reported the bright lights dream, when Tina emerged in a very frightened state, she was cowering and whimpering as she described being forced to do something bad. In her first-person narrative, she recounted an almost identical story of being taken by her uncle and a stranger to what sounded like an empty barn or a studio with bright lights, stripped naked, and made to submit to bestial practices. Her childlike report also suggested that the lights might have been used to take photographs of these pornographic scenes. As unbelievable or symbolic as it may have sounded at first, having heard and read about such exploitation of children (Gootman 2001), I was open to the possibility of the veracity of Tina's excruciatingly painful account, although it took months for Cindy as herself to even consider it. However, that was not our concern at the time, as I was primarily trying to help the patient understand how her mind worked. Interestingly, she had met with a surgeon previously who recommended an operation and he asked her if she would give permission for photographs to be taken for teaching purposes. This request was probably the day residue that was incorporated into the dream. What was especially significant at this point in our work was exploring the reciprocal amnesia and relationship between the dream in the third person and the narrative in her dissociated state in the first person. Cindy had no memory of Tina's account in the session but had remembered the nightmare. Conversely, Tina claimed to remember the incident as having happened to her but had no awareness or knowledge of Cindy's dream.

It appeared that in this case, as well as in others I have seen (Brenner 2001), an aspect of ego functioning during the dream state was recruited as an organizing influence in the creation of her personifications. This aspect is the so-called functional phenomenon, originally described by Silberer (1909), as the human mind's universal tendency to create symbols to represent its own alterations of consciousness. This autosymbolism is well known in hypnogogic and hypnopompic states, where dreamlike imagery may be metaphorical or somatic or take the form of people in these twilight states. Applying this principle to dissociation, I have postulated that children who retreat into such autohypnotic, defensive, altered states in response to severe overstimulation and pain may anthropomorphize these changes in consciousness also. These mental representations of this response to trauma would then be subject to re-representation in the patient's nightly dreams and add to her confusion over reality. Over time, especially with repetitive trauma and recurrent dreams, these personified altered states may become regular characters who populate the psyche whose function it is to contain intolerable affects, memories, and instinctual urges. As such, they become part of the patient's repertoire of symbols in her dream life and in her dissociative structures, having a common origin in early trauma but being kept separate from the patient's awareness for defensive reasons. This phenomenon could be seen as a dream within a dream.

The effect of such sessions on the analyst's own dream life provides further evidence of the dreamlike nature of analysis. In his work with a severely regressed woman with polymorphous perverse sexuality, Boyer (1977) describes falling into a trance during a session and dreaming about it that night. He then discovered through his self-analysis of the dream that he was unconsciously identifying with the woman's son who was traumatized by being forced to watch his mother's promiscuous escapades during her drunken states. Through this insight he was able to regain his analyzing function and listen better, which enabled the patient to remember her own dreams and hypnogogic fantasies of being forced to watch women being subject to sexually degrading acts. In this case, the voyeuristic element of her psychopathology appeared to induce a dream within a dream for the analyst.

In the course of my intensive work with someone who disowned anxiety-laden mental contents, I became subject to Cindy's powerful, autohypnotic, defensive mental processes, which induced me to enact a traumatic scenario from her childhood. Through projective identification (Grinberg 1962), I resonated with (Kelman 1982) and embodied the essence of her paternal object, the dreaded male relative who would lapse into a drunken stupor, wake up, and then rape her on a regular basis while her mother was working. As a result, we both lapsed into our respective dreamlike states as Cindy reexperienced how as a child her mind warded off the anxiety and terror at the time. Inasmuch as the analytic session itself has been likened to a dream and has roots in hypnosis, it could be considered that we enacted a dream within a dream. The analytic atmosphere, which is conducive to free association, encouraged her dream ego to express itself. The hypnotic effects of Cindy's dream ego induced me to become drowsy and literally sleep with her in the session. Sleeping in her presence apparently activated her personification, Tina, who, borne of trauma, owned and contained what Cindy could not. Tina's presence and participation in the therapeutic process was essential, and she developed her own transference as part of a complex mosaic transference seen in such patients. My unwitting participation in the dream within a dream was catalytic as long as I could regain my observing and work ego so I could continue to analyze. The emergence of Jack, the angry, transsexual protector, alarmed me and kept me awake so I could appreciate the significance of her populated inner life. As such, he functioned as a paternal superego who awakens the child from his blissful sleep at the mother's breast (Lewin 1954). Initially, I enacted Cindy's dream with her through my drowsiness. As I became more aware of the nature of the intersubjective processes between us, I was better able to stay more alert and continue analyzing. The enactments evolved more into first-person narratives with transference phenomena that were then more potentially analyzable and able to be worked through.

TECHNICAL CONSIDERATIONS

I have defined five stages of treatment in the analytically informed work with this population as well as considered a unique psychic structure whose purpose it is to disown intolerable mental contents and maintain the illusion that there are "others" who live in the mind and share the body. It has been described by some patients as feeling like time-sharing of the body. The unique psychic structure, the "It's not me!" self, is not a personification or alter personality per se, but would be more analogous to the man behind the curtain in *The Wizard of Oz* who creates the illusion of separateness with whatever defensive maneuvers are available. The ego in the dream state is a key organizing influence, as are perverse sexuality, the intergenerational effects of transmission of the perpetrator's own trauma, the seemingly bizarre effects of near-death experiences in children, and the divisive effects on the psyche of aggression and the death instinct (Brenner 2001). During the first phase, the development and maintaining of the therapeutic alliance with the patient during her various defensive altered states, the analyst's challenge is analogous to a group therapist trying to facilitate a group with an unknown number of participants who do not know the existence of the others. The next phase involves a delineation of the so-called mosaic transference, which considers the various transference configurations of each of the personifications taken as a totality, that is, a mosaic. Given the propensity of preoedipal issues, quite often the overall picture is one of a rapprochement quality transference with powerful forces seeking to flee and other powerful forces desperately clinging to the good object. In Cindy's case, for example, Tina, though terrified, would beg Cindy to bring her. Jack, on the other hand, rejected treatment and wanted to have as little to do with me as possible. Interestingly, as therapy progressed, he would be the one who would call and leave me messages berating me for leaving on vacation or otherwise being less than available for the children.

The third phase of treatment, challenging the "It's not me!" self, eventually results in its dissolution, which then reduces the divisive elements in the psyche promoting integrative processes to occur spontaneously. Interpreting the resistances and defenses that actively maintain the separateness and the illusion of separate people requires a great reduction of the very powerful autohypnotic underpinnings to the patient's cadre of inner people. Because of the strong amnestic barriers, the different thresholds of pain and the different experiences of bodily sensations during different states as well as different sexual developmental pathways and gender identities, the conviction that there are truly different people inhabiting the body can be very great and seem to reach delusional proportions. In Cindy's situation, there was sadomasochistic heterosexuality and transsexualism in her different female and male selves.

The patient needs a lot of clinical evidence to even consider beginning to give up this most formidable characterological defense. To help her observing ego develop at the outset, the patient needs to acquire the capacity to "stay there" while the various personifications are out, a phenomenon known as co-consciousness. This increased internal communication may be facilitated by the analyst's functioning analogously to being an auxiliary memory bank and an old-fashioned switchboard operator who helps make connections between one altered ego state and another. The very fact that the patient may become able to "listen in" and observe her other selves in and of itself challenges her conviction of disconnectedness and separateness of the selves. Functioning as an auxiliary memory bank and filling in the holes in her memory is an essential part of this function. As a result, the patient eventually is able to recognize that there is indeed a link between her and her selves, which weakens the "It's not me!" self. When this softening occurs, the patient's conviction of separateness can be challenged but she cannot reconcile her insight; she knows and does not know, concluding that "It's me but it's not me!" The anxiety can be overwhelming and the risk of self-injury may be considerable if "knowing" too quickly intensifies guilt and a sense of badness over one's impulses and past events.

Bringing the patient's attention to the clinical observations from her dreams and her personifications regarding their striking similarities can be a crucial form of interpretive activity. It helps provide an explanation not only for what is being kept separate but also for how it is being kept separate. In this regard, it can be helpful to educate the patient a bit about how the mind can be affected by early trauma. This approach provides evidence of the common origin of both mental products and bypasses the issue of veracity or accuracy of whatever traumatic experience may be represented by both of these mental products. Cindy was easily able to own her dream but not her dissociated personifications' first-hand account. Accepting one rendition but totally dismissing an almost identical version from another possible part of her mind required her to be able to trust and believe in my own honesty and good intentions since I had to relay it to her. As a result, relational elements of the therapy were essential to its success. Therefore, issues related to construction, recall of early experience, and the controversy surrounding possible false memories could wait until a later point in treatment.

CONCLUSION

By recognizing the patient's pattern and self-analyzing my intersubjective experience, I was eventually able to consider that I was living out the patient's posttraumatic dream with her in the session. The construction that was ultimately made was that she entered a defensive altered state as a child while being forced to sleep with her alcoholic uncle, and she dreamed about it. The session where I fell asleep was preceded by just such a dream of the patient running in fear from him, which suddenly shifted into a scene where she was being grabbed and pulled toward him while he was lying on a mattress. She then saw a little girl she did not know lying there, which was a dream representation of her depersonalization and dissociation at the time. This little girl expressed herself as Tina during the patient's waking dream as a dissociated self. As a sleeping participant in this enactment during the session, I was unable to maintain analytic ego functioning, which heightened the patient's sense of anxiety and danger. It prompted the emergence of her Tina self and then her rageful transsexual self, Jack, whose protective but self-destructive tendencies entered the therapeutic process. Jack was perhaps the most separate part of her mind, expressing her revulsion, disgust, and angry protest over her female genitalia and vulnerability to penetration by men, as well as her enormous separation anxiety. This personification was the most difficult state for her to own as part of her psyche, and much of the interpretative work centered around reconciling these disparate selves.

It can be clinically demonstrated and made useful to the patient at an appropriate point in treatment that there is a common origin to her posttraumatic dreams and the creation of separate selves in her dissociated mind. Recurrent posttraumatic dreams about experiences during which the patient enters an altered ego state at the time could be seen as a dream within a dream. The therapist's falling asleep during a session with such a patient and enacting a traumatic scenario is an enactment of this dream within a dream. By recognizing this phenomenon, it may then be possible to make important inferences about the structure of the dissociated mind that may be utilized in a clinically helpful manner for the patient. To do so, one must find a way to stay awake and continue to analyze in the presence of very powerful and infectious autohypnotic forces in the patient's mind.

9

Eye Movement Desensitization and Reprocessing (EMDR)?

To shorten analytic treatment is a justifiable wish, which as we shall hear is being sought after in various ways.

[Freud 1913, p. 130]

Long analyses are no longer rare and the treatment of those who have endured severe, early, sexual trauma may well exceed a decade in duration. Those who work with such patients know that the process cannot be rushed. Developmental fixations, ego boundary disturbances, severe anxiety, and dissociative features require time, empathy, and much patience. Modifications in analytic technique may be required (Brenner 2001), and openness to new ideas is warranted given the complexity and difficulties encountered in such patients. The cross-fertilization from interdisciplinary collaboration, such as the neurosciences, has provided much validation for what we do, but as yet has yielded little in the way of technical advances to facilitate the therapeutic process (Goldberg 2000). The question of whether the duration of treatment can be shortened is a complicated and worthy research issue, but the how and in what way is not clear. In the greater world of psychotherapy, there is much enthusiasm about eye movement desensitization and reprocessing (EMDR), a new procedure that may be unfamiliar to many analysts. After the following unusual clinical event, my curiosity about it was piqued and I pursued a study of it.

CASE VIGNETTES

A woman consulted me several years ago because she was unhappy with the progress she was making in therapy. She had been in various forms of treatment for almost twenty of her forty years and was still suffering from what she felt were vague, unintegrated memories of early sexual abuse. Though successful in her chosen profession, she lived a solitary life and was incapable of sustaining intimacy with either sex. Having spent more than a decade in psychoanalysis with a classically trained clinician, she finally left in great disappointment and frustration over not feeling believed nor taken particularly seriously about her past. Having heard this part of her history, I began to hypothesize that perhaps a treatment guided by an overvalued belief in the primacy of fantasy and psychic reality might have prevented her analyst from considering trauma, and perhaps he subtly discouraged the patient from exploring that avenue. Yet, when she revealed more of her treatment history, it became clear that there was much more than a possible countertransference enactment by an analyst denying her past and imposing his theoretical worldview upon her, not unlike the way an abusing father might have done.

As I listened further, the patient told me that she investigated a number of alternative treatment modalities and decided that EMDR was the best choice for her. Now she was looking for someone who would employ that technique because she needed something stronger—"a physiologic treatment to get the trauma out." I was curious about her conviction and about her expression "a physiologic treatment to get the trauma out," as though she were looking for some type of purgative, like a psychic laxative or enema. However, she was not interested at all in exploring the meaning of her choice of words, only in interviewing me for my qualifications. I was puzzled that she had consulted me in the first place because she informed me that she was already in treatment with a top expert in EMDR. I clearly had no such claim and immediately told her so. Apparently unfazed by my revelation, she continued, and reported that the treatment had initially been helpful but she soon became embroiled in conflicts with the therapist that interfered with her progress. She described the treatment as "intensive EMDR," consisting of at least three to four sessions a week, which, instead of facilitating things, had only seemed to aggravate her more! When I tried to point out to her in lay terms that perhaps elements of an unresolved negative transference carrying over from her former analyst might be posing a powerful resistance, she looked skeptical and uncomprehending. Her reaction disturbed me, given all of the years of her supposed exploration of such phenomena in her protracted analysis. She wanted to believe she could divorce the practitioner from the procedure and achieve her goals in treatment, the nature of which were becoming more and more nebulous to me as our conversation continued.

The more intrigued I became by the nature of her therapeutic problem, the more I inquired about her relationship with her current therapist, and at that point she insisted that I was not the right doctor for her. I maintained, however, that if, indeed, she felt something beneficial had accrued early on from the EMDR, wouldn't it be necessary to examine the nature of the conflict she was now experiencing? Could she not consider a psychodynamic view of the whole EMDR experience? Getting impatient with me, the woman then bluntly asked me if I would employ EMDR with her. I told her I would be happy to explore her request and think about how to incorporate this modality if she could tell me more about how she felt that it had worked for her. I also said that I would want to work collaboratively with her, so I asked her if she could tell me more about how it was implemented with her. I was concerned about rushing in and doing something to her without knowing what it meant, as I sensed her conflicted wish over passively submitting to a directive procedure and becoming cured. At this point, she politely thanked me, completely assured that I was the wrong doctor for her, and left uneventfully at the end of the hour. I felt that I had handled the situation appropriately because I did not allow myself to get drawn into a symbolic enactment that might have had countertherapeutic consequences, such as an unconscious revictimization of her. However, I did feel disappointed that I could not have found a way both to be of help to her and to learn more about her dilemma. At that time, I had had only limited exposure to EMDR from my days on the dissociative disorders unit at the Institute of Pennsylvania Hospital, felt somewhat skeptical about its efficacy, felt a bit silly about waving my hands in front of patients' eyes, and did not understand how such a technique could have gained such popularity in such a short time. As someone working with trauma patients, I began to feel that perhaps I needed to know a bit more about it.

While I was pondering these issues after the session, I let my mind become prepared for my next appointment, a woman in analysis who had suffered unresolved grief over the sudden death of an aunt who had raised her from infancy. The woman I had just seen had faded from the center of my attention and I expected never to see her again. I entered the waiting room to greet my analysand, an unchanging ritual that we had performed many hundreds of times before, but this time I was in for a shock. As I pushed the door open to find my patient in her usual spot, her eyes revealed nothing about what she, on some level, knew would happen a moment later. The motion of the door was suddenly stopped by a dull thud and a high-pitched scream. Feeling a bit unnerved, I peered around the corner and saw the woman I had just interviewed trying to button up her overcoat and wrap a scarf around herself just behind the door. It was a most unlikely spot for anyone to be standing and it had completely taken me by surprise. After being assured that she was not injured, I accompanied my next patient into the office who had witnessed the whole spectacle and appeared impassive and almost in a trance.

Despite her outward appearance, this event had a profound impact upon her analysis. It became a catalyst for her to conjure up an image of the circumstances around the death of her beloved aunt, a topic that, until that moment, was a black hole without words. It enabled her to think and fantasize about it (Britton 1998). The aunt left home one day and never returned, the victim of a freak accident involving a collision. My patient was frozen in the time around her death, unable to recall life with her before the tragedy, but also unable to appreciate the passage of time and life without her afterward. The news of her death and the funeral were a trance-like blur, complicated by her never seeing the aunt's dead body, an unfortunate set of conditions lending themselves to a pathological grief reaction (Volkan 1981). She never could truly believe the woman had died, nor could she address any elements of conflict around their relationship.

The design of my office enables patients who arrive early to sit in an enclosed waiting room off to the side of the entranceway so patients leaving a session do not have to pass them. In so doing, the patient's privacy is respected under usual circumstances because there would generally be no reason to return to the waiting room. This time, however, a mysterious woman suddenly "came back" and in the patient's unconscious mind, as revealed by a slip of the tongue, was getting "undressed" in front of her when this secret pleasure was traumatically interrupted by my hitting her with the door. As such, it became a "now moment" in the analysis, in which an action served as a powerful interpretation and advanced the therapeutic process (Stern et al. 1998). As we analyzed her associations over the subsequent weeks, it became clear that the woman represented the aunt's sudden return from the dead, and she was seductively undressing in front of her. It reawakened her very deeply repressed negative oedipal and adolescent homosexual longings for the aunt, which was how she felt before the tragedy. Subsequently, over the course of analysis, she then became able to construct a fuller image of her and recall their relationship in greater depth, essentially reviving her through memories emerging in the transference. This reconstructive step was necessary in order to begin to mourn for her aunt in a more healthy way (Brenner 1988a). What she was able to achieve in analysis was with the unwitting help of the frustrated woman looking for EMDR.

It appeared as though the analysis of the activity in the waiting room helped my patient move beyond a point of entrenched resistances. After this incident, I decided to investigate EMDR further to see for myself if, indeed, there might be some merit to this type of planned activity (Freud 1919a).

I realized that some colleagues might see my research into this issue as rather unanalytic and might even question my faith in the analytic method, as though I were straying from the flock. But psychoanalysis is not a religion, and there is no sacred text that cannot be questioned (Brenner 1999b). Nevertheless, the nature of Freud's character and his insistence upon loyalty to his brilliant ideas may continue to exert an influence on his followers, making some of us uneasy about looking beyond the couch for new answers to very old questions. My work with massively traumatized individuals, especially those who employ defensive, altered ego states, has repeatedly brought me back to some of the earliest controversies surrounding psychoanalysis, and in this case it is the issue of the role of active techniques

(Frank 1992). From Freud's rebuke of Ferenczi's "active technique" involving suggestion to induce change (Bibring 1954, Ferenczi 1919a, 1920, 1925) to the question of integrating cognitive/behavioral therapies (Gill 1984, Wachtel 1987) to the recognition of the importance of the new interpersonal experience (Greenberg and Mitchell 1983, Hoffman 1983, Jacobs 1986, Loewald 1960), analysts have studied the effects of their intentional and unintentional behavior on the therapeutic process. It was in this context that the frustrated woman looking for EMDR became a catalyst for me as well.

WHAT IS EMDR?

Eye movement desensitization and reprocessing (EMDR), is a cognitive/behavioral psychotherapy that incorporates alternating sensory stimulation to both halves of the brain. It was discovered by Francine Shapiro, a psychologist from the West Coast, who, as the now famous legend goes, was walking in a forest one sunny afternoon with a lot of issues on her mind. While preoccupied with her problems, her eyes started darting back and forth involuntarily following the strobe light patterns of light shining through the leafy canopy above. During this experience, she felt an unusual sense of calm and wondered what effect the alternating eye movements might have had on this dramatic change in her mental state. As a curious and disciplined thinker, she decided to research this issue, and conducted a series of experiments to learn more about this phenomenon. Through many refinements, it was then incorporated into a cognitive therapy paradigm, her theoretical orientation, which, in and of itself, had been shown to be helpful in reducing anxiety in posttraumatic states. As such, the standard EMDR protocol was developed (Shapiro 1989, 1995, Shapiro and Forrest 1997). In it, the patient is led through numerous sets of horizontal or diagonal eye movements while focusing on a particular aspect of his or her problem. For example, if patients are experiencing posttraumatic flashbacks and survivor guilt associated with an earthquake, they are helped to develop a "negative cognition" about themselves associated with the greatest distress. In such a situation, a typical negative cognition would be, "I do not deserve to live while others more worthy than I did not." Following the negative cognition, subjects are then asked to develop a positive cognition or goal as to how they would like to feel. An example might be "My life does have value and I did the best I could." These negative and positive cognitions are then rated in terms of the intensity of subjective distress and the validity with which the individual feels or believes each of these statements. The subject is then asked to focus on the cognition and an image of the trauma while following the stimulation by the therapist.

Throughout this process, which may take place over a series of sessions, patients may revisit the traumatic experience as though they were watching a video on visual fast forward, stopping at various points along the way to "reprocess" it, resolving the faulty cognitions about themselves and resolving the symptoms. Insight and connections with the past are not important in this protocol. On the way to achieving the new cognitions, such as "I am worthy and do deserve to have lived," the patient may report new memories and new thoughts about the traumatic event and develop a healthier perspective about one's own helplessness in such a situation.

This method has been studied by both combat-related posttraumatic stress disorder (PTSD) (Carlson et al. 1998) and civilian-related PTSD (Marcus et al. 1997) therapists, enthusiastic clinicians who have reported dramatic reduction of symptoms in astonishingly few visits, offering the hope of providing much to many with few resources in this era of managed care (Chambless et al. 1998). It would be the realization of the modern dream of rapid, drug-free access to the inner reaches of the mind to alleviate suffering and promote self-acceptance. Intensive training workshops on weekends are offered regularly throughout the country where upward of 200 therapists can be trained at a time and get their EMDR certificates. Advanced training sessions are also available for those seeking to acquire more customized ways of applying the methodology to work with complex clinical situations, such as character pathology, dissociative disorders, and addictions. For example, techniques known as cognitive interweaves were developed to help the therapist overcome the patient's unconscious resistances to the procedure. Of course, such situations come as no surprise to the psychodynamically sophisticated clinician, and, in fact, are encountered much more frequently than first thought by EMDR practitioners. Nevertheless, EMDR has been touted as one of the greatest psychotherapeutic breakthroughs in decades, seeming to promise to level the playing field for the less highly trained mental health professionals who become proficient in this procedure. Certainly, the enthusiasm and group excitement generated over a very full weekend of lectures and practical experiences can fill one with renewed confidence, energy, and optimism about what one can accomplish in short-term treatment with distressed individuals. Indeed, a quick look in the Yellow Pages will show how many therapists now advertise this modality.

Throughout my own training weekend, the instructors repeatedly emphasized that understanding and reflection were not necessary and perhaps would even slow down a reprocessing. Indeed, their subtle mockery of the psychoanalytic approach always produced chuckling in the newly initiated audience. Furthermore, they stressed that eye movements in and of themselves were not essential, but rather any sensory stimulation alternating between the hemispheres, such as lights at either end of a long bar, sounds in either ear, tactile cues to each hand in alternating fashion, and so on, would be equally as effective. Devices with lights and headphones were also designed and advertised as having the advantage of freeing up the therapist to take notes and being even less physically present to possibly interfere with the pure, active elements of the treatment. The instructors repeatedly mentioned that they regretted that the use of the term *EMDR* had taken hold because of the newer research about the importance of the interhemispheric stimulation. Earlier thinking about an unknown, unique, optico-cortico-limbic pathway enabling one to process trauma would, therefore, have to be discarded along with the theory that EMDR somehow replicated eye movements in REM sleep or activated some mysterious, conditioned reflex in the brain. With this new thinking in mind, they quickly tried to dispel any ideas about the therapist's hand gestures themselves having anything at all to do with the mechanism of action. Indeed, an early, skeptical psychodynamic theory suggested that the rapid pointing and shaking of a finger back and forth in the patient's face gave the unconscious message that one's thinking was wrong and had to be corrected by suggestion, threat, or some other use of one's role as an authority figure. However, I felt they were unwittingly reinforcing this point about the symbolic importance of the raised hand by curiously issuing a cautionary note to the large group to the contrary: in using the standard EMDR technique, one should refrain from suggestive hand gestures, such as fancy flourishes, the middle finger, signs of the cross, and the like. In other words, they certainly gave the impression that they knew EMDR practitioners could unintentionally communicate something to the patient with one's hand but then denied its significance if one stuck to the basic movements that they were teaching. Although it seemed that the explicit references to unconscious influences were taboo in the official rhetoric and paradigmatic thinking, it was an unavoidable fact of mental life.

In the small group experiences where we got to practice our new skills on each other, the more sophisticated instructors did, indeed, acknowledge, however quietly, that they realized such factors. For instance, one aspect of the physical arrangement, that is, the dyad, is to sit closer to each other with knees almost touching. Since this proximity could deeply affect the patient, especially a sexually traumatized one, it should be talked about first, and perhaps for as long as necessary, as well as adjusting the standard protocol for the sake of the individual's anxiety. In fact, we were taught that the most seasoned EMDR clinicians modify the protocol to comfortably incorporate it into their preexisting styles of therapy so it does not feel so much like a foreign, mechanical procedure superimposed on one's existing style. This bit of wisdom was at great variance with a more purist approach that implied that the clinician is an interference and that perhaps the use of devices like light sticks would be the ideal technique. In my own experience during the training weekend, I could not help but see the ubiquitous role of unconscious factors and was especially struck by the development of an instant negative maternal transference in a woman with whom I was practicing. During our EMDR session, she wanted to develop a better self-image and free herself from her mother's hypercritical domination when she was a child. She was hypercritical of everything I tried to do with the EMDR technique. I was either moving my hand too fast or too slow or too horizontally or too diagonally. She then wanted me to tap on her hands using tactile cues and wanted me to speak a little differently to her. When I eventually accommodated all of her wishes in this structured exercise, she was able to work on her issue and felt better. When I offered to share my observation with her afterward that there might have been an enactment of her feeling controlled by me, like her mother, and wanting to fight that off by dominating me in return, she gave a smile of recognition. A rapid transference phenomenon appeared to be operative the colored her experience of me as the EMDR practitioner, and part of her feeling better might have been due to her gratification of being able to control all of my actions, which she could not do with her mother.

Interestingly, the divergence of opinion among the instructors during the EMDR weekend seemed analogous to one of the central debates in contemporary psychoanalysis, that is, whether it is a one-person or a two-person psychology. Those at the extreme end of the one-person view deemphasize the importance of the person of the analyst and the analytic relationship. Since the patient's problem is seen as almost solely intrapsychic, the active ingredients are free association and interpretation of the transference projected onto an essentially anonymous and almost interchangeable analyst. Countertransference would be seen as an interference and a sign of disturbance in the analyst. In contrast, those at the opposite end of the spectrum would view the process as a collaborative effort and all mental products would be seen as a coconstructed phenomenon. The use of self-disclosure, countertransference, and an ongoing emphasis on the here-and-now relationship would take precedence over genetic construction of one's past, and regression might be seen as an unnecessary and perhaps undesirable side effect of archaic technique. It seems that we trainers were subtly exposed to the same controversy in the EMDR culture, but it was not acknowledged and perhaps not fully recognized by those in charge.

Despite the failure of agreement on why it works, there was no doubt that many believe that, indeed, it does work (Van Etten and Taylor 1998). The enthusiasm, optimism, and hope for this modality were bolstered by the claim that, despite its recent entry into the clinical world, it has nevertheless been the most studied treatment approach ever (Parnel 1999, Shapiro and Forrest 1997). So rapid have some of the patient responses been the we were asked to reconsider our own sense of propriety and respect for time with regard to, for example, how long must it take for mourning of the dead to occur. It was therefore quite a blow for the proponents of EMDR when it was rated lower than expected as a recommended treatment for trauma in a special issue devoted to PTSD in the *Journal of Clinical Psychiatry* (Expert Consensus Guideline Series 1999). Ironically, it was rated on a par with psychoanalysis.

I will offer clinical material where EMDR was incorporated into the psychoanalytically informed treatment of three patients with dissociative psychopathology and histories of early sexual trauma. In keeping with the idea that elements of the standard protocol may be modified and possibly dovetail into a psychodynamic therapeutic approach (Wachtel 1999), case 1 deals with a recurrent nightmare, case 2 with unintegrated memories, and case 3 with artist's block.

CASE 1

Rachel, a woman who had been in psychoanalytic treatment with me five times a week for about a decade, had done quite well for a number of years after termination until serious health problems contributed to a regression characterized by crying spells, hopelessness, and a very disturbing recurring dream. She had had severe dissociative psychopathology, fulfilling diagnostic criteria for DID (APA 1994) and was a survivor of long-standing paternal sexual abuse throughout her childhood. She was very reluctant to resume intensive therapy, hoping that her depressive symptoms would resolve with a short course of psychotherapy with me. Given the complexity of all of her circumstances, I agreed with her plan as long as we both kept an open mind to the possibility that her condition might warrant deeper exploration than she preferred. Already having been on antidepressant medication prescribed by her internist, the patient proceeded cautiously with a once-a-week schedule as she feared a full-blown deterioration of her dissociative disorder, which, interestingly, never did recur.

As we resumed therapy, it became clear that she had lost her observing ego and capacity for self-analytic exploration. She would sigh and groan as she recalled my incessant encouragement of her saying whatever comes to mind, at times feeling that she had failed a course and had to return for remedial sessions. Furthermore, as is known in postanalytic follow-up, there were elements of an unresolved transference (Hurn 1973, Norman et al. 1976). I was seen as an idealized rescuer-father, but her wish for a rapid cure crashed headlong into the weekly reality that I did not possess such magic. Her nightly dream, a nightmare that often awoke her in a panicky, cold sweat, was of her being tied down and locked in a basement. Her captor, a sadistic professor from college whom she felt was punishing her for something, would walk by and glare at her but offered no explanation of her alleged offense nor how long she would have to suffer. Rachel's medical problems, which at times were disabling and made her feel like a prisoner in her own body, felt like a curse to her. She was loath to consider any psychodynamic contribution to either their onset or her delayed recovery, despite the fact that we had extensively explored her mind–body connection and had seen numerous demonstrations of both conversion and psychophysiological symptoms during her near-decade of treatment. This time, however, she reverted to an old attitude, "You don't believe me," alluding not only to her symptoms but also to her incest and her father's threat that since no one would believe her, she would be locked up in a mental hospital for being crazy if she ever told anyone.

Years before, our work had been complicated by the sudden death of her boyfriend, an unstable but loving man whose own troubled childhood made them feel like they were soul mates. However, they were pathologically attached; one day, Rachel's mood swings and suicidal despair incited a panic in him, which she was convinced had precipitated his own very reckless behavior, resulting in his death. Unresolved grief and a deep sense of guilt haunted her as she clung to a secret memorial of linking objects (Volkan 1981), such as his necktie and car keys, which were kept hidden but never far from her. Despite all of the available information to the contrary, not the least of which was his own long history of poor judgment and daredevil behavior tempting fate, she was absolutely convinced that his death was her fault. Despite much work in her analysis, especially around a termination phase lasting over two years, she seemed to have been more able to reconcile her profound ambivalence over the incest than the death of her lover. Nevertheless, mourning the loss of the analyst enabled her, to some extent, to work through both losses. She remembered her unfinished business but was unsure of the extent to which further analysis was warranted at this juncture, so I gently pointed out the dilemma when it seemed appropriate to the material that was emerging.

Therapy was increased to twice weekly after about two months, and we continued in a typical dynamic and expressive mode with careful attention to the reality of her medical problems and the ongoing need for supportive affirmation of her valiant efforts to regain healthy functioning. Rachel surprised herself with her capacity to work in this mode again, freely acknowledging, however, how much it pained her to revisit old wounds that did not readily seem relevant to her current plight. However, she trusted me to guide her, and urged me to be vigorous and confronting, lest her acknowledged resistance keep her in treatment for many more years again. About six months later, an external, unavoidable circumstance arose that would put a stop to our work in four months unless she were to have taken drastic steps, which could have caused considerable morbidity and risk for her. At that point, I decided to mention EMDR to her.

Knowing me and my dedication to the analytic model after so many years of working together, she was also aware of my flexibility in the service of continuing the process of self-understanding. We had maintained continuity throughout inpatient hospitalizations for suicidal regressions at which times she had needed high doses of medication, yet throughout I tried to maintain a stance of empathy and to convey the message that virtually all of her symptoms were potentially understandable and resolvable. Nevertheless, she gave me a wide-eyed look and laughed when I described the technique of moving my fingers across her range of vision. I told her that I was not at all sure it would help her but was willing to try it with her if she were open to it. After thinking about it for a week, she decided to proceed and we agreed to start during the next session.

I asked her to think of that aspect of her current problem that caused her the most distress and she quickly mentioned her recurrent dream, which interrupted her sleep and filled her with terror. In a sense, we shifted to more of a symptom-oriented, focused therapy at this point, such as is endorsed by Luborsky (1996). Rachel was quite apprehensive about what effect this strange procedure might have on her psyche, increasing her fear all along that our work would have revealed her underlying "craziness" replete with hallucinations and disabling memory loss once again. While offering no promises, I did remind her that, as yet, I saw no evidence of a flare-up of her dissociative psychopathology, although I could not guarantee that she might not regress with the EMDR. With this caveat in mind, I suggested that we start slowly and examine her responses all along the way. During these times, I moved my seat closer to her, but not as close as recommended. I was also very attentive to her facial expressions and body language as well as my own, which we explored in detail.

Much to our surprise, she felt that the guided eye movements loosened up her mind, allowing thoughts, feelings, and memories to come to the fore more easily. She got anxious after the first set of movements, or saccades, feeling light-headed and dreamy the way she would feel before involuntary "switching" to one of her dissociated self-states or alter personalities. This time, however, things rushed to her consciousness that she had not thought about for years, and she did not lose any continuity of the self. This response to the eye movements happened almost every time during the approximately ten EMDR sessions that I conducted with her. It appeared to me as a rapid de-repression of the material once dissociated, reorganized, and then re-forgotten after the analysis (Brenner 2001) which was reexamined during this course of psychotherapy.

Typically, Rachel would sit silently during each set, which might last anywhere from ten seconds to several minutes until there was a significant change in her facial expression or until she stopped tracking my fingers. I would then ask her where her mind went and how she felt and we would discuss it further, making connections with her past work and her current problems. Depending on qualitative factors, such as the depth of our exploration, her curiosity, and my intuition, we might repeat the eye movements again or simply pursue our psychotherapeutic conversation until the end of the hour. In this regard, the eye movements seemed to "prime the pump," as it were, allowing her more rapid access to repressed material and bypassing some of her resistance. It was striking to sit with her when, for example, seemingly out of the blue, she would suddenly report a vivid image of her father quietly opening her bedroom door, walking in, grabbing her and leading her to his room to rape her. Such reflections were part of our daily work years before but not explicitly sought in this installment as I deferred to Rachel's feelings that it had all been reasonably well put to rest. It appeared that her response to this activity (Ferenczi

1919a,b) provided deeper associations to her dreams, which until then usually pertained only to the lover's death. It was also noteworthy, I thought, that this time she had made a point of emphasizing how her father would tightly grab her by her wrist and pull her toward him. I asked her to say more about which hand he used, alluding to my own use of the hand to guide her eyes and flow of associations. Rachel thoughtfully replied that her father's strong right hand was used to hurt her and, while she still felt intimidated and still felt intermittent waves of fear with me, she felt that, in here, a strong, right hand was being used to help her.

Rachel's dream evolved during the last several months of treatment after focusing on it during the EMDR. It initially became more terrifying as she found herself shackled in the basement, now in darkness, listening to a woman's voice condemning her for her behavior and blaming her for the boyfriend's death. Then the lights were dimly put back on and the professor berated her also. As our work progressed and she revisited the issue of her guilt over not refusing her father's advances long after she thought she was old enough to have said no, once again she was amazed at the suddenness with which such ideas came back into awareness during the EMDR. Her conscious belief that she was toxic because she was the cause of her boyfriend's death had deeper, unconscious determinants in her rejection by her mother and becoming her father's "little whore." Once brought back into treatment, we reanalyzed this material and she felt some relief.

Her dreams changed further in that she now found herself untied in the basement but could not find the door. Her malicious captor continued to lurk about, silently mocking her, as she remained trapped in his lair. Her reality notwithstanding, Rachel's conflicted fear of a long, exhausting re-analysis while trapped in the clutches of a sadomasochistic, transference configuration appeared to provide some of the fuel for this dream as we reminisced about some of the more painful moments from our work in the past. With the appointed termination date rapidly approaching, Rachel decided, with my encouragement, to revisit her boyfriend's grave, a site she had dared not return to since the horrendous funeral where she felt shunned by his family. The grave was overgrown with weeds and neglected by the living, according to the cemetery caretakers. Rachel trimmed, pruned, and planted around the headstone. She sat for hours and cried as she imagined what might have been—"If only . . . " (Akhtar 1996). Then, in a moment she would treasure forever, a soft wind blew by and she thought she heard her boyfriend's voice telling her that it was "okay," as he gently caressed her hair. Following his "forgiveness" of her, she was able to forgive herself and had a peaceful, uninterrupted sleep.

Shortly thereafter, Rachel had a dream in which the door to the basement finally appeared but she could not unlock it. Material about her father, her boyfriend, and the transference converged as she anticipated an ambivalent but necessary parting from me. We agreed to a follow-up session two months later. In the last two weeks before termination, Rachel was able to open the door to the basement in her dream but then found herself locked outside of my office. She then found herself in my office, but it was vacated and she felt abandoned. One day after our last session, Rachel left me a message stating that she found herself outside and knew where she was going.

At the follow-up appointment two months later, she felt considerably relieved, was functioning much better, and her dreams rarely woke her. We agreed to periodic follow-up every several months and she continued to be doing well.

CASE 2

Carla had been in five-time-a-week analysis for many years and functioned well for several years after termination. She had experienced depression, anxiety, and dissociative phenomena that were consistent with an intermediate-level dissociative character (Brenner 1994a, 1996b, 2001) or Dissociative Disorder, Not Otherwise Specified (APA 1994). A recurrence of paralyzing guilt associated with exaggerated fears of punishment due to an ambiguous situation at work prompted her to consult with me again. She also had lost her capacity to self-analyze, and her observing ego seemed nonexistent. As in case 1, we agreed to meet in an expressive, supportive mode, not knowing how deeply our work would take us. In contrast to Rachel, however, Carla's negative transference was not as well worked through, and a mixture of deep fear coupled with rage was covered over by a self-effacing pseudo-compliance. She bitterly complained that she once again felt guilty over things that she did not completely believe, or own, as her own memories, and her trust in judgment for such matters was very limited. Although she had come to the inescapable conclusion about early sexual trauma and her mother's complicity in it, she still could not truly "feel" what had been coming to mind about an incestuous relationship with her uncle, a surrogate father. In particular, she was fixated on a scenario of a small girl being in a shed where some sort of sexual torture and overstimulation had taken place. Her sister was looking up or hiding in a corner at the time. In her loneliness, fear, and pain, she would focus on a design on the wall, creating an imaginary girlfriend who kept her company. She had fragmentary images of bright lights in her face, being restrained, and something rubbing against her genitals which had burned. Her rage and tantrums had been characterized by kicking and destructive behavior in the office, often accompanied by dissociative amnesia and the desperate protest—"Get the fuck off me!" She knew, but did not know (Laub and Auerhahn 1993) that her fixation on this material was very significant but could not own and accept that her uncle could do such things to her. It would change her life and possibly cause an irreparable break with her mother.

One day she told me that she heard about the use of EMDR in the treatment of acute trauma and wondered if I thought it could be helpful for her. Considering how long she had been struggling with her issues of trauma, however, she had had some doubts. I encouraged her to read up on EMDR, and we explored the issues relating to the complexity of her situation and the long-standing nature of how we had been working together analytically. At this time, she confessed that given how resistant and fearful she had always been, any short-term method would most certainly have failed and/or driven her away if it had been tried in the past. Lacking deep curiosity for defensive reasons, her wish not to know was an ongoing issue. She had always hoped that if she just felt good enough about herself, then perhaps she did not need to remember every bad thing that had ever happened to her.

While back in treatment for less than a year, an event with her family revived the affects of her childhood, which resulted in a further regression, the severity of which she had not experienced in years. Despite being in tight financial straits, she vowed that she would never ask her family for money, feeling as though she were either being paid off to be silent or fearing her request would be ignored. Yet, she felt continued rage, a sense of injustice, and a wish for restitution for all of her mistreatment, which she believed had contributed to her severe masochistic trends, high-risk behavior, and frank self-destructive activity. Feeling that she was finally far enough along in her understanding of herself, having accepted her uncle's limitations and believing that underneath it all he truly loved her, she fortified herself and asked for financial assistance. He then readily complied, much to her relief, but access to the money required a complex, potentially illegal procedure that might have resulted in negative repercussions for her sister. She felt utterly flabbergasted and duped once again when she realized the implications of this offer. She might benefit at someone else's expense, and she could not accept this "Sophie's choice." She berated herself for believing that he had changed and started to deteriorate. Her backslide accelerated when her mother, who encouraged her to give her uncle another chance, did not go to bat for her and left her to fend for herself. Feeling betrayed, unprotected, and neglected by her mother while she was trusting in her uncle, she became overwhelmed once again. It was during this time, after we had examined the situation and made as many connections as we could, that EMDR was discussed. I told her that I was open to her idea, which, perhaps like medication (Brenner 2001), might be incorporated into our therapeutic relationship. Similarly, we would attempt to analyze the meaning, effects, and implications of it for our work in light of her past.

Knowing how enactment-prone and easily startled she remained, I emphasized the importance of both collaboration and becoming as informed about it as possible before reaching any decision. After a period of time and a thorough discussion, we agreed that it would be helpful to arbitrarily set a date on which to commence the EMDR. Furthermore, we discussed the standard protocol, that one focuses on a particular memory or mental construct associated with intense unpleasurable affect, in the hope that through some unknown mechanism one might be able to rapidly work the issue through desensitization and reprocessing. Given her propensity for a negative therapeutic reaction, I was very low-key about the prospects of its usefulness in cases like hers where severe, repetitive childhood trauma from decades past might be less likely to benefit relative to a more recently experienced, single traumatic experience.

On the appointed day, a preplanned double session, she was very anxious, giddy, and ambivalent. I reviewed the simple instructions of following the movement of my hand for a brief period of time while she focused on a predetermined memory about which she hoped to feel better. As with Rachel (see case 1), given the analytic model with which we had been working for so long, I felt it would be even more foreign, artificial, and interfering to ask her to rate her affective experience on a Subjective Units of Distress Scale (SUDS) or a Validity of Cognition (VOC) scale, used in the very structured, cognitively based standard EMDR model (Shapiro 1995, Shapiro and Forrest 1997). Furthermore, in this case, I decided not to move closer as is recommended in the standard protocol. The patient, who for all of her years in treatment with me had only occasionally sat up on the couch during especially regressive and terrifying moments, had recently taken to sitting up more and trying to maintain some eye contact with me. Had she not, I think the demand of dramatically modifying the arrangement, that is, not only sitting up but also following my moving hand, would have been even more anxiety-provoking than it was. Perhaps she would not have even brought it up. Nevertheless, we spent weeks talking about her feelings of looking in my direction and how strange it might feel during EMDR. I assured her that she could stop it whenever she wanted and we would take our time to discuss all of her reactions to this innovation, thinking of it as a parameter (Eissler 1953). To bind her anxiety, she decided in advance on a topic on which to focus but then decided, interestingly, at the last moment to let whatever comes to mind come to mind. Motorically expressing her ambivalence over this new activity, every time she said she was ready and I would raise my hand, she would turn in my direction and then squeeze her eyes shut as tightly as possible. After about ten tries and our good-naturedly laughing together about her clearly recognizing how much she did not want to see anything, we proceeded.

During the first set, she almost immediately said that she was very tired of doing it and realized the absurd humor in her statement, having spent months contemplating EMDR and yet feeling tired of it in moments. She could not associate further to this clearly loaded statement, and we continued for about another minute or so. At the same time, she was struck by the newness of her statement—"tired of doing it"— and also noted that during the course of several more sets of eye movements that she had other seemingly new thoughts. However, what was most new for her was her actually visualizing scenarios from her childhood, which she likened to seeing a movie inside her mind. While she was viewing it, she was unable to speak and even afterward found it difficult to narrate what she had seen. In keeping with the data of positron emission tomography (PET) scan studies of brain profusion during reactivation of traumatic material, I wondered if such images were being activated in her right hemisphere while her speech center in Broca's area in the left hemisphere was being inhibited (Rauch et al. 1996, van der Kolk 1996). If so, then was there, indeed, something "new" happening in her mind/brain that facilitated her seeing something new during the session, or was it merely a provocative activity with an overstimulated patient? We continued with several more sets of eye movements, allowing much more time for her to regain her speech and describe what she could. What was especially striking to her were several new visualizations, one of being held upside down with her legs apart while her uncle masturbated her and performed oral sex. In the past, she could not figure out her body position for these sexual acts to occur and was always confused. The uncle's use of his hands also figured in his positioning of her body. Also, seeing her sister in the scenario with her uncle made her wonder for the first time, consciously, if she, too, were made to participate in any sexual activity. This was a very anxiety-laden topic, which we subsequently explored in detail. Furthermore, she heard and saw someone walk into the shed, thinking that it had been her mother. Throughout this session, the patient was surprised over how overtly in control she was, an observation in contrast with her fantasy that EMDR would liberate so much hostile destructiveness (Parens 1979) that she would destroy my office. In fact, she was so much in control that she seemed inappropriately muted given the intense nature of her "pictures."

During the next session, she reported a difficult time over the weekend with waves of panic that something terrible was going to happen. The panic escalated during the session until she revealed that she was apprehensive that we were simply going to launch into another EMDR session, that is, do it again without any further discussion. When this was explored further, she relaxed when she realized that we had not planned to do more EMDR work, and therefore would not, unless discussed and mutually agreed upon, but her transference fears prevailed. Furthermore, she expressed worry that my hand must have gotten very tired the first time and would certainly get tired again today if we "did it." In our usual analytic mode, we then explored the meaning of her concerns, which eventually linked to her fears of and wishes for either or both of us doing something sexual to the other or to ourselves with our hands. Fantasies of parallel masturbation, mutual masturbation, and rape had been analyzed in the transference during her first analysis and these issues had been revived during the guided eye movements this time. She became very anxious about knowing more too quickly and felt that the eye movements might be opening something up by facilitating her seeing sexually arousing memories. In addition, she was becoming more aware of an enactment in the transference, that I would expect her to comply and force something upon her with which she was quite familiar and something she was very, very tired of. After about ten sessions over several months in which guided eye movements were used for anywhere from 1 or 2 minutes up to a series of sets throughout the hour, she felt she had seen enough for the time being. It was as though there were a catalytic effect of the procedure that fueled productive exploration and vital linkages of affect, memory, and insight. It seemed self-limited and something that perhaps we might consider again at some point in the future. Therapy then continued in our usual exploratory manner and, when relevant, we would analyze the experience like anything else that had come up in our work.

CASE 3

Several months into a psychotherapy treatment that has spanned more than a decade and a half, Mary (see Chapters 2 and 3) penciled a detailed sketch and quietly showed it to me (Figure 9–1). She was unable to associate to it and was quite anxious when I asked her anything about it. Although she was curious about any observations I made and would share with her, she would become very self-conscious and felt transparent. Initially, she presented for help in an acutely suicidal state related to a homosexual panic and was hospitalized for several weeks. At that point, she revealed very little about herself or her family except that she was a struggling artist and that alcoholism ran rampant throughout her family. She was desperate to speak, but had few words and tried to tell me her story through her art.

The steps leading nowhere, the mask being manipulated by teams of little people, the mysterious sphinx, the stage on which to perform, and the anatomically correct foot pierced by a rectangular, metal rod were powerful, evocative images. We later came to recognize that this work was a self-portrait revealing her severe dissociative psychopathology replete with a socially

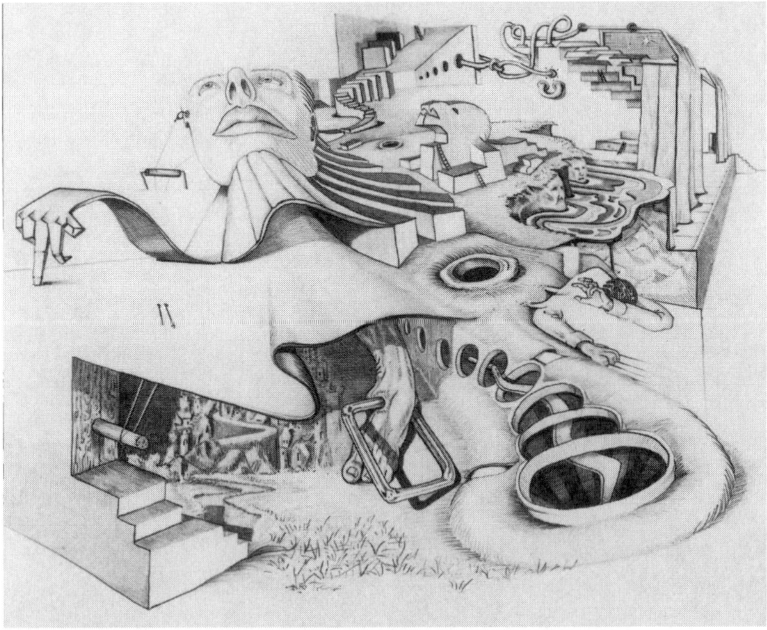

Figure 9–1 ***"M.C. Escher–Like" Mask and Sphinx***

compliant self, that is, the mask, her many inside people working behind the scenes, and the painful secrets of her childhood, which were compartmentalized and kept from awareness.

A year-and-a-half into treatment following a near-fatal overdose, her inability to give a safety contract and her being committed to a state hospital after a several-month hospitalization where she was in a daze and said very little, she painted *A New Idea* (Figure 9–2).

She brought it in after rededicating herself to working with me following an angry hiatus due to her commitment. Again, she said very little about it at the time, as the fetus emanating from the subject's right temporal area in this garishly colored acrylic left much to my imagination. Much later, she revealed that during her confinement and time spent with the

Figure 9–2: *A New Idea (Fetus)*

chronically mentally ill, she saw how her life would deteriorate if she did not take treatment seriously. The fetus represented not only such a new idea but also the idea that her neglect and mistreatment began in utero with her mother's smoking, drinking, and poor diet. At the time, the only sexual molestation she had spoken about began as a teen, at the hands of several older boys and men.

A month later, she painted another acrylic (Figure 9–3) but did not bring it in until about thirteen years later! Her

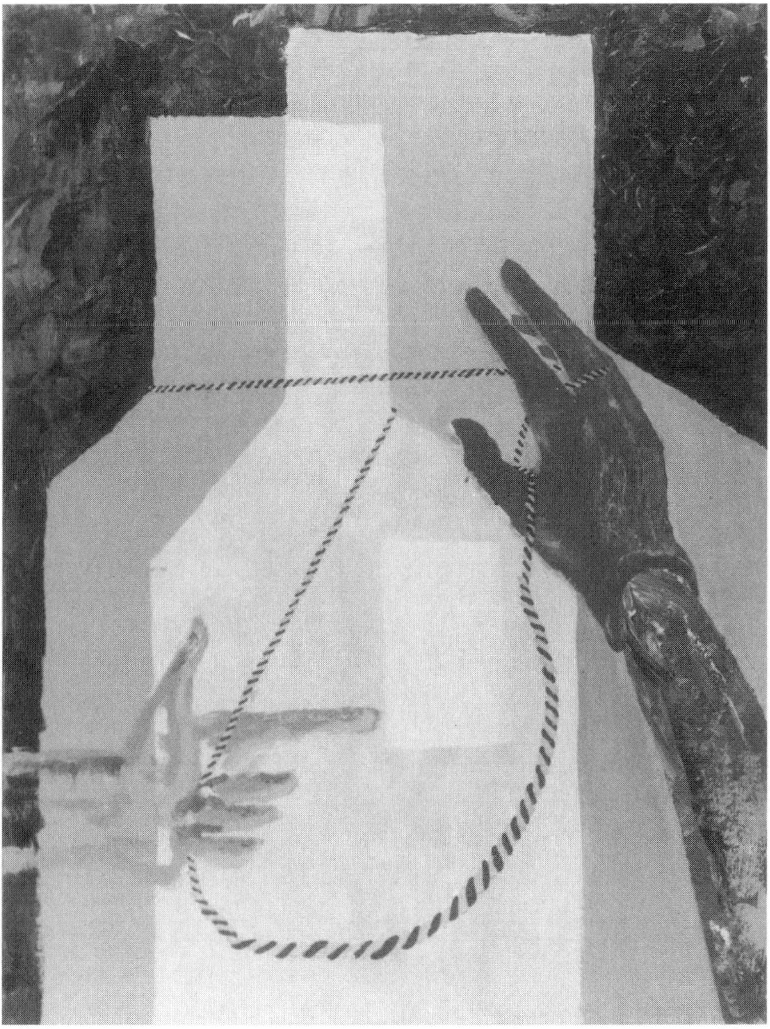

Figure 9–3 *The Noose Tightens*

capacity to keep things to herself, and to keep the secrets of her incestuous relationship with her mother are reflected in the time elapsed before she brought in this piece. The fear and pressure she felt mounting inside during each session as she struggled with telling me are depicted in this stylized work by the cord being wrapped around her neck by disembodied hands.

Two months later, feeling as though she were dying inside, she produced a frenetic and chaotic acrylic (Figure 9–4) of a hapless figure being choked by a very powerful hand. This work also did not find its way into therapy until thirteen years later when she regained her ability to paint again. At the time, she was feeling more out of control, disintegrated, and utterly terrified.

A companion piece (Figure 9–5), created a month later, expressed her ego boundary disturbance in the form of her

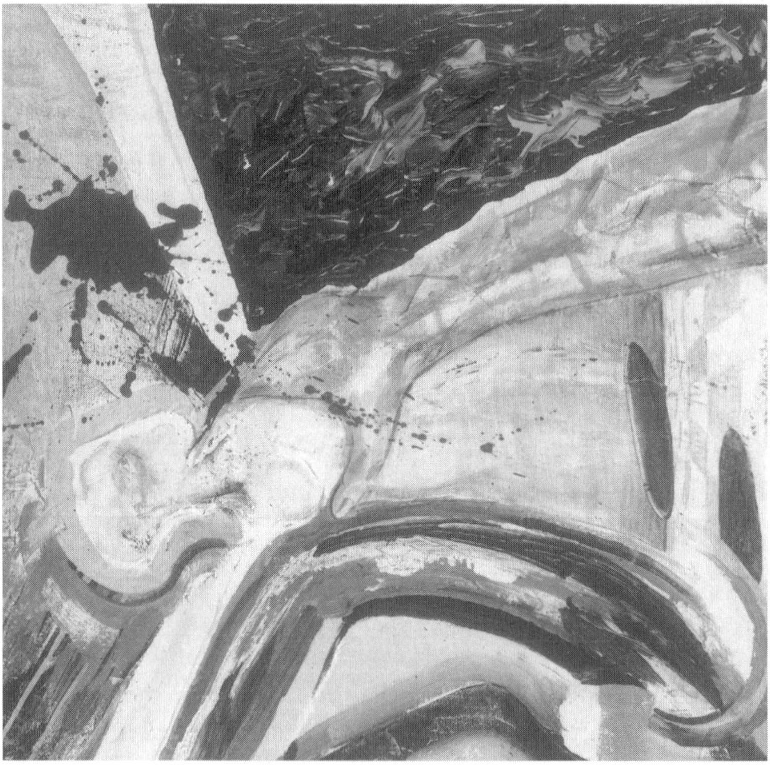

Figure 9–4 *Bloody Choke*

Figure 9–5 *Exploding Guts*

intestines and her organs exploding through her body as she sat in the chair in my office trying to talk to me. To the outside observer, she frequently appeared almost catatonic at times, moving very slowly and deliberately while showing virtually no facial expression except an ineffable, vacant sadness with an unfocused gaze. She drank heavily to sedate herself and also felt so quietly paranoid that the slightest movement of a chair from one session to the next took on great personal meaning. Much later, she confided that she believed I was testing her and trying to drive her crazy by making subtle changes in the chair's position. It never occurred to her that other patients might have shifted in the chair or that the housekeeping staff might have inadvertently moved it while vacuuming. In Mary's mind, everything had to be kept perfectly still or she would, indeed, explode into hundreds of fragments and, like Humpty Dumpty, would not be able to be reassembled. We had been meeting at least twice a week when she was an outpatient, which would increase to five times a week during her several hospitalizations.

About a year later, which was about three years into treatment, she simply stopped painting and drawing. It completely overwhelmed her, and she developed an almost complete inhibition that lasted over ten years. Expressing herself through art had a countertherapeutic effect that destabilized her and made her see certain truths that were intolerable. The last piece she did (Figure 9–6), which was done in colored pencils, bothered her so much that she was unable to take it back home, so I kept it in the office for her. The bald, ambiguously gendered figure enigmatically gesturing to the viewer, the naked body on its back with legs spread apart, and the figure in the box holding a knife in one hand and covering the eyes with the other were revealing too much that she was not ready to see, both literally and figuratively.

Mary's alcoholism, depression, and suicidal despair continued, but she remained stubbornly committed to our

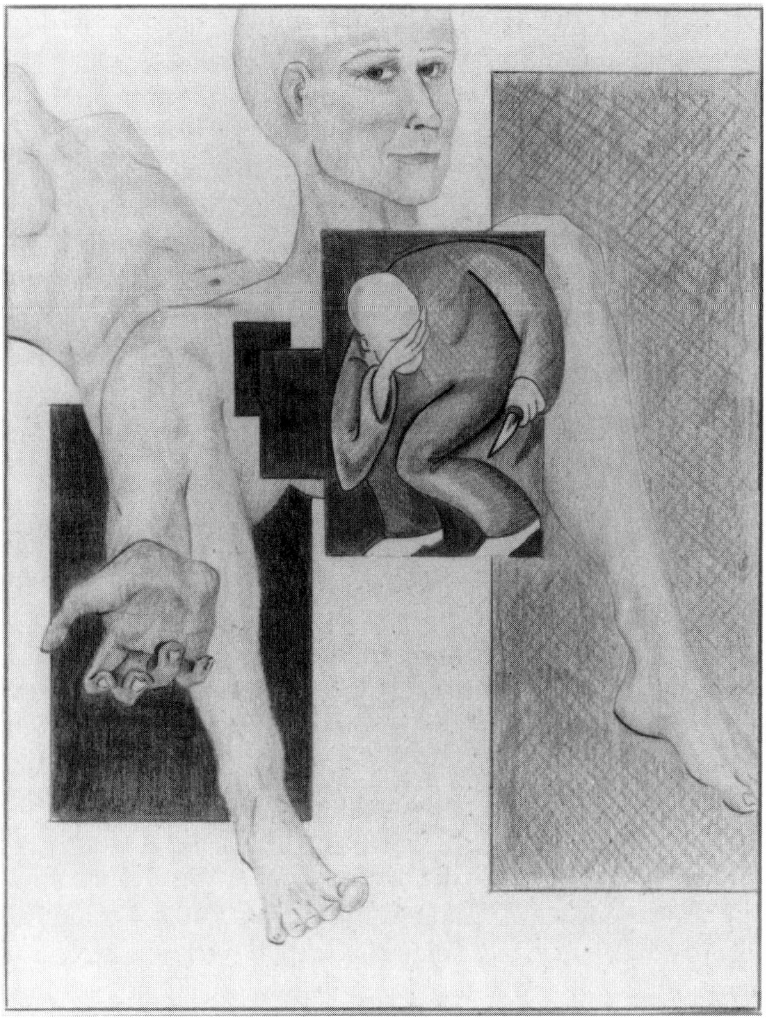

Figure 9–6 *Can't See/In a Box*

biweekly visits, living an ascetic life and working two jobs to make ends meet. Her reticence and negativism belied her unswerving dedication to therapy. She never missed an appointment. Several years later, during a hospitalization, she reacted very strongly to a benign picture on the wall of a mother braiding her daughter's hair. The mother was straddling the girl with her legs spread out, and Mary became visibly agitated by the scene. She left me an urgent message that she wanted to speak with me, which was most uncharacteristic of her. At that time, she cautiously admitted that she thought I should know about the very unnatural relationship she had with her mother. The nature and duration of the incest took years for her to describe, which required the help of her inner cadre of selves. Excruciating memories, primitive aggression, homosexuality, sadomasochistic heterosexuality, transsexualism, and bestiality were encapsulated by her dissociated selves. In these various amnestic states, she lived out several sexual pathways. The intensity of her rage at her mother in the transference was chilling and frightening to me at times; eventually the words and the narrative began to take form through her construction of her childhood. When she finally decided to stop drinking and fight for her life, she embraced the Alcoholics Anonymous (AA) program, feeling a sense of belonging to this group that became her new surrogate family. She never thought she could reveal the secret because her mother told her that God would kill her if she told. Interestingly, one of her most agonizing hallucinations was eventually understood, her "hearing" a frightened, young boy, an alter personality, who would cry out, "God is trying to kill me!" In her despair, the patient would simply report, "I'm hearing God's trying to kill me. God's trying to kill me." She would hear his cries quite frequently during the sessions when she was trying to talk about her mother, and this dissociated, personified resistance took many years to analyze.

Figure 9–7 *Silent Scream with a Red "V"*

With the exception of a never-brought-in acrylic done five years before the EMDR (Figure 9–7), and ten years after the colored pencil drawing in Figure 9–6, she essentially produced no artwork during this time. Even attempts to make something as mundane as holiday greeting cards were scuttled, as such work reminded her of the importance of family, which she never had. The painting in Figure 9–7 had troubled Mary very much as it portrayed a silhouetted woman silently mouthing a bloodcurdling scream, which was depicted by the red *V*. Recognizing how choked off from the intensity of her affect she felt, she preferred to take as little medication as possible in order to feel something and, she hoped, feel real. Indeed, she sensed the alienation from the inner workings of her mind, as Mary was the pseudo-compliant social mask being manipulated by her other selves. What she did know was that there was deep terror and anguish, so that if she were ever to learn how to scream, she feared she would never stop. Yet, she desperately did want to feel and remember simultaneously without losing time and maintaining continuity of her sense of self.

It is not entirely clear to me why I offered EMDR to Mary but I suspect that I, too, shared her unconscious fantasy that an abreaction would be curative for her. Even though the standard EMDR protocol is not based on a therapeutic catharsis model, perhaps on some level I had hoped that that would happen in a safe way for her. Again, I did not see her silent-scream painting until well into the EMDR work but certainly sensed her frustration. As in the other cases, I discussed the idea in a very low-key way, but the mere fact that I offered it immediately raised Mary's hope for a breakthrough. Furthermore, my apparent display of increased interest in her by leaning forward in the chair, sitting a little closer, and actively focusing on the procedure with her was quite gratifying and made her feel special. Similarly, I was struck by her immediate first reaction to it as she suddenly recalled certain details of her chosen issue, a rape at knifepoint while hitchhiking, which was a murky event she had told me about several times before. In this initial session, I did not want to launch right into maternal incest issues, so we agreed on a less highly charged trauma.

These memories were linked to her senses (Brenner 1988a), that is, the color of his clothing, the texture of the mud, and, as she lay on the ground, the wet stains on her pants after she got dressed in a daze as she was left in an isolated, wooded area. For the first time, she realized how poor her judgment had been, how easily she could have been killed, and how such events helped obliterate memories of her mother's exploitation of her, serving the function of screening one trauma with another (Glover 1929). She felt so affectively stirred up and liberated afterward that I was initially concerned about a suicidal regression and uncontrollable dissociative switching. What I did not anticipate was an urge to start painting again. While I did encourage her to express herself with painting as I had many times before over the years, I did not know what effect it would have, since she was usually so afraid of becoming more out of control after seeing what came out of her.

Figure 9–8, done within a day of the first EMDR session, illustrates how stimulated and electrified she felt. In this large, acrylic painting, the subject has an aura that looks like hundreds of pins sticking in or coming out of her body, and her right hand curiously resembles the configuration of my hand during an EMDR set. It also resembles a *V* for victory and a hand gesture used by the Pope. There is a regressive fusion of our bodies. Interestingly, my/her hand is being held in place by a band tightly secured from an unseen location, and a body part being controlled by strings is a theme throughout her work (see Figure 9–1). In addition, we discovered later on that bound hands were also associated with the bondage of her limbs by her mother when she was a child. Furthermore, the subject is holding a blood-red spear/phallus as it threatens to come up out of her in the form of a murderously rageful expression of emotion toward her perpetrators. Mary's mind continued to be stimulated for hours after the EMDR, and we considered that that might be

Figure 9–8 *EMDR—Aura*

analogous to food in a microwave that continues to cook after the power is turned off.

About a week after the first EMDR session, she painted another rendition of her experience. This time, our bodies were differentiated and it is viewed from behind me (Figure 9–9).

Figure 9–9 *Powerful Hand & Back of Head*

The aura and electricity are still there, as is the scream, which remains stuck in her throat. The powerful, outstretched right arm and oversized EMDR hand are prominently outlined in this figure, and one cannot help but notice the back of my head, which I am told is rendered quite realistically here. As a result, attention is perhaps also drawn to what is in the back of my mind, as well as what is going on in the back of Mary's mind. She pointed out that the thirteen curved reverberations painted above her head represent her "inside people," all of whom came forward and simultaneously participated in the procedure. As such, it had the quality of an integrative experience (Brenner 2001).

About two weeks after this EMDR session, Mary portrayed herself as alone and sinking back into the therapy chair, hiding her face, and covering her genital area in shame

Figure 9–10 *EMDR—Sinking Into Chair*

(Figure 9–10). Receding into the distance and withdrawing from me, the powerful affects and hoped-for scream have also diminished as per the greatly reduced, jagged, red vertical line in her chest. She is losing the spark, the intensity, and the hope generated by the EMDR, as she feels herself giving into helplessness and despair once again. She asks for another EMDR session and we agreed to repeat this procedure during the next hour.

Following the second EMDR session, she quickly produced two more large acrylics (Figures 9–11 and 9–12). In one (Figure 9–11), she is depicted as a very large, androgynous figure full of despair and hopelessness. Her heart, shaped like a clenched fist and outlined in smeared blood-red paint, is aching as she feels pressure on her left shoulder. The pressure comes from the green, claw-like fingers belonging to an unseen monster standing behind her in the shadows. She cannot escape her

Figure 9–11 *EMDR—Helpless Giant*

Figure 9–12 *EMDR—Mother's Black Hand*

mother's grip and awaits the monster's next move. I pointed out to her that from the viewer's perspective of the painting, she appears to be a giant who does not seem to know her own strength. She looked at me quite quizzically when I said this. In the next painting (Figure 9–12), the patient's head is being gripped by two hands and pulled toward the other figure, who is reclining with knees bent and legs spread apart. Mary's tongue is obediently outstretched, knowing, after literally decades of conditioning, exactly how her mother likes to be pleasured as she is about to perform cunnilingus on her. Her mother's right hand, interestingly, is very prominent here and painted black, symbolizing a gloved hand that leaves no fingerprints or incriminating evidence behind after a crime.

During this period of time, Mary's despair intensified, and she had not felt such strong suicidal feelings in several years. Ambivalent longings for her mother, with whom she had finally broken off contact several years previously, were expressed in the form of an interpersonal conflict among her different selves: the "children" cried for their mother, an idealized figure who would finally love them and not hurt them; her violent, male transsexual self made sadistic threats with a knife to Mary's lover, displacing his rage and craving one more chance to be with "the mother." The alter had found a way of mastering the situation by becoming the active one and seducing the mother, putting her at his mercy sexually. He especially enjoyed her occasionally pushing him away and eventually submitting. In so doing, he became the initiator, not the victim, and learned to like it. He imagined having a penis as he penetrated her with whatever he could insert into the mother's vagina. This revelation in an amnestic, defensive, altered state illustrated her identification with the aggressor and added an important perspective to such an incestuous relationship, which persisted into adulthood (see Chapter 2).

After the third EMDR several weeks later, she produced a self-portrait that more clearly depicted her symbiosis with her mother (Figure 9–13). In it, she tries to extricate herself by pulling her taffy-like body apart from her mother's naked body, as she is focused on painting on a canvas. Interestingly, she is painting a hand with two fingers outstretched, signifying the EMDR hand that, curiously, is a left hand, not the right hand I was using. Mary herself is left-handed, and perhaps this reversal of handedness signifies the merging she experiences with me in the regressive, maternal transference. Mary's expression reveals a slight smile and a sense of purpose.

The last painting of the series, Figure 9–14, done shortly after the self-portrait (Figure 9–13), appears to summarize her experience of the three sessions of EMDR which were inter-

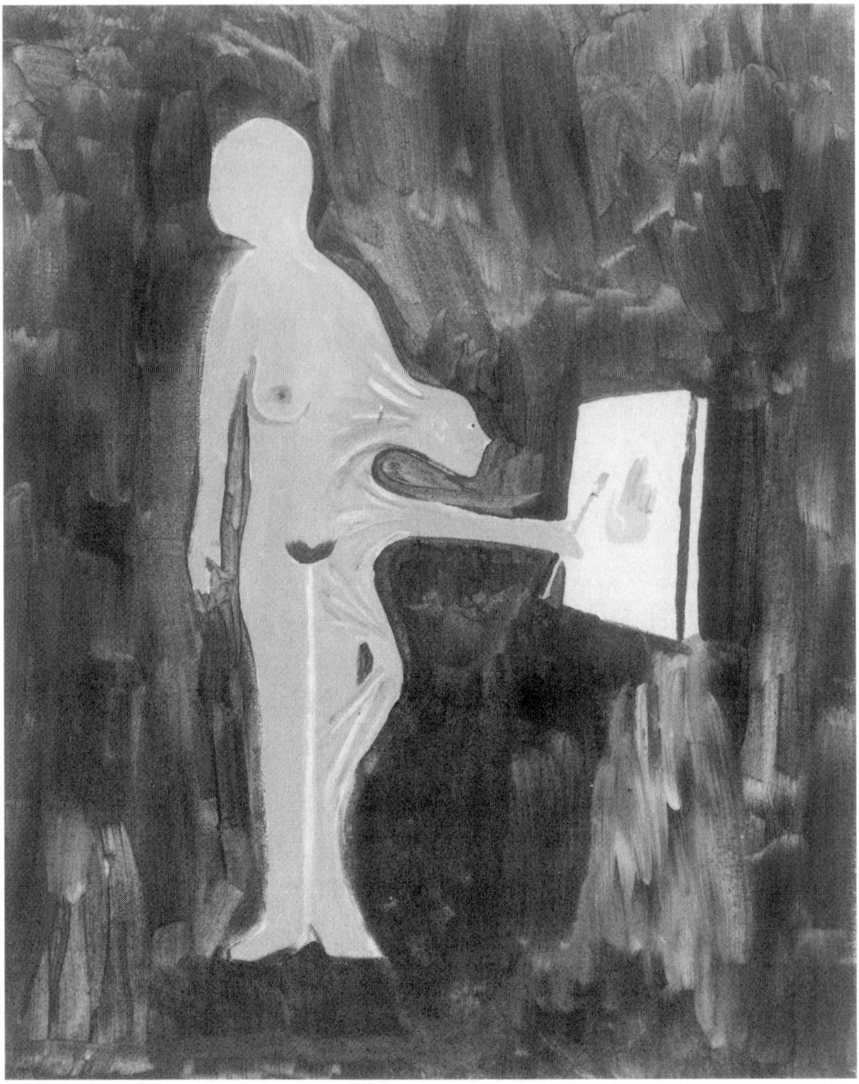

Figure 9–13 *EMDR—Self Portrait Painting Hand*

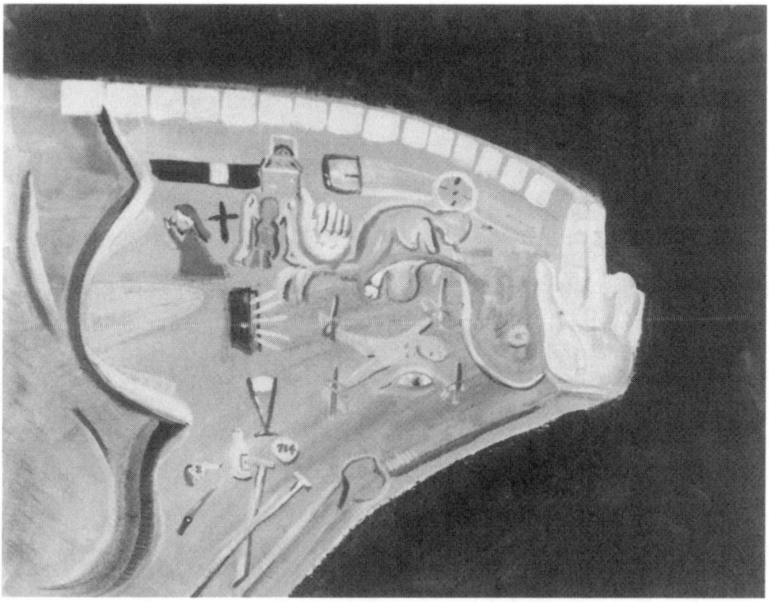

Figure 9–14 *EMDR—B&W Coming out of the Mouth*

spersed over a period of about two months. The profile of her open mouth spews forth many figures depicting aspects of her abuse, which appear to be drawn out by the EMDR hand. In this collection, there is a nun kneeling in prayer in a cluster of religious symbols, which appear to be on the tip of her tongue. Interestingly, one of the first things Mary talked about when she first began treatment was a period of elective mutism when she was 5 years old while attending Catholic preschool. She hinted at inappropriate touching of her body and harsh punishments meted out by the nuns. Moving clockwise, one sees a hand with a raised thumb, symbolizing her rape when she was hitchhiking. Her wristwatch denotes the passage of time and the long-standing nature of her abuse. Then there is a woman with pendulous breasts leaning over, a penis, a breast, and a figure lying on her back with all four limbs tied down. Under this figure is an eye, an eye that sees all and knows all. This eye is "I," her very fragile, true self who knows that whatever happened, happened to all of her, not an alter personality. Below the eye is a toothbrush her mother used to scrub her "dirty" genitals clean, along with a wooden broom handle and knitting needles that she inserted into the patient's vagina. The knife, handgun, beer bottle, glass of beer, and pill are symbols of her violent impulses and self-destructive efforts to self-medicate, numb herself, and forget all that had happened to her. To complete the cycle, there is an open door, which represents her long-standing, recurrent nightmare of being awakened in the middle of the night by a mysterious woman who opens her bedroom door and is about to harm her.

All of this material had already emerged over the years in therapy. What was striking about it this time was that the patient was able to develop more of a chronological narrative and further the construction of her life. With all of her alters participating in the EMDR, Mary's co-consciousness was increased, allowing her to hear their voices more clearly while maintaining more of a sense of continuity of her own self.

DISCUSSION

Mary's artistic rendering of her experience with the guided eye movements graphically illustrates how stimulated and activated she felt. As with the other two patients who also reported new thoughts, recollections, visualizations, and feelings, Mary, during the first session when focusing on her rape, blurted out, "I should have screamed!" This idea never crossed her mind before, as she grew up with the silence of her incestuous relationship with her mother. While Mary could visualize her memories and had a photographic memory of images, she could not speak or feel the experiences in her usual state of consciousness. One of the recurrent images in her art depicts her scream rising up from her body and getting stuck in her throat. Carla (case 2), on the other hand, lived in perpetual, psychic torment, and reported that she had never visualized her early, traumatic experience until she started seeing pictures of it during the eye movements. In contrast, Rachel (case 1) had visualized, felt, and made thought connections during her analytic work but had forgotten much of what she had integrated. During her guided eye movements, it had appeared as though we could work through her resistances to remembering more quickly, as material rushed back into her awareness. In none of the three cases did the patient appear to lapse into a hypnotic trance or react solely to suggestion. Clearly, however, there were enactments in all, which were analyzed as best as possible given the limitations of the depth and the intensity of the work at the time, that is, two times a week, three times a week, and one time a week, respectively. These enactments seemed to involve the EMDR hand, which was evident in all three cases and associated with an emphasis on material related to the role of hands in their trauma. Most specifically in the artist's case, my hand guiding her eyes seemed to represent, unconsciously, her mother's hands guiding her head and mouth to perform oral sex upon her. A cathexis of the hand as a part of the patient and of the other was a prominent finding.

In addition to the myriad symbolic possibilities pertaining to the hand, the link between hand gestures and language has also been appreciated by both evolutionary biology and comparative neuroanatomy. For example, Deacon (1997) suggests that early language in our Paleolithic ancestors derives from both guttural sounds and gestures. As a result, the hand would have been used for important communication long before the arrival of our species. To corroborate this theory, Pally (1999), citing Rizzolati and Arbib (1998) emphasizes the importance of the presence of "mirror neurons" in Broca's area in the human brain, as well as in the homologue of the monkey brain known as F-5, located in the ventral premotor area of the frontal cortex. Significantly, when monkeys imitate hand gestures, this part of their brains is activated, suggesting that their action/recognition system may represent a rudimentary component that underlies language development. Such a mechanism may also be involved in the preverbal facial attunement of the mother and infant, and in empathic connections in adulthood. In addition, it might be tempting to speculate that Mary's reversal of my EMDR hand from right to left in Figure 9–13 might in part be due to the mirror neurons in her Broca's area being recruited in the service of a regressive dedifferentiation of our bodies, as she was left-handed. Consequently, if one were to consider this complex psychotherapeutic interaction from a neurosciences standpoint also, it might deepen our understanding of the role of our "hard wiring" in such relationships with severely traumatized patients.

FROM NEUROSCIENCE TO PSYCHOANALYSIS

Edelman and Tononi (2000) explain an essential human phenomenon this way:

> To support conscious experience, a large number of groups of neurons must interact rapidly and reciprocally through the process called reentry. [p. 36] . . . Perhaps the most direct indication of how important rapid reentrant neural interactions are for generating a unified conscious experience are disconnection syndromes in neurology and dissociation disorders in psychiatry . . . in which one or more areas of the brain were anatomically or functionally disconnected from the rest of the brain owing to some pathological process, traumatic event or surgery while the areas themselves are

> relatively unchanged. The most dramatic and certainly best-studied form of [anatomical] disconnection is the split brain syndrome in which persons with intractable epilepsy undergo surgery that severs the large numbers of reciprocal connections between the two halves of the brain (i.e., via the corpus callosum and, in a few cases, the anterior commissure). [p. 63]

A functional disconnection syndrome, while by no means agreed upon by experts in the field of dissociative disorders, has been theorized as an etiological factor in multiple personality or dissociative identity disorder (Benner and Evans 1984, Braun 1984, Brende 1984). Because of the complexity of the symptomatology and the fact that many such cases are not merely dual personalities that could be assigned to each hemisphere, a simplified view of the manifestations of a disconnection syndrome can easily be discounted (Ross 1997, Sidtis 1986). Nevertheless, certain features of these cases do warrant a deeper look at their neural connections. In my own experience, a majority of such DID patients have had at least one alter personality with different handedness (Brenner 1994a, 2001). In these lower-level dissociative characters, as I have described them, quite often this alter is one of the most disturbed and is psychologically disconnected from the others. An anecdotal incident that illustrated the potential importance of this observation occurred when a right-handed patient sustained a left-sided stroke from an embolus in the right middle cerebral artery. Although rapid medical treatment enabled her to regain almost full recovery after several months, she was initially hemiparetic on the left side. Curiously, when her left-handed alter personality was accessed, she was able to use her left hand, much to the astonishment of her neurologists. In addition, when Rachel in case 1 became integrated as a result of treatment, she lost the capability of using her left hand. However, in case 3, where the alter personalities were still operative, Mary's very disturbed and isolated little children were indeed of opposite handedness. While certainly in need of extensive neurobiological corroboration, the possibility of different parts of the brain controlling handedness for different alters in such patients raises important questions about unusual neural circuitry affecting psychological defenses in those severely traumatized in childhood.

Experimentally, a functional disconnection may be created by the so-called Wada test, in which the left carotid artery is injected with sodium amytal to paralyze the right side of the body and narcotize the left hemisphere. The subject is then asked to hold an object blindly in his left hand. When the left hemisphere recovers, he is asked to identify the object that he cannot articulate but successfully points to. Once visualized, he then becomes able to remember it and verbalize it, suggesting that the left hemisphere initially had no access to the information, which would have freely traveled bilaterally under normal circumstances. It is not until the right hemisphere points to the object, reactivating the information, that it is then transmitted to the left where it can be reprocessed and ultimately put into words (Risse and Gazzaniga 1979).

Developmentally, the corpus callosum begins to mature at 18 months and continues through latency until about the age of 6 to 8, thus limiting direct, internal interhemispheric communication until then (Pally 2000). For this reason, it has been theorized that when young children talk to themselves, that is, their "egocentric speech," it is in order for the hemispheres to better communicate with each other. Since the right hemisphere is typically dominant and directs behavior at this point, speaking aloud enables the child to hear what is being planned and to re-encode the information in the left hemisphere through an external circuit (Joseph 1996). Under normative conditions, the internal transfer of information from right to left occurs when maturation is completed. Even after maturation, however, psychic trauma may induce hyperarousal and a functional shutdown of the left hemisphere, resulting in a one-sided encoding of the affective memory on the right.

Recent neuroimaging studies measuring regional cerebral blood flow (rCBF) and oxygen consumption through positron emission tomography (PET) provide intriguing evidence for this effect. In one study, Rauch and colleagues (1996) studied eight subjects with PTSD who reacted to hearing their own narratives being read to them. Their scans revealed increased brain activity in the right hemispheres, specifically in the right medial orbitofrontal cortex, right insular cortex, right anterior temporal lobe, anterior cingulate gyrus, right amygdala, right medial temporal cortex, right secondary visual cortex, and bilateral sensory motor cortex. Furthermore, there were decreases in the activity of the left middle temporal cortex and the left inferior frontal cortex (Broca's area). In co-investigator van der Kolk's (1996) words, "Perhaps most significantly, Broca's area 'turned off' . . . [and] this reflects the tendency in PTSD to express emotions as physical states rather than as verbally encoded experiences. Our findings suggest that PTSD patients' difficulties with putting feelings into words are mirrored in actual changes in brain activity" (p. 233). Using a similar research design with a comparison group, Shin and colleagues (1999) studied sixteen survivors of early sexual abuse. Of the eight with PTSD, there was a greater autonomic response and a greater activation of the orbitofrontal cortex and anterior temporal poles. Once again, the PTSD group showed decreases in Broca's area. In their review of such studies, Pitman and colleagues (2000) conclude that "PTSD symptoms may be conceptualized as the products of fear conditioning. . . . Results of PTSD functional neuroimaging studies point to the amygdala and associated anterior paralimbic activation during traumatic reexperiencing" (p. 53). If this is so and if, indeed, Broca's area shuts down, these findings would appear to support treatments that promote interhemispheric communication and verbal expression.

Psychoanalysis is the ultimate therapy that promotes making connections in the mind—thoughts and feelings, conscious and unconscious, past and present—and verbalizing them. Such connections are facilitated by a particular type of mental functioning that requires integrated activity and is well known to analysts, that is, metaphorical thinking. Sharpe (1940), for example, noted that "metaphor fuses sense experience and thought in language" (p. 156). Shengold (1981) observed that "metaphor leads to memory and the experiential" (p. 303). Rizzuto (2001) has focused on the limbic system's involvement in the processing of experience, emphasizing the importance of "affectively valued body perception" (p. 535) in metaphorical thinking. But, especially pertinent to this discussion, are Levin (1997) and Modell (1997), who point out that using metaphors promotes the concerted functioning of both hemispheres as such mental processes require linkages of those areas of the brain involved in affective, somatic, sensory, and verbal activity. Consequently, the analyst's empathic appreciation of patients' metaphors and his use of metaphor in interpretative interventions is essentially integrative. It is not surprising, therefore, that severely traumatized patients, especially those traumatized in childhood, not only may experience difficulties in abstract and metaphorical thinking but also may even be quite impaired in this area (Herzog 1982). Could it be, therefore, that a procedure like guided interhemispheric stimulation implemented at certain times in the therapeutic process with especially refractory patients could facilitate integrated mental activity? If so, could such a procedure be thoughtfully brought into the analytically informed therapeutic situation? At least one very senior analyst does not think so. Even though Paul Ornstein, according to Genova (2001), found EMDR to be quite interesting, he doubted he would ever use it for fear that introducing the technique would cause a great interference: "I won't interrupt a person's process. . . . I'm a purist" (p. 40).

PARAMETER OR PARIAH?

Neuroscientists have cautioned us not to make too speculative a leap by drawing one-to-one correspondences from their findings to psychological processes. The brain is much too complex and the "decade of the brain" has merely opened the door to what we will eventually learn. It would be an error if we were simply "reifying our metaphors" (Brenner 1994a, p. 840), especially with the dissociative disorders, but one nevertheless needs to keep an open mind (Rapaport 1951). A number of psychoanalysts, however, seem to take an extreme position, insisting that we must never take our pictorial images of the psyche literally because "they have no grounding in reality" (Goldberg 2000, p. 67). Furthermore, as Goldberg wryly contends, "to say that psychotherapeutic changes do change one's PET scan is no different than saying that learning the cello does so as well" (p. 67). He concludes that "the inaccessibility of the unconscious is a fundamental feature of psychoanalysis. It is not a place nor a structure, and treating it as such robs *it* of its essence and us of its value" (p. 68).

Nevertheless, reports in the literature are appearing in which neurobiological findings are being linked to the clinical situation. Yovell (2000), for example, tells of his increased empathy for a patient sexually abused in childhood who, despite all of her efforts at remembering being raped at age 4, simply could not. He notes, "I allowed for the possibility that many or all of Tara's difficulties in remembering her past were due to chronic hippocampal damage and, hence, would not be reversed by even the most illuminating interpretation." (p. 179). The author considers that "her difficulties remembering could be viewed both psychologically and neurobiologically as 'the result of a damaged hippocampus coupled with a hypersensitive amygdala' . . . [which might] describe the same phenomenon in two different languages" (p. 180). Of course, given the limited clinical data presented, one might also skeptically wonder if the author is actually offering a neurologically informed rationalization for his therapeutic fatalism. And so the question remains as to what impact our increased knowledge of brain functioning will have on the technical issues confronting psychoanalytically informed therapies.

It may very well be that the putative interhemispheric stimulation induced by actions, such as the guided eye movements in EMDR, will ultimately prove to be a psychological artifact of dubious clinical value. If so, it will eventually lose its popularity and wash to shore along with the flotsam and jetsam of other faddish treatments. But even if this were to be so, other neurobiologically informed discoveries may inspire some clinicians to consider other relatively simple maneuvers that could affect one's psychic equilibrium and defensive operations. How might one think about incorporating such actions into therapy?

Freud's revolutionary technique required patients to lie on the couch out of their view of him. It was a vestige of his days as a hypnotist, which also freed him up from the social issues of face-to-face contact. He did not have to worry about betraying emotion through his facial gestures or body language while listening with "evenly suspended attention" to his patients' associations. After abandoning hypnotherapy, he did, however, stop touching his patients' foreheads and hands, but the arrangement on the couch has remained as the standard (Freud 1913, 1925a) even though contemporary proponents of the relational approach question its use (Greenberg and Mitchell 1983). As a result, it would be a great challenge for a patient if she, at some point in analysis, would be asked to do something different other than sit or lie on a couch and talk. The specific procedure under inquiry here, guided eye movements, which, incidentally, have reportedly been used for centuries by yoga masters for relaxation (Parnel 1999), would pose an especially great challenge to patients using the couch. Clearly, much clinical research would be needed to determine its potential value in psychodynamically informed work, but to even consider introducing such a thing, as I mentioned earlier, felt silly and dubious to me; I suspect other analysts might feel that way as well. However, each of my three patients was convinced that it did something that facilitated their treatment, and I found it helpful to think about the introduction of this modification in light of Eissler's (1953) classic contribution on parameters.

Eissler, a staunch supporter of Freud's ideas, adhered to the notion of the supremacy of the interpretation as the ultimate agent of change in psychoanalysis. Although he acknowledged that perhaps he was too rigorous in his views, he was very concerned about "wild analysis" (Freud 1910). He was critical of Alexander and French's (1946) principle of flexibility, which endorsed adjusting the frequency of sessions and manipulation of the transference to reduce the patient's anxiety and promote behavioral change. Eissler used his influence to challenge these and other would-be heirs to Ferenczi's controversial legacy, which endorsed flexibility to the point of extreme gratification as per his principle of indulgence (Ferenczi 1919a, 1920, 1925, 1928, 1930). In his landmark work, Eissler set forth four criteria: "(1) A parameter must be introduced only when it is proved that the basic model technique does not suffice; (2) The parameter must never transgress the unavoidable minimum; (3) A parameter is to be used only when it finally leads to it self-elimination (p. 112) and (4) The effect of the parameter on the transference relationship must never be such that it cannot be abolished by interpretation" (p. 113). Freud (1919a) hinted at the limits of interpretation in the treatment of phobias at the Budapest Congress in 1918 when he stated, "One can hardly master a phobia if one waits until the patient lets the analysis influence him to give it up. . . . One succeeds only when one can induce them by the influence of the analysis to . . . go into the street and struggle with their anxiety" (pp. 165–166). In his work with the "Wolfman," an obsessive-compulsive, he introduced two additional parameters, setting a fixed termination date and omnipotently promising the patient that his intestinal problems would completely resolve (Freud 1918). Eissler points out that Freud's innovation in the latter case never became standard practice by others, perhaps in part because these parameters did not fulfill his criteria due to the mandated termination, which did not allow time to analyze and abolish them.

In keeping with psychoanalytic efforts to treat the most disturbed, (Fromm-Reichman 1950), Eissler also addressed the technical challenges of working with schizophrenic and delinquent patients in which the former cannot free-associate while the latter will not. Emphasizing the greater importance of ego organization over the specific set of symptoms and defenses, he builds on Freud's observation by adding that those patients whose ego integrity has, for example, been modified by severe trauma may not derive the maximal benefit of analysis from interpretation alone. In Freud's (1937) words, "Every normal person is only approximately normal on the average. His ego approximates that of the psychotic in some part or another and to a greater or lesser extent; and the degree of its remoteness from one end of the series and of its proximity to the other will furnish us with a provisional measure of what we have indefinitely termed an 'alteration of the ego'" (p. 235). Consequently, the impingement of both internal and external pressure on the developing ego and immature brain may lead to symptoms and ego deformation. Therefore, according to Eissler

(1953), "The intervening variety of ego modifications to which a variety of techniques must be correlated provide, in my estimation, a system which is ideally flexible and superbly adaptable to actual clinical work" (p. 130).

Interestingly, some of the problems described by Eissler in working with schizophrenics may be applicable to DID also, a condition that often may be confused with the former (Kluft 1987). For example, hearing voices and the inability to distinguish external reality from mental events warrant the parameters of reducing symptoms and setting the goal of building a healthy ego. In addition, the problem of secondary resistance or resistance against the exploration of resistance (Freud 1920, 1937) needs to be recognized in such patients also. For example, patients with severe dissociative psychopathology have enormous amnestic gaps and often do not recognize them. It may take considerable therapeutic work to bring these to the patient's attention only to have her continually "forget" that she even has such a problem in the first place. Ferenczi's (1933) descriptions of his severely traumatized patients are remarkably similar, and his technical experimentation becomes comprehensible in this context (Brenner 2001).

CONCLUSION

During the course of an analytically informed treatment of a patient with severe early trauma that results in a modification of the ego, such as dissociative character pathology, it may be determined that the standard technique does not suffice. Certain parameters would then be warranted. The construction of one's childhood may be very difficult or seemingly impossible owing to the inaccessibility of early memories because of insurmountable resistances, very deep repression or dissociative defenses, and the effects of severe, early trauma on the developing brain, such as an interference in interhemispheric communication. At some point in the treatment, the introduction of a technical innovation, such as guided eye movements, may loosen up the psyche and facilitate the therapeutic process. In my limited sample of three patients, this modification was very time-limited, which coincides with informal reports of other analysts (K. Frantz, M.D., personal communication, 2000). After the patient decides she has had enough, therapy then may return to a more typical mode of exploration. Furthermore, the employment of this technique did appear to be analyzable and not greatly affect the overall transference configuration of my three long-term patients. These observations are based on a limited sample of three, long-term patients with severe, early trauma and varying degrees of dissociative psychopathology at different stages of integration and different degrees of intensity of their treatment. Although multiply determined (Waelder 1936), all seemed to benefit from a period of guided eye movements and the benefit was associated with a cathexis of the hand. The question is asked as to whether more analysts would consider reporting on their clinical experiences and determining what, if any, objective value there is in introducing such a procedure into treatment. Could something like guided eye movements become a parameter that might enhance the efficacy of analytic therapy in certain patients or will it be a pariah of the analytic community? As the analyst's clinical field of vision continues to grow, we need to be receptive to new findings, while retaining our heritage of providing the optimum experience for self-exploration, understanding, growth, and healing.

References

Abraham, B. (1986). *The Angel of Death—The Mengele Dossier*. Brazil: Sherit Haplieta.

Akhtar, S. (1992). *Broken Structures: Severe Personality Disorders and Their Treatment*. Northvale, NJ: Jason Aronson.

———. (1996). "Someday . . . " and "if only fantasies." *Journal of the American Psychoanalytic Association* 44:723–753.

———. (1999). *Immigration and Identity*. Northvale, NJ: Jason Aronson.

Alexander, F., and French, T. M. (1946). *Psychoanalytic Therapy: Principles and Application*. New York: Ronald Press.

Alexander, L. (1948). The sociopsychologic structure of the S.S. *Archives of Neurology and Psychology* 59:622–634.

Alexander, R. (1981). On the analyst's 'sleep' during the psychoanalytic session. In *Do I Dare Disturb the Universe—A Memorial to Wilfred R. Bion*, ed. J. S. Grotstein, pp. 46–57. London: Marefield.

Allegro, L. A. (1992). On the formulation of interpretation. *International Journal of Psycho-Analysis* 71:421–434.

American Psychiatric Association. (1994). *Diagnostic and Statistical Manual of Mental Disorders* (DSM-IV), 4th ed. Washington, DC: American Psychiatric Press.

Apprey, M. (1991). Psychical transformations by a child of incest. In *The Trauma of Transgression*, ed. S. Kramer and S. Akhtar, pp. 115–148. Northvale, NJ: Jason Aronson.

———. (1993). The African-American experience: forced migration and transgenerational trauma. *Mind and Human Interaction* 4:70–75.

Arlow, J. (1979). Metaphor and the psychoanalytic situation. *Psychoanalytic Quarterly* 48:363–385.

Aron, L. (1991). The patient's experience of the analyst's subjectivity. *Psychoanalytic Dialogue* 2:475–507.

Bach, S. (in press). *A mind of one's own: some observations on thinking disorders.* In *Symbolization and Desymbolization: Essays in Honor of Norbert Freedman,* ed. R. Lasky. New York: Other Books.

Bak, R. C. (1968). The phallic woman: the ubiquitous fantasy in perversion. *Psychoanalytic Study of the Child* 23:15–36. New York: International Universities Press.

Balint, A., and Balint, M. (1939). On transference and countertransference. *International Journal of Psycho-Analysis* 20:223–230.

Balter, L., Lothane, Z. and Spence, J. H. (1980). On the analyzing instrument. *Psychoanalytic Quarterly* 49:474–504.

Benner, D. G., and Evans, C. (1984). Unity and multiplicity in hypnosis, commisurotomy, and multiple personality disorder. *Journal of Mind and Behavior* 5:423–432.

Beres, D., and Arlow, J. (1974). Fantasy and identification in empathy. *Psychoanalytic Quarterly* 43:26–50.

Bergmann, M., and Jucovy, M., eds. (1982). *Generations of the Holocaust.* New York: Basic Books.

Berman, E. (1981). Multiple personality: psychoanalytic perspective. *International Journal of Psycho-Analysis* 62:283–300.

Bibring, E. (1954). Psychoanalysis and the dynamic psychotherapies. *Journal of the American Psychiatric Association* 2:745–790.

Bibring, G. L. (1954). The training analysis and its place in psychoanalytic training. *International Journal of Psycho-Analysis* 35:169–173.

Bion, W. (1959). Attacks on linking. *International Journal of Psycho-Analysis* 40:308–315.

Blos, P. (1967). The second individuation process of adolescence. *Psychoanalytic Study of the Child* 22:162–186. New York: International Universities Press.

Blum, H. (1985). Superego formation, adolescent transformation, and the adult neurosis. *Journal of the American Psychoanalytic Association* 33:887–909.

———. (1986). On identification and its vicissitudes. *International Journal of Psycho-Analysis* 67:267–276.

———. (1987). The role of identification in the resolution of trauma. *Psychoanalytic Quarterly* 56:609–627.

———. (1989). The concept of termination and the evolution of psychoanalytic thought. *Journal of the American Psychoanalytic Association* 37:275–295.

———. (1994). The confusion of tongues and psychic trauma. *International Journal of Psycho-Analysis* 71:871–882.

———. (1996). Seduction trauma and pathogenesis. *Journal of the American Psychoanalytic Association* 44:1147–1164.

Bollas, C. (1987). *The Shadow of the Object.* London: Free Association.

Bonomi, C. (1999). Flight into sanity: Jones's allegations of Ferenczi's mental deterioration reconsidered. *International Journal of Psycho-Analysis* 80:507–542.

Borch-Jacobsen, M. (1996). *Remembering Anna O.: A Century of Mystification.* New York: Routledge.

Borkin, J. (1978). *The Crime and Punishment of I. G. Farben.* New York: Free Press.

Bowlby, J. (1973). *Attachment and Loss, Vol. 2: Separation: Anxiety and Anger.* New York: Basic Books.

Boyer, L. B. (1977). Working with a borderline patient. *Psychoanalytic Quarterly* 46:386–424.

Braun, B. G. (1984). Towards a theory of multiple personality and other dissociative phenomena. *Psychiatric Clinics of North America* 7:171–193.

Brende, J. O. (1984). The psychophysiologic manifestations of dissociation. *Psychiatric Clinics of North America* 7:41–50.

Brenner, C. (1982). *The Mind in Conflict.* New York: International Universities Press.

Brenner, I. (1988a). Multisensory bridges in response to object loss during the Holocaust. *Psychoanalytic Review* 75:573–587.

———. (1988b). *Unconscious fantasies of the selection in children of*

Holocaust survivors. Paper presented at the First Jerusalem International Conference of Children of Survivors, December.

———. (1994a). The dissociative character: a reconsideration of multiple personality and related phenomena. *Journal of the American Psychoanalytic Association* 42:819–846.

———. (1994b). Letter to the editor. *Journal of the American Psychoanalytic Association* 43:300–303.

———. (1996a). On trauma, perversion, and multiple personality. *Journal of the American Psychoanalytic Association* 44:785–814.

———. (1996b). The characterological basis of "multiple personality." *American Journal of Psychotherapy* 50:154–166.

———. (1999a). Deconstructing DID. *American Journal of Psychotherapy* 53:344–360.

———. (1999b). *Remembering, repeating and keeping separate: reflections on the gospel according to Freud*. Paper presented at the International Psychoanalytic Association, Santiago, Chile, July.

———. (1999c). Returning to the fire: surviving the Holocaust and "going back." *Journal of Applied Psychoanalytic Studies* 1:145–162.

———. (2000a). Stacheldraht in der Seele. In *Das Ende-der Sprachlosigkeit?*, ed. L. Opher-Cohn, J. Pfafflin, B. Sontag, B. Klose, and P. Ponagy-Whendt, pp. 113–139. Giessen: Psychosozial-Verlag.

———. (2000b). *Transmission of trauma in children of survivors: a review of cases*. Paper presented at the American Psychoanalytic Association Holocaust Discussion Group, New York, December.

———. (2001). *Dissociation of Trauma: Theory, Phenomenology and Technique*. Madison, CT: International Universities Press.

Breuer, J., and Freud, S. (1893–1895). Studies on hysteria. *Standard Edition* 2:1–323.

Britton, R. (1998). *Belief and Imagination: Explorations in Psychoanalysis*. London: Routledge.

Bromberg, P. (1998). *Standing in the Spaces: Essays on Clinical Process, Trauma, and Dissociation*. Hillside, NJ: Analytic Press.

Brown, D. G. (1977). Drowsiness in the countertransference. *International Review of Psycho-Analysis* 4:481–492.

Calef, V., and Weinshel, E. M. (1980). The analyst as the conscience of the analysis. *International Review of Psycho-Analysis* 7:279–290.

———.(1981). Some clinical consequences of introjection: gaslighting. *Psychoanalytic Quarterly* 50:44–65.

Carlson, J. G., Chemtob, C. M., Rusnak, K., et al. (1998). Eye movement desensitization and reprocessing treatment for combat related posttraumatic stress disorder. *Journal of Traumatic Stress* 11:3–24.

Carroll, J. (2000). *The Church and the Jews: A History*. Boston: Houghton Mifflin.

Chambless, D., Baker, M. J., Baucom, D. H., et al. (1998). Update on empirically validated therapies. *Clinical Psychology* 51:3–16.

Clifft, M. (1986). Writing about psychiatric patients. *Bulletin of Mental Disorders* 50:511–524.

Cohen, M. (1952). Countertransference and anxiety. *Psychiatry* 15:231–243.

Cooper, A. M. (1986). Summary. In *The Termination of the Training Analysis: Process, Expectations, and Achievements*, ed. A.M. Cooper, pp. 53–57. International Psychoanalytic Association Monograph 5. London: I. P. A. Secretariat.

Cooper, S. H. (1998). Analyst subjectivity, analyst disclosure, and the aims of psychoanalysis. *Psychoanalytic Quarterly* 67:379–406.

Cornwell, J. (1999). *Hitler's Pope—The Secret History of Pius XII*. New York: Viking Penguin.

Cowell, A. (1998). Berlin, still a fateful city. *New York Times*, May 24, 1998, p. 3.

Czech, D. (1990). *Auschwitz Chronicle 1939–1945*. New York: Henry Holt.

Danieli, Y. (1981). Countertransference in the treatment and study of Nazi Holocaust survivors and their children. *Victimology: An International Journal* 5:3-4.

Davidowicz, L. (1975). *The War Against the Jews 1933–1945*. New York: Holt, Rinehart & Winston.

Deacon, T. W. (1997). *The Symbolic Species*. New York: Norton.

Dean, E. S. (1957). Drowsiness as a symptom of countertransference. *Psychoanalytic Quarterly* 26:246–247.

Dennett, D. (1987). *The Intentional Stance.* Cambridge, MA: MIT Press.

DeWind, E. (1968). Symposium: psychic traumatization through social catastrophe. *International Journal of Psycho-Analysis* 49: 302–305.

———. (1972). Persecution, aggression, and therapy. *International Journal of Psycho-Analysis* 53:173–177.

Dickes, R. (1965). The defense function of an altered state of consciousness: a hypnoid state. *Journal of the American Psychoanalytic Association* 13:356–403.

Dickes, R., and Papernik, D. S. (1977). Defensive alterations of consciousness, hypnoid states, sleep and the dream. *Journal of the American Psychoanalytic Association* 25:635–654.

Edelman, G. M., and Tononi, A. (2000). *A Universe of Consciousness: How Matter Becomes Imagination.* New York: Basic Books.

Ehrenberg, D. B. (1992). Self-disclosure: therapeutic tool or indulgence? Countertransference disclosure. *Psychoanalytic Dialogue* 31:213–228.

Eissler, K. R. (1953). The effect of the structure of the ego on psychoanalytic technique. *Journal of the American Psychoanalytic Association* 20:104–143.

———. (1955). *The Psychiatrist and the Dying Patient.* New York: International Universities Press.

Ellenberger, H. F. (1970). *The Discovery of the Unconscious.* New York: Basic Books.

Elsass, P. (1997). *Treating Victims of Torture and Violence.* New York: New York University Press.

Emde, R. N. (1999). Moving ahead: integrating influences of affective processes for development and for psychoanalysis. *International Journal of Psycho-Analysis* 80:317–339.

Escoll, P. (1999). The "silent" parent and the unprotected, scapegoated child. In *Proceedings of At the Threshold of the Millennium,* vol. 2, ed. M. R. Brescia and J. Lemlij, pp. 125–130. Lima: Peru.

Eshel, O. (2001). Whose sleep is it anyway? Or "night moves." *International Journal of Psycho-Analysis* 82:545–562.

Expert Consensus Guideline Series. (1999). Treatment of post-traumatic stress disorder. *Journal of Clinical Psychiatry* 60:1–76.

Faimberg, H. (1988). The telescoping of generations. *Contemporary Psychoanalysis* 23:99–118.

Fairbairn, W. R. D. (1952). *On Object-Relations Theory of the Personality*. New York: Basic Books.

Falk, A. (1996). *A Psychoanalytic View of the Jews*. Cranbury, NJ: Associated Press.

Federn, E. (1990). *Witnessing Psychoanalysis: From Vienna Back to Vienna Via Buchenwald and the USA*. London: Karnac.

Federn, P. (1952). *Ego Psychology and the Psychoses*. New York: Basic Books.

Fenichel, O. (1942). Symposium on neurotic disturbances of sleep. *International Journal of Psycho-Analysis* 23:49.

Ferencz, B. B. (1979). *Less Than Slaves*. Cambridge, MA: Harvard University Press.

Ferenczi, S. (1919a). On the Technique of Psychoanalysis. In *Further Contributions to the Theory and Technique of Psycho-Analysis 1926*, ed. J. Rickman, pp. 177–189. London: Hogarth Press, 1950.

———. (1919b). Technical difficulties in the analysis of a case of hysteria. In *Further Contributions to the Theory and Technique of Psycho-Analysis*, ed. J. Rickman, pp. 189–197. London: Hogarth Press, 1950.

———. (1920). The further development of an active therapy in psychoanalysis. In *Further Contributions to the Theory and Technique of Psycho-Analysis*, ed. J. Rickman, pp. 198–217. London: Hogarth Press, 1950.

———. (1925). Contraindications to the "active" psychoanalytic technique. In *Further Contributions to the Theory and Technique of Psycho-Analysis*, ed. J. Rickman, pp. 217–230. London: Hogarth Press, 1950.

———. (1928). The elasticity of psychoanalytic technique. In *Final Contributions to the Problems and Methods of Psychoanalysis*, ed. M. Balint, pp. 87–102. New York: Basic Books, 1955.

———. (1929). The unwelcome child and his death instinct. In *Final Contributions to the Problems and Methods of Psychoanalysis*, ed. M. Balint, pp. 102–107. New York: Basic Books, 1955.

———. (1930). The principles of relaxation and neocatharsis. In *Final Contributions to the Problems and Methods of Psychoanalysis*, ed. M. Balint, pp. 108–125. New York: Basic Books, 1955.

———. (1932). Diary entries: January 19, June 3, July 21, 1932. *The Clinical Diary of Sandor Ferenczi*, ed. J. Dupont, transl. M. Balint and N. Z. Jackson. Cambridge, MA: Harvard University Press, 1988, pp. 13–16, 115, 162–166.

———. (1933). Confusion of tongues between the adult and the child. In *Final Contributions to the Problems and Methods of Psychoanalysis*, ed. M. Balint, pp. 155–167. New York: Basic Books, 1955.

Firestein, S. K. (1978). *Termination in Psychoanalysis*. New York: International Universities Press.

Fischer, R. M. S. (1991). The unresolved rapprochement crisis: an important constituent of the incest experience. In *The Trauma of Transgression*, ed. S. Kramer and S. Akhtar, pp. 39–56. Northvale, NJ: Jason Aronson.

Fliess, R. (1953). The hypnotic evasion: a clinical observation. *Psychoanalytic Quarterly* 22:497–516.

Fodor, N. (1951). *New Approaches to Dream Interpretation*. New Hyde Park, NY: University Books.

Fogelman, E., and Savran, B. (1979). Therapy groups for children of Holocaust survivors. *International Journal of Group Psychotherapy* 29:211–236.

Fonagy, P. (1999). *Attachment, the Holocaust, and the outcome of child psychoanalysis: the third generation*. Paper presented at the Philadelphia Psychoanalytic Institute, June.

Fonagy, P., Steele, H., Moran, G., et al. (1991). The capacity for understanding mental states: the reflective self in parent and child and its significance for security of attachment. *Infant Mental Health Journal* 13:200–217.

Fonseca, I. (1995). *Bury Me Standing: The Gypsies and Their Journey.* New York: Vintage.

Frank, K. A. (1992). Combining action techniques with psychoanalytic theory. *International Review of Psycho-Analysis* 19:57–79.

Freud, A. (1936). The ego and the mechanisms of defence. In *The Writings of Anna Freud, vol. 2.* New York: International Universities Press. 1966.

———. (1968). The problem of training analysis. In *The Writings of Anna Freud, vol. 4*, pp. 407–421. New York: International Universities Press.

Freud, S. (1886). Letter to Martha, February 2, 1886. In *Cocaine Papers,* ed. R. Byck. New York: Stonehill. (1974), pp. 163–166.

———. (1900). The interpretation of dreams. *Standard Edition* 4/5:1–626.

———. (1910). Observations on "wild" analysis. In *Collected Papers,* Vol. 2, 297–304. London: Hogarth Press.

———. (1912). Recommendations to physicians practicing analysis. *Standard Edition* 12:111–120.

———. (1913). Further recommendations in the technique of psychoanalysis: on beginning the treatment. *Standard Edition* 12:121–144.

———. (1914). On Narcissism. *Standard Edition* 14:69–102.

———. (1916). Some character-types met in psychoanalytic work. *Standard Edition* 14:312–324.

———. (1918). From the history of an infantile neurosis. *Standard Edition* 17:3–122.

———. (1919a). Lines of advance in psychoanalytic therapy. *Standard Edition* 17:123–204.

———. (1919b). The uncanny. *Standard Edition* 17:217–256.

———. (1920). Beyond the pleasure principle. *Standard Edition* 18:7–64.

———. (1923a). The ego and the id. *Standard Edition* 19:1–59.

———. (1923b). A short account of psychoanalysis. *Standard Edition* 19:191–209.

———. (1925a). An autobiographical study. *Standard Edition* 20: 3–74.

———. (1925b). On negation. *Standard Edition* 19:233–239.

———. (1926). Inhibitions, symptoms and anxiety. *Standard Edition* 20:75–175.

———. (1930). Civilization and its discontents. *Standard Edition* 21:59–145.

———. (1937). Analysis terminable and interminable. *Standard Edition* 23:209–253.

———. (1939). Moses and monotheism. *Standard Edition* 23:1–139.

———. (1940a). An outline of psycho-analysis. *Standard Edition* 23:139–207.

———. (1940b). Splitting of the ego in the process of defence. *Standard Edition* 23:271–278.

Fromm-Reichman, F. (1950). *Principles of Intensive Psychotherapy.* Chicago: University of Chicago Press.

Furst, S. S. (ed.) (1967). *Psychic Trauma.* New York: Basic Books.

Gabbard, G. D. (2000). Disguise and consent: problems and recommendations concerning the publication and presentation of clinical material. *International Journal of Psychotherapy* 81:1071–1086.

Gampel, Y. (1982). A daughter of silence. In *Generations of the Holocaust,* ed. M. Bergmann, and M. Jucovy. New York: Basic Books, pp. 120–136.

Ganzarain, R. (1991). Extra-analytic contacts: fantasy and reality. *International Journal of Psycho-Analysis* 72:131–140.

Gay, P. (1988). *Freud—A Life For Our Time.* New York: Norton.

Genova, P. (2001). Rabbi among the mechanics. *Psychiatric Times,* May, pp. 34–40.

Gill, M. M. (1984). Psychoanalytic, psychodynamic, cognitive behavior and behavior therapies compared. In *Psychoanalytic Therapy and Behavior Therapy: Is Integration Possible?,* ed. W. Ankowitz and S. B. Messer, pp. 179–187. New York: Plenum.

Glover, E. (1929). The screening function of traumatic memories. *International Journal of Psycho-Analysis* 10:90-93.

Goldberg, A. (2000). Gaps, barriers and splits: the psychoanalytic search for connection. *Neuro-Psychoanalysis* 2:61–68.

Gootman, E. (2001). Father sought to "swap" girl, 4, for sexual abuse. *The New York Times,* October 12, p. 4.

Greaves, G. (1993). A history of multiple personality disorder. In

Clinical Perspectives on Multiple Personality Disorder, ed. R. P. Kluft and C. G. Fine, pp. 355–380. Washington, DC: American Psychiatric Press.

Greenberg, J. (1995). Psychoanalytic technique and the interactive matrix. *Psychoanalytic Quarterly* 64:1–22.

Greenberg, J., and Mitchell, S. (1983). *Object Relations in Psychoanalytic Theory*. Cambridge, MA: Harvard University Press.

Greenson, R. (1966). That "impossible" profession. *Journal of American Psychological Association* 14:9–27.

Greyson, B. (1983). The psychodynamics of near-death experiences. *Journal of Nervous and Mental Disorders* 171:376–381.

Grinberg, L. (1962). On a specific aspect of countertransference due to the patient's projective identification. *International Journal of Psycho-Analysis* 43:436-440.

Grinberg, L., and Grinberg, R. (1989). *Psychoanalytic Perspectives on Migration and Exile*. New Haven, CT: Yale University Press.

Gross, L. (1988). *The Last Jews in Berlin*. New York: Simon and Schuster.

Grubrich-Simitis, E. (1981). Extreme traumatization as cumulative trauma: psychoanalytic investigation of the effects of concentration camp experiences on survivors and their children. *Psychoanalytic Study of the Child* 36:415–450. New Haven, CT: Yale University Press.

———. (1984). From concretism to metaphor—children of Holocaust survivors. *Psychoanalytic Study of the Child* 39:301–319. New Haven, CT: Yale University Press.

———. (1986). Six letters of Sigmund Freud and Sandor Ferenczi on the interrelationship of psychoanalytic theory and technique. *International Review of Psycho-Analysis* 13:259–277.

Gutman, Y., and Berenbaum, M., eds. (1994). *Autonomy of the Auschwitz Death Camp*. Washington, DC: Holocaust Memorial Museum.

Hammer, M. F., Redd, A. J., Wood, E. J. et al. (2000). Jewish and Middle Eastern non-Jewish populations share a common pool of y-chromosome biallelic haplotypes. *Proc. Nat. Acad. Sci. USA* 97:6769–6774 (June 6).

Hardtmann, G. (1982). The shadows of the past. In *Generations of the Holocaust*, ed. M. Bergmann and M. Jucovy, pp. 228–244. New York: Basic Books.

Hart, K. (1981). *Return to Auschwitz: The Remarkable Life of a Girl Who Survived the Holocaust.* Saddle Brook, NJ: Athenaeum.

Hartmann, H. (1939). *Ego Psychology and the Problems of Adaptation*, trans. D. Rapaport. New York: International Universities Press, 1958.

Herzog, J. (1982). World beyond metaphor: thoughts on the transmission of trauma. In *Generations of the Holocaust*, ed. M. S. Bergmann and M. E. Jucovy, pp. 103–119. New York: Basic Books.

Hesse, E., and Main, M. (1999). Second generation effects of unresolved trauma in nonmaltreating parents: dissociated, frightened and threatening parental behavior. *Psychoanalytic Inquiry* 19:481–540.

Hilberg, R. (1971). *Documents of Destruction: Germany and Jewry, 1933–1945.* Chicago: Quadrangle.

———. (1985). *The Destruction of the European Jews,* revised edition, vol. 3. New York: Holmes & Meier.

Hodge, A. (2000). *A report of an unusual case of incest between a mother and a daughter.* Paper presented at the American Psychoanalytic Association, New York, December.

Hoffer, A. (1985). Toward a definition of psychoanalytic neutrality. *Journal of the American Psychoanalytic Association* 33:771–795.

———. (1990). Book review. The clinical diary of Sandor Ferenczi. *International Journal of Psycho-Analysis* 71:723–727.

Hoffer, P. T., and Hoffer, A. (1999). Ferenczi's fatal illness in historical context. *Journal of the American Psychoanalytic Association* 47:1257–1268.

Hoffman, I. Z. (1983). The patient as interpreter of the analyst's experience. *Contemporary Psychoanalysis* 19:389–422.

Hurn, H. T. (1973). Panel: fate of the transference after the termination of analysis. *Journal of the American Psychoanalytic Association* 21:182–192.

Inderbitzin, L., and Levy, S. (1994). External reality as defense. *Journal of the American Psychoanalytic Association* 42:763–788.

Jacobs, T. (1986). On countertransference enactments. *Journal of the American Psychoanalytic Association* 34:289–308.

———. (1991). *The use of the self.* Madison, CT: International Universities Press.

———. (1999). On the question of self-disclosure by the analyst: error or advance in technique? *Psychoanalytic Quarterly* 68:159–183.

Jacobson, E. (1957). Normal and pathological moods: their nature and function. *Psychoanalytic Study of the Child* 12:73–113. New York: International Universities Press.

Janet, P. (1889). *L'Automatisme Psychalogique.* Paris: Baillienc.

———. (1907). *The Major Symptoms of Hysteria.* New York: Macmillan.

Johnson, P. (1987). *A History of the Jews.* New York: Harper & Row.

Jones, E. (1953). *The Life and Work of Sigmund Freud,* vol. 1. New York: Basic Books.

Joseph, R. (1996). *Neuropsychiatry, Neuropsychology and Clinical Neuroscience.* Baltimore: Williams & Wilkins.

Josephus, F. (1984). The Jewish war. In *Josephus: Complete Works.* Grand Rapids, MI: Kregel.

Jucovy, M. (1986). The Holocaust. In *The Reconstruction of Trauma—Its Significance in Clinical Work,* ed. A. Rothstein. Madison, CT: International Universities Press, pp. 153–169.

Katan, A. (1961). Some thoughts about the role of verbalization in early childhood. *Psychoanalytic Study of the Child* 16:184–188. New York: International Universities Press.

Kelman, H. (1982). On resonant cognition. *International Review of Psycho-Analysis* 14:111–123.

Kestenberg, J. (1972). Psychoanalytic contributions to the problem of children of survivors from Nazi persecution. *Israel Annals of Psychiatry and Related Disciplines* 10:311–325.

———. (1980). Psychoanalyses of children of survivors from the Holocaust: case presentations and assessment. *Journal of the American Psychiatric Association* 28:775–804.

———. (1982). The persecutor's children: introduction. In *Generations of the Holocaust,* ed. M. Bergmann and M. Jucovy, pp. 161–166. New York: Basic Books.

Kestenberg, J., and Brenner, I. (1986). Children who survived the Holocaust. *International Journal of Psycho-Analysis* 67:309–316.

———. (1988). Le narcissisme au service de la survie. *Revue Francaise de Psychoanalysis* 6:1393–1408.

———. (1995). Narcissism in the service of survival. In *Vulnerable Child*, vol. 2, ed. T. Cohen, M. H. Etezady, and B. L. Pacella, pp. 35–50. Madison, CT: International Universities Press.

———. (1996). *The Last Witness*. Washington, DC: American Psychiatric Press.

Kestenberg, J., and Gampel, Y. (1983). Growing up in the Holocaust culture. *Israel Journal of Psychiatry* 29:129–146.

Khan, M. M. R. (1963). The concept of cumulative trauma. *Psychoanalytic Study of the Child* 18:286–306. New York: International Universities Press.

Klein, H. (1973). Children of the Holocaust: mourning and bereavement. In *The Child in His Family, the Impact of Disease and Death*, ed. E. J. Anthony and C. Koupernik, pp. 393–409. New York: Wiley.

Klein, M. (1935). A contribution to the psychogenesis of manic-depressive states. In *Love, Guilt and Reparation and Other Works, 1921–1945*, pp. 262–289. New York: Free Press. 1975.

———. (1940). Mourning and its relation to the manic-depressive states. In *Love, Guilt and Reparation and Other Works, 1921–1945*, pp. 344–369. New York: Free Press. 1975.

Kluft, R. P. (1984). Treatment of multiple personality disorder: a study of 33 cases. *Psychiatric Clinics of North America* 7:9–29.

———. (1987). First rank symptoms as a diagnostic clue to multiple personality disorder. *American Journal of Psychiatry* 144:293–298.

Kogan, I. (1995). *The Cry of Mute Children: A Psychoanalytic Perspective of the Second Generation of the Holocaust*. London: Free Association.

Kohut, H. (1971). *The Analysis of the Self*. New York: International Universities Press.

———. (1977). *The Restoration of Self*. New York: International Universities Press.

Kramer, S. (1983). Object-coercive doubting: a pathological defense response to maternal incest. *Journal of the American Psychoanalytic Association* 31:325–351.

———. (1991). Psychopathological effects of incest. In *The Trauma of Transgression*, ed. S. Kramer and S. Akhtar, pp. 1–12. Northvale, NJ: Jason Aronson.

———. (1994). Further considerations of somatic and cognitive residues of incest. In *Victims of Abuse*, ed. A. Sugarman, pp. 69–96. Madison, CT: International Universities Press.

Kris, E. (1956). The recovery of childhood memories in psychoanalysis. *Psychoanalytic Study of the Child* 11:54–88. New York: International Universities Press.

Krystal, H. (1968). *Massive Psychic Trauma*. New York: International Universities Press.

———. (1988). *Integration and Self-Healing: Affect-Trauma-Alexythymia*. Hillsdale, NJ: Analytic Press.

Laskey, R. (1978). The psychoanalytic treatment of a case of multiple personality. *Psychoanalytical Review* 65:353–380.

Laub, D. (1998). Unpublished manuscript. Children of perpetrators.

Laub, D., and Auerhahn, N. (1993). Knowing and not knowing massive psychic trauma: forms of traumatic memory. *International Journal of Psycho-Analysis* 74:287–302.

Lazar, S. (2001). Knowing, influencing, and healing: paranormal phenomena and implications for psychoanalysis and psychotherapy. *Psychoanalytic Inquiry* 21:113–131.

Levi, P. (1986). *Survival in Auschwitz: The Awakening*. New York: Summit.

Levin, F. (1997). Integrating some mind and brain views of transference: the phenomena. *Journal of the American Psychoanalytic Association* 45:1121–1152.

Levine, H. (1982). Toward a psychoanalytic understanding of children of survivors of the Holocaust. *Psychoanalytic Quarterly* 51:76–92.

Lewin, B. D. (1954). Sleep, narcissistic neurosis, and the analytic situation. *Psychoanalytic Quarterly* 23:487–510.

———. (1955). Dream psychology and the analytic situation. *Psychoanalytic Quarterly* 24:169–199.

Lichtenberg, J. D, Lachman, F. M., and Fosshage, J. L. (1992). *Self and Motivational Systems: Toward a Theory of Psychoanalytic Technique.* Hillsdale, NJ: Analytic Press.

Lifton, R. J. (1986). *The Nazi Doctors: Medical Killing and the Psychology of Genocide.* New York: Basic Books.

Liotti, G. (1992). Disorganized attachment in the etiology of the dissociative disorders. *Dissociation* 5:196–200.

Lipton, S. D. (1961). The last hour. *Journal of the American Psychoanalytic Association* 9:325–330.

Loewald, W. (1960). On the nature of therapeutic action in psychoanalysis. *International Journal of Psycho-Analysis* 58: 463–472.

Loomis, C. J. (1998). Everything in history was against them. *Fortune,* April 13, pp. 66–84.

Luborsky, L. (1964). A psychoanalytic research on momentary forgetting during free association. *Bulletin of the Philadelphia Association for Psychoanalysis* 14:119–137.

———. (1967) . Momentary forgetting during psychotherapy and psychoanalysis: a theory and research method. In *Motives and Thought: Psychoanalytic Essays in Honor of David Rapaport,* ed. R. R. Holt, monograph 18/190, pp. 175–217. New York: International Universities Press.

———. (1996). *The Symptom Context Method: Symptoms as Opportunities in Psychotherapy.* Washington, DC: American Psychoanalytic Association.

Madow, L. (1997). On the way to a second symbiosis. In *The Seasons of Life,* ed. S. Kramer and S. Akhtar, pp. 157–170. Northvale, NJ: Jason Aronson.

Mahler, M., Pine, A., and Bergman, A. (1975). *The Psychological Birth of the Human Infant.* New York: Basic Books.

Marcus, S., Marquis, P., and Sakai, C. (1997). Controlled study of treatment of PTSD using EMDR in an HMO setting. *Psychotherapy* 34:307–315.

Mark, B. (1985). *The Scrolls of Auschwitz.* Tel Aviv: Am Oved.

Marmer, S. S. (1980). Psychoanalysis of multiple personality. *International Journal of Psycho-Analysis* 61:439–459.
Marrus, M. R. (1987). *The Holocaust in History.* New York: Meridian.
Masson, J. M. (1984). *The Assault on Truth.* New York: Farrar, Straus & Giroux.
Mayer, E. L. (1996). Subjectivity and intersubjectivity of clinical facts. *International Journal of Psycho-Analysis* 77:709–738.
———. (2001). On "telepathic dreams?" An unpublished paper by Robert J. Stoller. *Journal of the American Psychoanalytic Association* 49:629–657.
McLaughlin, J. T. (1975). The sleepy analyst: some observations on states of consciousness in the analyst at work. *Journal of the American Psychoanalytic Association* 23:363–382.
Meri, L. (1984). *Hõbevalgem* Tallin: Eesti Raamat. [Unpublished translation by J. Kangilaski]
Michel, E. W. (1993). *Promises to Keep.* New York: Barricade.
Michels, R. (1983). The scientific and clinical functions of psychoanalytic theory. In *The Future of Psychoanalysis*, ed. A. Goldberg, pp. 125–135. New York: International Universities Press.
———. (1999). Looking back: the history of psychiatry in the 20th century. *Archives of General Psychiatry* 56:1153–1154.
Mitchell, S. A. (1988). *Relational Concepts in Psychoanalysis: An Integration.* Cambridge, MA: Harvard University Press.
Modell, A. (1997). Reflections on metaphors and affects. *Annals of Psychoanalysis* 25:219–233.
Moses, R. (1978). Adult psychic trauma: the question of early predisposition and some detailed mechanisms. *International Journal of Psycho-Analysis* 59:353–364.
Muller-Paisner, V. (1998). *From Steeple to Star.* Unpublished manuscript.
Niederland, W. G. (1961). The problem of the survivor. *Journal of Hillside Hospital* 10:233–247.
———. (1981). The survivor syndrome: further observations and dimensions. *Journal of the American Psychoanalytic Association* 29:413–425.

Nir, Y. (1989). *The Lost Childhood.* New York: Harcourt Brace Jovanovich.

Noll, R. (1997). *The Aryan Christ: The Secret Life of Carl Jung.* New York: Random House.

Norman, H., Blacker, K., Oremland, J., and Barrett, F. (1976). Fate of the transference neurosis after termination. *Journal of the American Psychoanalytic Association* 24:471–498.

Novey, S. (1985). *The Second Look: The Reconstruction of Personal History in Psychiatry and Psychoanalysis: Monograph 3.* New York: International Universities Press.

Oliver, M. (2000). In memoriam—Sigi Ziering; survived Nazi camps. *American Gathering of Jewish Holocaust Survivors* 15:20.

Olsson, P. A. (1986). Complexities in the psychology and psychotherapy of the phenomenally wealthy. In *The Last Taboo—Money as Symbol and Reality in Psychotherapy and Psychoanalysis,* ed. D. W. Kruger, pp. 55–69. New York: Brunnel Mazel.

Ornstein, A. (1986). The Holocaust: reconstruction and the establishment of psychic continuity. In *The Reconstruction of Trauma—Its Significance in Clinical Work,* ed. A. Rothstein, pp. 171–191. Madison, CT: International Universities Press.

Pally, R. (1999). Monkey see, monkey do. *American Psychoanalyst* 33:34–35.

———. (2000). *The Mind-Brain Relationship.* London: Karnac.

Parens, H. (1979). *The Development of Aggression in Early Childhood.* New York: Jason Aronson.

Parnel, L. (1999). *EMDR in the Treatment of Adults Abused as Children.* New York: Norton.

Pick, D. (2000). *Svengali's Web: The Alien Encounter in Modern Culture.* New Haven, CT: Yale University Press.

Pine, F. (1997). *The Diversity and Direction in Psychoanalytic Technique.* New Haven, CT: Yale University Press.

Pitman, R. K., Shin, L. M., and Rauch, S. L. (2000). Investigating the pathogenesis of posttraumatic stress disorder with neuroimaging. *Journal of Clinical Psychiatry* 62:47–54.

Poland, W. (1977). Pilgrimage: actions and traditions in self-analysis. *Journal of the American Psychoanalytic Association* 25:399–416.

Pollack, G. (1961). Mourning and adaptation. *International Journal of Psycho-Analysis* 42:314–361.

Pressac, J. (1989). *Auschwitz: Technique and Operation of the Gas Chambers.* New York: Beatte Klarsfeld Foundation.

Putnam, F. W. (1989). *Diagnosis and Treatment of Multiple Personality Disorder.* New York: Guilford.

Rachman, A. W. (1989). Confusion of tongues: the Ferenczian metaphor for childhood seduction and emotional trauma. *Journal of the American Academy of Psychoanalysis* 17:182–205.

———. (1997). The suppression and censorship of Ferenczi's "Confusion of Tongues" paper. *Psychoanalytic Inquiry* 17:459–485.

———. (1998). Judicious self-disclosure by the analyst. *International Forum of Psychoanalysis* 7:263–269.

Racker, H. (1957). The meanings and uses of countertransference. *Psychoanalytic Quarterly* 26:303–357.

Rank, O. (1936). *Will Therapy and Truth and Reality.* New York: Knopf, 1945, 1-vol. ed.

Rapaport, D. (1951). *Organization and Pathology of Thought.* New York: Columbia University Press.

Rauch, S. L., van der Kolk, B. A., Fisler, R., et al. (1996). A symptom provocation study using positron emission tomography and script driven imagery. *Archives of General Psychiatry* 53:380–387.

Redlich, F. (1998). *Hitler—Diagnosis of a Destructive Prophet.* New York: Oxford University Press.

Renik, O. (1991). One kind of negative therapeutic reaction. *Journal of the American Psychoanalytic Association* 39:87–105.

———. (1993). Analytic interaction: conceptualizing technique in light of the analyst's irreducible subjectivity. *Psychoanalytic Quarterly* 62:559–571.

———. (1995). The idea of the anonymous analyst and the problem of self-disclosure. *Psychoanalytic Quarterly* 64:466–495.

———. (1996). The perils of neutrality. *Psychoanalytic Quarterly* 65:495–517.

———. (1999). Playing one's cards face up in psychoanalysis: an approach to the problem of self-disclosure. *Psychoanalytic Quarterly* 68:521–539.

Risse, G. L., and Gazzaniga, M. S. (1979). Well kept secrets of the right hemisphere: a carotid amytal study of restricted memory transfer. *Neurology* 28:950–953.

Rittenberg, S. M. (1987). On charm. *International Journal of Psycho-Analysis* 68:389–396.

Rizzolati, G., and Arbib, M. A. (1998). Language within our grasp. *Trends in Neuroscience* 21:188–194.

Rizzuto, A. (2001). Metaphors of a bodily mind. *Journal of the American Psychiatric Association* 49:535–568.

Rosenblum, S. (1998). Abstinence, anonymity and the avoidance of self-disclosure. *Psychoanalytic Inquiry* 18:538–549.

Rosenkotter, L. (1982). The formation of ideals in the succession of generations. In *Generations of the Holocaust,* ed. M. Bergmann and M. Jucovy, pp. 176–182. New York: Basic Books.

Ross, C. A. (1989). *Multiple Personality Disorder: Diagnosis, Clinical Features and Treatment.* New York: Wiley.

———. (1997). *Dissociative Identity Disorder*. New York: Wiley.

Ross, D. R., and Lowenstein, R. J. (1992). Multiple personality and psychoanalysis: an introduction. Perspectives on multiple personality. *Psychoanalytic Inquiry* 12:3–48.

Sandler, J. (1976). Countertransference and role-responsiveness. *International Journal of Psycho-Analysis* 3:43–47.

Sandler, J., and Freud, A. (1983). Discussions in the Hamstead Index of *The Ego and the Mechanisms of Defense, Journal of the American Psychoanalytic Association*, vol. 31, suppl., pp. 19–146.

Sar, V., and Tutkun, H. (1997). Treatment of dissociative identity disorder in Turkey: a case study. *Dissociation* 10:148–156.

Schachter, J., and Luborsky, L. (1998). Who's afraid of psychoanalytic research? *International Journal of Psychoanalysis* 77:709–737.

Schafer, R. (1983). *The Analytic Attitude.* New York: Basic Books.

Scott, W. C. (1975). Remembering sleep and dreams. *International Review of Psycho-Analysis* 2:253–354.

Searles, H. F. (1965). *Collected Papers on Schizophrenia and Related Subjects.* London: Maresfield.

Shapiro, F. (1989). Efficacy of eye movement desensitization procedure in the treatment of traumatic memories. *Journal of Traumatic Studies* 2:199–223.

———. (1995). *Eye Movement Desensitization and Reprocessing: Basic Principles, Protocols and Procedures.* New York: Guilford.

Shapiro, F., and Forrest, M. S. (1997). *E.M.D.R.—The Breakthrough Therapy for Overcoming Anxiety, Stress and Trauma.* New York: Basic Books.

Sharfstein, S. S. (1999). In the year 2099. *Archives of General Psychiatry* 56:1151–1152.

Sharpe, E. F. (1940). Psycho-physical problems revealed in language: an examination of metaphor. In *Collected Papers on Psycho-Analysis,* pp. 155–169. New York: Brunner/Mazel, 1950.

Shengold, L. (1981). Insight as metaphor. *Psychoanalytic Study of the Child* 36:289–306. New Haven, CT: Yale University Press.

———. (1989). *Soul Murder: The Effects of Childhood Abuse and Deprivation.* New Haven, CT: Yale University Press.

———. (1999). *Soul Murder Revisited.* New Haven: Yale University Press.

Shin, L. M., McNally, R. J., Kosslyn, S. M., et al. (1999). Regional cerebral blood flow during script-driven imagery in childhood sexual abuse-related post traumatic stress disorder: a PET investigation. *American Journal of Psychiatry* 156:574–584.

Shirer, W. L. (1984). *The Nightmare Years—1930–1940.* Boston: Little, Brown.

Sichrovsky, P. (1986). *Strangers in Their Own Land: Young Jews in Germany and Austria Today.* Philadelphia: Jewish Publication Society.

Sidtis, J. J. (1986). Can neurological disconnection account for psychiatric dissociation? In *Split Minds, Split Brains,* ed. J. M. Quen, pp. 127–147. New York: New York University Press.

Silberer, H. (1909). Report on a method of eliciting and observing certain symbolic hallucination phenomena. In *Organization and Pathology of Thought,* ed. D. Rapaport, pp. 195–207. New York: Columbia University Press, 1957.

Simenauer, E. (1982). The return of the persecutor. In *Generations of the Holocaust*, ed. M. Bergmann and M. Jucovy, pp. 167–175. New York: Basic Books.

Singer, M. (1977). The fiction of anonymity. In *The Human Dimension in Psychoanalysis*, ed. K. A. Frank, pp. 181–192. New York: Grune & Stratton.

Singer, M. (1996). *The borderline dilemma—the underlying unity with neurosis and perversions.* Paper presented at the American Psychoanalytic Association Meetings, New York, December.

Smith, H. F. (1995). Analytic listening and the experience of surprise. *International Journal of Psycho-Analysis* 76:67–78.

Spezzano, C. (1993). *Affects in Psychoanalysis—A Clinical Synthesis.* Hillsdale, NJ: Analytic Press.

Steele, B. F. (1970). Parental abuse of infants and small children. In *Parenthood, Its Psychology and Psychopathology*, ed. E. J. Anthony and T. Benedek, pp. 449–477. Boston: Little, Brown.

———. (1991). The psychopathology of incest participants. In *The Trauma of Transgression*, ed. S. Kramer and S. Akhtar, pp. 13–38. Northvale, NJ: Jason Aronson.

Stern, D., Sander, L. W., Nahum, J., et al. (1998). Non-interpretive mechanisms in psychoanalytic therapy: the "something more" than interpretation. *International Journal of Psycho-Analysis* 79:903–922.

Strean, H. (1981). Extra-analytic contacts: theoretical and clinical considerations. *Psychoanalytic Quarterly* 50:238–259.

Sullivan, H. S. (1953). *The Interpersonal Theory of Psychiatry.* New York: Norton.

Tarnower, W. (1966). Extra-analytic contacts between the psychoanalyst and the patient. *Psychoanalytic Quarterly* 35:399–413.

Tischler, G. L., and Astrachan, B. M. (1999). Psychiatry 2099. *Archives of General Psychiatry* 56:1155–1156.

Tutkun, H., Sar, V., Yargic, L. I., et al. (1998). Frequency of dissociative disorders among psychiatric inpatients in a Turkish university clinic. *American Journal of Psychiatry* 155:800–805.

Tutkun, H., Yargic, L. I., and Sar, V. (1996). Dissociative identity disorder presenting as hysterical psychosis. *Dissociation* 9:244–252.

van der Kolk, B. A. (1996). The body keeps the score—approaches to the psychobiology of post-traumatic stress disorder. In *Traumatic Stress—The Effects of Overwhelming Experience in Mind, Body and Society*, ed. B. van der Kolk, A. McFarland, and L. Weisseth, pp. 214–241. New York: Guilford Press.

van der Kolk, B. A., and Greenberg, M. S. (1987). The psychobiology of the trauma response: hyperarousal, constriction, and addiction to traumatic reexposure. In *Psychological Trauma*, ed. B.A. van der Kolk, pp. 63–87. Washington, DC: American Psychiatric Press.

van der Kolk, B., and Kadish, W. (1987). Amnesia, dissociation and the return of the repressed. In *Psychological Trauma*, ed. B. van der Kolk. Washington, DC: American Psychiatric Press.

Van Etten, M. L., and Taylor, S. (1998). Comparative efficacy of treatments for posttraumatic stress disorder: a meta-analysis. *Clinical Psychological Psychotherapy* 5:126–144.

van Leeuwen, K. (1988). Resistances in the treatment of a sexually molested six year old. *International Review of Psycho-Analysis* 15:149.

Volkan, V. (1981). *Linking Objects and Linking Phenomena*. New York: International Universities Press.

———. (1987). *The Need to Have Enemies and Allies: From Clinical Practice to International Relationships*. Northvale, NJ: Jason Aronson.

———. (1995). Intergenerational transmission and "chosen" traumas: a link between the psychology of the individual and that of an ethnic group. In *Psychoanalysis at the Political Border: Essays in Honor of Rafael Moses*, ed. L. Rangell and R. Moses, pp. 251–276. Madison, CT: International Universities Press.

———. (1996) Bosnia-Herzegovina: ancient fuel of a modern inferno. *Mind and Human Interaction* 7:110–127.

———. (1997). *Bloodlines: From Ethnic Pride to Ethnic Terrorism*. New York: Farrar, Straus and Giroux.

Volkan, V. D., Ast, G., and Greer, W. (2002). *The Third Reich in the Unconscious*. New York: Routledge.

Wachtel, P. L. (1987). *Action and Insight*. New York: Guilford.

———. (1999). *E.M.D.R. and psychoanalysis: an intriguing interface. EMDRIA Audiotape* C114.

Waelder, R. (1936). The principle of multiple function: observations on overdetermination. *Psychoanalytic Quarterly* 5:45–62.

Waite, R. G. (1977). *The Psychopathic God—Adolf Hitler.* New York: Basic Books.

Wangh, M. (1968). A psychogenetic factor in the recurrence of war: symposium on psychic traumatization through social catastrophe. *International Journal of Psycho-Analysis,* 49:319–323.

Weiss, S. (1975). The effect on the transference of "special events" occurring during psychoanalysis. *International Journal of Psycho-Analysis* 56:69–75.

Werman, D. S. (1977). Normal and pathological nostalgia. *Journal of the American Psychoanalytic Association* 25:387–399.

Wiesel, E. (1961). *Dawn.* New York: Bantam.

Winnik, H. Z. (1968). Contributions to the symposium on psychic traumatization through social catastrophe. *International Journal of Psycho-Analysis,* 49:298–301.

Winnicott, D. W. (1935). The manic defense. In *Collected Papers: Through Pediatrics to Psychoanalysis,* pp. 129–144. London: Tavistock.

———. (1963). The psychotherapy of character disorders. In *The Maturational Processes and the Facilitating Environment.* Madison, CT: International Universities Press, 1965.

———. (1967). Mirror-role of the mother and family in child development. In *The Predicament of the Family: A Psycho-Analytic Symposium,* ed. P. Lomas, pp. 26–33. London: Hogarth.

Wolfenstein, E. V. (1985). Three principles of mental functioning in psychoanalytic theory and practice. *International Journal of Psycho-Analysis* 66:77–94.

Wolfenstein, M. (1966). How is mourning possible? *Psychoanalytic Study of the Child* 21:92–126. New York: International Universities Press.

Yahil, L. (1990). *The Holocaust.* New York: Oxford University Press.

Yehuda, R. (1999). Parental PTSD as a risk factor for PTSD. In *Risk Factors for Posttraumatic Stress Disorder,* ed. R. Yehuda, pp. 93–123. Washington, DC: American Psychiatric Press.

Yovell, Y. (2000). From hysteria to posttraumatic stress disorder: psychoanalysis and the neurobiology of traumatic memories. *Neuro-Psychoanalysis* 2:171–182.

Zetzel, E. R. (1965). Depression and the incapacity to bear it. In *Drives, Affects, Behavior*, ed. M. Schur, pp. 243–274. New York: International Universities Press.

Index

About the Author

Dr. Ira Brenner is a Clinical Professor of Psychiatry at Jefferson Medical College, and Training and Supervising Analyst as well as Director of the Psychotherapy Program for the Psychoanalytic Center of Philadelphia. Dr. Brenner is the recipient of the Simon Gratz Research Prize for 2000 from Jefferson Medical College for his work in psychic trauma, and the recipient of the Pierre Janet Award for 2001 from the International Society for the Study of Dissociation, for the best publication of the year on the subject for his book *Dissociation of Trauma: Theory, Phenomenology and Technique.* Dr. Brenner received the Practitioner of the Year Award from the Philadelphia Psychiatric Society in 2003, and he maintains a private practice in the Philadelphia area.